Casebook on Contract Law

Casebook
on Contract Law

W .T. Major

PITMAN
PUBLISHING

Pitman Publishing
128 Long Acre, London WC2E 9AN
A Division of Longman Group UK Limited.

First published 1990
Reprinted 1991, 1993

© Longman Group UK Ltd. 1990

British Library Cataloguing in Publication Data
Major, W.T. (William Thomas)
　Casebook on contract law.
　1. England. Contracts. Law
　I. Title
　344.206'2

ISBN 0 273 03082 5

Typeset by FDS Ltd, Penarth
Printed and bound in Singapore

To Alison, William, Katie and Thomas

Contents

Preface

This compilation is a direct development from *Cases in Contract Law* in the M & E Casebook series. Its publication provides the opportunity to revise and update the original selection of cases. Some recent cases of substantial importance are now included, particularly in the field of agreement and terms (the *Harvela* case and the *Interfoto* case), and in the field of exclusion clauses (*Smith v. Eric S. Bush* and *Harris v. Wyre Forest District Council*).

Each chapter contains a summary of its subject-matter and the cases are annotated wherever this might prove helpful. The main purpose of this casebook is to provide a companion to the recommended textbooks for students preparing for law papers at 'A' Level and the various professional examinations. It may also serve as a pocket-size *aide-mémoire* for first-year law students, who will know that there is no substitute for reading the actual reports

The publisher and the compiler are grateful to the Incorporated Council of Law Reporting and to Butterworths who kindly gave permission to include extracts from the Law Reports and the All England Reports respectively. Our thanks are also due to *The Times* newspaper for permission to include the report on the *Wyre Forest* case and *Smith v. Eric S. Bush*.

WTM

Table of cases

1. Agreement

> It must, to constitute a contract, appear that the two minds were at one, at the same moment of time, that is, that there was an offer continuing up to the time of acceptance: Dickinson v. Dodds, per JAMES, L.J.

Summary

1. Definition

Agreement is an essential element in the formation of a contract. It is made when an offeree accepts the offer made to him by the offeror. The cases in this chapter are concerned with the nature of the offer and the rules governing acceptance.

2. The offer

The terms of the offer must be certain: *Scammell* v. *Ouston* [1941]; *Chillingworth* v. *Esche* [1924]. An invitation to treat is not an offer: *Pharmaceutical Soc.* v. *Boots* [1953]; *Harris* v. *Nickerson* (1873); *Gibson* v. *Manchester Council* [1979].

3. Acceptance

Generally, an acceptance does not take effect unless and until it is communicated to the offeror: *Felthouse* v. *Bindley* (1863). But, in the case of unilateral contract, acceptance need not be communicated: *Carlill* v. *Carbolic Smoke Ball Co.* [1893]; *Harvela Investments Ltd* v. *Royal Trust of Canada* [1985]. Also, where acceptance is duly made by post, agreement is deemed to have been concluded before the acceptance actually reaches the offeror; *Henthorn* v. *Fraser* (1842); *Household Fire Insurance Co.* v. *Grant* [1879].

Acceptance must be unconditional so as to correspond exactly with the offer, and where it is at variance with the offer, the purported acceptance operates as a counter-offer: *Davies* v. *William Old* [1965]; *Hyde* v. *Wrench* [1840]. Only an offeree is capable of accepting an offer: *Boulton* v. *Jones* [1857].

The offeror may stipulate, or the circumstances may imply, that the communication of acceptance be made in some particular manner: *Holwell Securities* v. *Hughes* [1974]; *Quenerduaine* v. *Cole* [1883].

4. Unilateral contracts

In the case of unilateral contracts, the offer is accepted by the offeree's compliance with the terms of the offer: *Carlill* v. *Carbolic Smoke Ball Co.* [1893]. The offeror may be bound from the time when the offeree begins to comply: *Errington* v. *Errington and Woods* [1952].

5. The end of an offer

There are three ways in which an offer may come to an end so as to become incapable of acceptance. They are:

(*a*) revocation: *Byrne* v. *Van Tienhoven; Dickinson* v. *Dodds* [1876];

(*b*) lapse: *Ramsgate Victoria Hotel Co.* v. *Montefiore* [1886]; *Quenerduaine* v. *Cole* [1883] and

(*c*) rejection: *Hyde* v. *Wrench* [1840].

Scammell v. Ouston

[1941] A.C. 251; [1941] 1 All E.R. 14

House of Lords

The parties entered into negotiations for the supply of a motor lorry, giving an old lorry in part exchange. The parties were agreed as to the new lorry to be supplied, the price and the rebate in respect of the old lorry and further, they were agreed that the balance of the purchase price was to be had on hire-purchase terms over a period of two years. The precise terms of the hire-purchase agreement were not settled. The prospective hirer subsequently repudiated the transaction contending that there never was any concluded agreement between the parties because the terms of the prospective hire-purchase agreement had not been settled. HELD, by VISCOUNT SIMON L.C., VISCOUNT MAUGHAM, LORD RUSSELL and LORD WRIGHT, the expression 'on hire-purchase terms' was too vague to be given any definite meaning. Therefore there was no concluded agreement.

VISCOUNT SIMON, L.C. . . . it appears to me that the crucial sentence, 'This order is given on the understanding that the balance of purchase price can be had on hire-purchase terms over a period of two years,' is so vaguely expressed that it cannot, standing by itself, be given a definite meaning. That is to say, it requires further agreement to be reached between the parties before there would be a complete *consensus ad idem*. If so, there was no contract, and, therefore, no breach.

NOTE

It was not unusual for judges to use the expression *consenus ad idem* to mean contractual agreement, as did Viscount Simon in *Scammell* v. *Ouston*. Nevertheless, in this connection, the courts are not concerned with the subjective intentions of the parties, but rather with what they said, what they wrote and what they did. The question of agreement is tested objectively. See, e.g., *Harvey* v. *Facey* (1893); *Bigg* v. *Boyd Gibbins* [1971].

There are two ways in which an agreement may fail for lack of certainty: first, the terms may be too vague; secondly, the terms may be obviously incomplete, e.g., where the offer or its acceptance was expressed to be 'subject to contract'.

In *Chillingworth* v. *Esche* [1924] the parties agreed on the sale of certain property 'subject to a proper contract to be prepared by the vendor's solicitors'. It was held by the Court of Appeal that there was no contract. In this case, Sargent L J said: 'The words "subject to contract" or "subject to formal contract" have by this time acquired a definite ascertained legal meaning. The phrase is a perfectly familiar one in the mouths of estate agents and other persons accustomed to deal with land; and I can quite understand a solicitor saying to a client: "Be sure that to protect yourself you introduce into any preliminary contract you may think of making, the words *subject to contract*". I do not say that the phrase makes the contract containing it necessarily and whatever the context a conditional contract. But they are words appropriate for introducing a condition, and it would require a very strong and exceptional case for the clear *prima facie* meaning to be displaced.' *Alpenstow* v. *Regalian Properties* [1985] is such a strong and exceptional case.

Harvey v. Facey

[1983] A.C. 552
Privy Council
The following telegraph messages passed between the parties:
Harvey to Facey: 'Will you sell us Bumper Hall Pen? Telegraph lowest cash price — answer paid.'

Facey to Harvey: 'Lowest price for Bumper Hall Pen £900.'

Harvey to Facey: 'We agree to buy Bumper Hall Pen for the sum of nine hundred pounds asked by you. Please send us your title deed in order that we may get early possession.'

Facey's telegraph form was signed by him. Harvey, contending that the three telegrams constituted a binding contract for the sale of the property known as Bumper Hall Pen, sought specific performance. The Supreme Court of Jamaica held that the telegrams constituted a binding contract. Facey appealed.

HELD, by the Judicial Committee of the Privy Council (present: THE LORD CHANCELLOR, LORD WATSON, LORD HOBHOUSE, LORD MACNAGHTEN, LORD MORRIS and LORD SHAND), that Facey's telegram was not an offer and, accordingly, the last message from Harvey could not be a binding acceptance. There was no contract between the parties.

LORD MORRIS. The first telegram asks two questions. The first question is as to the willingness of L.M. Facey to sell to the appellants; the second question asks the lowest price, and the word 'Telegraph' is in its collocation addressed to that second question only, and gives his lowest price. The third telegram from the appellants treats the answer of L. M. Facey stating his lowest price as an unconditional offer to sell to them at the price named. Their Lordships cannot treat the telegram from L. M. Facey as binding in any respect, except to the extent it does by its terms, *viz.*, the lowest price. Everything else is left open, and the reply telegram from the appellants cannot be treated as an acceptance of an offer to sell to them; it is an offer that required to be accepted by L. M. Facey. The contract could only be completed if L. M. Facey had accepted the appellant's last telegram. It has been contended for the appellants that L. M. Facey's telegram should be read as saying 'yes' to the first question put in the appellant's telegram, but there is nothing to support that contention. L. M. Facey's telegram gives a precise answer to a precise question *viz.*, the price. The contract must appear by the telegrams, where as the appellants are obliged to contend that an acceptance of the first question is to be implied. Their Lordships are of opinion that the mere statement of the lowest price at which the vendor would sell contains no implied contract to sell at that price to the persons making the inquiry.

Bigg v. Boyd Gibbins Ltd.

[1971] 1 W.L.R. 913; [1971] 2 All E.R. 183
Court of Appeal, Civil Division
The plaintiffs and the defendants were negotiating by exchange of letters for the sale of a freehold property called Shortgrove Hall belonging to the plaintiffs. In one letter, the plaintiff wrote: 'As you are aware that I paid £25,000 for this property, your offer of £20,000 would appear to be at least a little optimistic. For a quick sale I would accept £26,000.' The defendants replied: 'I accept your offer', and asked the plaintiffs to contact the defendant's solicitors. Finally, the plaintiffs wrote: 'I thank you for your letter . . . accepting my price of £26,000 for the sale of Shortgrove Hall. I am putting the matter in the hands of my solicitors . . . My wife and I are both pleased that you are purchasing the property.' The plaintiffs brought this action for specific performance, alleging that

the exchange of letters constituted a contract for the sale of the property. Pennycuik, V. C., ordered specific performance of the agreement. The defendants appealed.

HELD, by RUSSELL, FENTON ATKINSON and CROSS, L.JJ., that although an agreement on price did not necessarily mean an agreement for sale and purchase, and the word 'offer' did not always mean offer in the sense of offer for actual sale but might be related to a particular term of the agreement whilst other negotiations in respect of the agreement continued, in the present case it was clear from the terms of the letters that the plaintiffs' first letter constituted an offer the acceptance of which constituted a binding agreement; accordingly, the plaintiffs were entitled to specific performance.

RUSSELL, L.J. It seems to me that in fact — and I am not dissuaded by the Privy Council case of *Harvey* v. *Facey* which had a particularity which I need not bother with—the defendants were correct in treating the first letter of 22nd December 1969, as an offer to sell the property at £26,000 when they write 'I accept your offer.' Further than that, it seems to me that the last letter of 13th January is a recognition, an affirmation indeed, that the parties have come to agreement on the sale of the property. 'I thank you for your letter . . . accepting my' offer to sell Shortgrove Hall at the 'price of £26,000.' Then again the phrase 'My wife and I are both pleased that you are purchasing' suggests to my mind that the plaintiffs regarded that which had passed up to then as having put the defendants in the position of the purchasers. I cannot escape the view, having read the letters, that the parties would regard themselves at the end of the correspondence, and would regard themselves quite correctly, as having struck a bargain for the sale and purchase of this property.

We were warned at an early stage in the argument quite rightly, that agreement on price does not necessarily mean agreement for sale and purchase, and we were referred to the warning phrases used by LORD GREENE, M. R. in *Clifton* v. *Palumbo*, where it was stated that 'offer' does not always mean offer in the sense of an offer for actual sale, but might be related to a negotiation continuing, but with agreement on one element of the contract which would or might subsequently be concluded. But bearing in mind those warnings, I am bound to say for myself the impression conveyed to my mind by these letters, and indeed the plain impression, is that the language used was intended to and did achieve the formation of an open contract.

Pharmaceutical Society of Great Britain v. Boots Cash Chemists (Southern), Ltd.

[1953] 1 Q.B. 401; [1953] 1 All E.R. 482
Court of Appeal

The defendants operated a self-service shop in the chemist's department of which certain drugs and medicines specified in Part I of the Poisons List compiled under *s.* 17 (1) of the Pharmacy and Poisons Act 1933, were displayed with retail prices marked. When the shop was open there was always a registered pharmacist in personal control of the chemist's department. It is the duty of the Pharmaceutical Society to take all reasonable steps to secure the enforcement of the provisions of the Pharmacy and Poisons Act 1933, s. 18 (1) of which provides that ' . . . it shall not be lawful — (*a*) for a person to sell any poison included in Part I of the Poisons List, unless . . . (*iii*) the sale is effected by, or under the supervision of, a registered pharmacist.' The plaintiff Society contended that the sales of the listed poisons took place when the customers took the goods from the open shelves and put them in the wire baskets provided and that, accordingly, the sales took place otherwise than according to s. 18 (1) of the Act. GODDARD, C.J., found for the defendants. The plaintiffs appealed.

HELD, by SOMERVELL, BIRKETT and ROMER, L.JJ., that the display of goods on the open shelves was an invitation to treat. No offer was made until the customer presented the goods selected at the cashier's desk. At that stage, a sale was effected when the customer's payment was accepted, the sale being conducted under the supervision of the registered pharmacist on duty.

SOMERVELL, L.J. Whether the plaintiffs' contention is right depends on what are the legal implications of the arrangements in this shop. Is the invitation which is made to the customer to be regarded as an offer which is completed so that both sides are bound when the article is put into the receptacle, or is it to be regarded as a more organised way of doing what is already done in many types of shops — and a bookseller is, perhaps, the best example — namely, enabling customers to have free access to what is in the shop, to look at the different articles, and then ultimately, having taken the one which they wish to buy, to come to the assistant and say: 'I want this'? Generally speaking, the assistant will say: 'That is all right,' the money passes, and the transaction is completed. I agree entirely with what the Lord Chief Justice says and the reasons he gives for his conclusion that in the case of the ordinary shop, although goods are displayed and it is intended that customers should go and choose what they want, the contract is not complete until the customer has indicated the article which he needs and the shopkeeper or someone on his behalf accepts that offer. Not till then is the contract completed, and, that being the normal position, I can see no reason for drawing any different inference from the arrangements which were made in the present case.

The Lord Chief Justice expressed what I consider one of the most formidable difficulties in the way of the plaintiffs' case when he pointed out that, if they were right, once an article has been placed in the receptacle the customer himself is bound and he would have no right, without paying for the first article, to substitute an article which he saw later of the same kind and which he preferred. I can see no reason for implying from this arrangement any position other than that which the Lord Chief Justice found, namely, that it is a convenient method of enabling customers to see what there is for sale, to chose, and possibly, to put back and substitute, articles which they wish to have, and then go to the cashier and offer to buy what they have chosen. On that conclusion the case fails, because it is admitted that in those circumstances there was supervision in the sense required by the Act and at the appropriate moment of time. For these reasons, in my opinion, the appeal should be dismissed.

NOTE
The Boots case should be compared with *Fisher* v. *Bell* [1960] in which a shopkeeper displayed a flick-knife in his shop window. By the knife was a ticket bearing the words, 'Ejector knife − 4s.' He was charged with offering a flick-knife for sale contrary to the provisions of the Restriction of Offensive Weapons Act 1959. The defendant was not guilty − the displaying of the knife with the ticket amounted to an invitation to treat. It was not an offer of sale.

Harris v. Nickerson

[1873] L.R. 8 Q.B. 286
Court of Queen's Bench

The defendant, an auctioneer, advertised that he would hold an auction sale of certain brewing materials, plant and office furniture on a specified date and the days following. The furniture was advertised for sale on the third day. The plaintiff, a London commission broker, obtained a commission to buy the office furniture and attended the sale. The defendant withdrew the office furniture from the sale and the plaintiff (who had purchased lots other than the office furniture) brought this action contending that the advertisement was akin to an advertisement for reward, *i.e.* general in its inception, but becoming a promise to the particular person who acts upon it before it is withdrawn.

HELD, by BLACKBURN, QUAIN and ARCHIBALD, JJ., that there was no contract, the advertisement being a mere declaration of intention.

QUAIN, J. When a sale is advertised as without reserve, and a lot is put up and bid for, there is ground for saying, as was said in *Warlow* v. *Harrison*, that a contract is entered into between the auctioneer and the highest bona fide bidder; but that has no application to the present case; here the lots were never put up and no offer was made by the plaintiff nor promise by the defendant, except by his advertisement that certain goods would be sold. It is impossible to say that that is a contract with everybody attending the sale, and that the auctioneer is to be liable for their expenses if any single article is withdrawn.

ARCHIBALD J. This is an attempt on the part of the plaintiff to make a mere declaration of intention a binding contract.

NOTE

For a House of Lords case on the distinction between an offer and an invitation to treats see *Gibson* v. *Manchester City Council* [1979]. The City Treasurer wrote to a tenant saying that the Council 'may be prepared to sell the house to you at the purchase price of £2725 less 20 per cent = £2180 (freehold)'. The letter continued: 'If you would like to make formal application to buy your council house please complete the enclosed application form and return it to me as soon as possible'. The tenant completed the form and returned it. The Council then changed its policy on the sale of council houses and the tenant was advised that the Council was unable to proceed with his application. The tenant brought this action claiming that the Council's letter was an offer which he had accepted by returning the application form. It was held by the House of Lords: there was no binding contract because there never was an offer made by the Council. The letter stating that the Council 'may be prepared to sell' was merely an invitation to treat.

Felthouse v. Bindley

[1862] 6 L.T. 157; 11 C.B. (N.S.) 869
Court of Common Bench
The plaintiff wished to buy a horse belonging to his nephew and, not having reached agreement as to price, wrote on 2nd January 1862 as follows:
'Dear Nephew,

Your price, I admit, was 30 guineas. I offered £30 — never offered more: and you said the horse was mine. However, as there may be a mistake about him, I will split the difference — £30 15s. — I paying all expenses from Tamworth. You can send him at your convenience, between now and the 25th of March. If I hear no more about him, I consider the horse mine at £30 15s.

Paul Felthouse.'

The nephew did not reply to this letter. But having a sale of his animals shortly afterwards, he instructed the defendant, an auctioneer, to keep that horse out of the sale. The auctioneer forgot his instructions and sold the horse. The plaintiff brought this action for conversion of the horse.
HELD, by WILLES, BYLES and KEATING, JJ., that, with regard to the question whether ownership had vested in the plaintiff, there was no contract for the sale of the horse.

WILLES, J. It is perfectly clear that there was no agreement for the sale of the horse on 2 January, and also that the uncle had no right to put upon the nephew that he should consider his offer accepted if he did not write. On 25 February the nephew had a sale of some of his effects, but prior to the sale he told the auctioneer not to sell the horse in question, which shows that he intended his uncle to have the horse according to the terms of his letter; but as he had not returned an answer he had not bound himself to accept the offer. On 25 February the horse, by mistake, was sold by the defendant, and on 27 February the nephew wrote to his uncle, which letter shows that he intended to accept the offer, and as far as he could did then accept it. Now, it appears to me that there was no binding acceptance by the nephew of the uncle's offer. Nor that he did anything to vest the property of the horse in him until 27 February; and that being so, it is perfectly clear that the plaintiff cannot recover as against the defendant.

[Decision affirmed by Exchequer Chamber, (1863) 7 L.T. 835]

NOTE

The general rule is that no contract is formed unless the acceptance is communicated to the offeror. The exceptions are unilateral contracts (*Carlill* v. *Carbolic Smoke Ball Co.* [1892] and postal acceptances (*Henthorn* v. *Fraser* [1892]).

Carlill v. Carbolic Smoke Ball Co.

[1893] 1 Q.B. 256; [1891-4] All E.R. Rep. 127

Court of Appeal

The defendants published the following advertisement in a newspaper: '£100 reward will be paid by the Carbolic Smoke Ball Co. to any person who contracts the increasing epidemic influenza, colds, or any disease caused by taking cold, after having used the ball three times daily for two weeks according to the printed directions supplied with each ball. £1,000 is deposited with Alliance Bank, Regent Street, showing our sincerity in the matter. During the last epidemic of influenza many thousand Carbolic Smoke Balls were sold as preventives against this disease, and in no ascertained case was the disease contracted by those using the Carbolic Smoke Ball. One Carbolic Smoke Ball will last a family several months, making it the cheapest remedy in the world at the price − 10s. post free. The ball can be refilled at a cost of 5s. Address: Carbolic Smoke Ball Co., 27, Princes Street, Hanover Square, London W.1.'

On the faith of this advertisement, the plaintiff bought a smoke ball and used it three times daily according to the printed directions from mid-November, 1891, to 17th January, 1892, when she contracted influenza. She then claimed the £100 regard and the defendants refused to pay.

HELD, by LINDLEY, BOWEN and A.L.SMITH, L.JJ., that (*i*) the deposit of £1,000 showed that the company intended to create legal relations – that the promise was not mere advertising puff, (*ii*) the advertisement was an offer made to all the world, and a contract was made with that limited portion of the public who came forward and performed the condition on the faith of the advertisement, and (*iii*) the offer contained an intimation that performance of the condition was sufficient acceptance and that there was no need for notification of acceptance to be given to the offeror.

LINDLEY, L.J. . . . We are dealing with an express promise to pay £100 in certain events. There can be no mistake about that at all. Read this how you will, and twist it about as you will, here is a distinct promise expressed in language which is perfectly unmistakeable, that £100 regard will be paid by the Carbolic Smoke Ball Co. to any person who contracts influenza after having used the ball three times daily, and so on. One must look a little further and see if this is intended to be a promise at all; whether it is a mere puff – a sort of thing which means nothing. Is that the meaning of it? My answer to that question is 'No,' and I base my answer upon this passage: '£1,000 is deposited with the Alliance Bank, Regent Street, showing our sincerity in the matter.' . . .

Then it is said that it is a promise that is not binding. In the first place it is said that it is not made with anybody in particular. The offer is to anybody who performs the conditions named in the advertisement. Anybody who does perform the conditions accepts the offer. I take it that if you look at this advertisement in point of law, it is an offer to pay £100 to anybody who will perform these conditions, and the performance of these conditions is the acceptance of the offer. That rests upon a string of authorities, the earliest of which is that celebrated advertisement case of *Williams* v. *Carwardine*, which has been followed by a good many other cases concerning advertisements of rewards. But then it is said: 'Supposing that the performance of the conditions is an acceptance of the offer, that acceptance ought to be notified.' Unquestionably as a general proposition when an offer is made, you must have it not only accepted, but the acceptance notified. But is that so in cases of this kind? I apprehend that this is rather an exception to the rule, or, if not an exception, it is open to the observation that the notification of the acceptance need not precede the performance.

This offer is a continuing offer. . . .But I doubt very much whether the true view is not, in a case of this kind, that the person who makes the offer shows by his language and from the nature of the transaction that he does not expect and does not require notice of the acceptance apart from notice of the performance.

NOTE

It is clear that, in the case of a bilateral contract, the offeror is contractually bound from the moment of acceptance. In the case of a unilateral contract it seems that the offeror is bound from the time when the offeree began to perform as required by the terms of the offer. In *Errington* v. *Errington and Woods* [1952], a man promised to give his house to his son and daughter-in-law provided they paid off the building society mortgage. The man died leaving all his property to his widow. The son then left his wife and went to live with his widowed mother, his wife [the man's daughter-in-law] remaining in the house in question. She continued to make regular payments to the building society. The widow later sought to recover possession of the house. It was held that the promise had led to the formation of a unilateral contract—a promise of the house in return for their act of paying the instalments. The promise could not be revoked after the couple had started to pay the mortgage instalments.

For a penetrating examination of the formation and nature of unilateral contracts see Lord Diplock's speech in *Harvela Investments* v. *Royal Trust Co. of Canada* [1985].

Harvela Investments Ltd. v. Royal Trust Co. of Canada

[1986] A.C.207; [1985] 3 W.L.R.276; [1985] 2 All E.R. 966
House of Lords

The first defendants held a parcel of shares for which the plaintiff and the second defendant were rival offerors. The parcel of shares would give to either purchaser control of the company. On 15 September 1981 the defendants invited the prospective purchasers to submit by sealed offer or confidential telex a 'single offer' for the whole parcel by a stipulated date. The defendants stated that 'we bind ourselves to accept the highest offer' which complied with the

terms of the invitation. On 16 September the plaintiff tendered a
bid of $2,175,000. The second defendant tendered (also on 16
September) a bid of $2,100,000 or $101,000 in excess of any other
offer expressed as a fixed money amount, whichever is the higher'.
On 29 September, the defendants accepted the second defendant's
bid as being a bid of $2,276,000 and entered into a contract for the
sale of the parcel of shares. The plaintiff contended that there was
a binding contract between the defendant vendors and the plaintiff
for the sale of the shares for the price of $2,175,000. After
succeeding at first instance and failing in the Court of Appeal, the
plaintiff appealed to the House of Lords:

HELD, by LORD FRASER, LORD DIPLOCK, LORD
EDMUNDS-DAVIES, LORD BRIDGE and LORD
TEMPLEMAN, that the appeal would be allowed because the
referential bid was invalid as being inconsistent with the purpose of
fixed bidding. Whether an invitation from a vendor was to be
construed as an invitation to participate in a fixed bidding sale or in
an auction sale depended on the presumed intention of the vendor
as deduced from the provisions of the invitation to bid.

The facts (a) that the vendors had undertaken to accept the
highest offer, (b) that the same invitation was extended to both
parties, and (c) that they had insisted that offers were to be
confidential, were only consistent with the intention to sell by fixed
bidding. The facts were inconsistent with the intention to create an
auction sale by referential bids.

LORD DIPLOCK. The construction question turns on the wording
of the telex of 15 September 1981 . . . addressed to both Harvela
and the second defendant. It was not a mere invitation to negotiate
for the sale of the shares in Harvey & Co. Ltd., of which the
vendors were the registered owners in the capacity of trustees. Its
legal nature was that of a unilateral or 'if' contract, or rather two
unilateral contracts in identical terms to one of which the vendors
and Harvela were the parties as promisor and promisee
respectively, while to the other the vendors were promisor and the
second defendant was promisee. Such unilateral contracts were
made at the time when the invitation was received by the promisee
to whom it was addressed by the vendors; under neither of them
did the promisee, Harvela and the second defendant respectively,
assume any legal obligation to anyone to do or refrain from doing
anything.

The vendors, on the other hand, did assume a legal obligation to the promisee under each contract. That obligation was conditional on the happening, after the unilateral contract had been made, of an event which was specified in the invitation; the obligation was to enter into a synallagmatic contract to sell the shares to the promisee, the terms of such synallagmatic contract being also set out in the invitation. The event on the happening of which the vendors' obligation to sell the shares to the promisee arose was the doing by the promisee of an act which was of such a nature that it might be done by either promisee or neither promisee but could not be done by both. The vendors thus did not, by entering into the two unilateral contracts, run any risk of assuming legal obligations to enter into conflicting synallagmatic contracts to sell the shares to each promisee.

The whole business purpose of unilateral contracts inviting two or more promisees to submit sealed tenders of a purchase price for property which are not to be disclosed to any competing promisee and imposing on the promisor a legal obligation to transfer the property to the promisee whose tender specifies the highest price is that each promisee should make up his mind as to the maximum sum which he estimates the property is worth to him, not a sum of money the amount of which cannot be determined except by reference to amounts specified in sealed tenders received from other promisees of which, under the terms of the unilateral contract, he is to be denied all knowledge before the time for making his own tender has expired. That business purpose would be defeated by a tender which took the form of an offer to purchase the property not for a specified fixed sum of money but for a sum greater by some specified amount than the fixed sum specified in the sealed tender lodged by some other promisee by the terms of a unilateral contract in identical terms. What other sensible reason could there be for making it a term of each unilateral contract that the promisee should be kept in ignorance of the amounts offered by any other promisees?

The second defendant claims that a fresh synallagmatic contract coming into existence on 29 September 1981 was made by his offer of 16 September 1981 to buy the shares at a price of $101,000 more than whatever fixed price was bid by Harvela and an acceptance of that offer by the vendors' telex of 29 September 1981 to the second defendant. To create such a fresh contract there must have been an intention on the part of each party, manifested to the other, to assume fresh contractual obligations to the other party which he had not hitherto been under any legal liability to perform. It seems to me to be clear beyond argument that there was no such intention by either party and none was manifested by either party to the other. The second defendant's only intention in making his offer of 16 September 1981 was to comply with the condition subsequent specified in the unilateral contract of 15 September and by so doing to convert it into the synallagmatic contract, the terms of which were contained in the invitation, which he asserted gave rise to the contractual obligation on the part of the vendors to transfer the shares to him, while the vendors' only intention, as the wording of their telex of 29 September makes clear, was to perform the legal obligation to the second defendant by which they were already bound under the synallagmatic contract into which the unilateral contract they had made with him had, as they believed, been converted. That each had misconstrued that unilateral contract cannot transform their common intention *to perform* an existing contract into an intention *to make* a fresh and different one.

Henthorn v. Fraser
[1892] 2 Ch. 27
Court of Appeal

An appeal from the decision of the Vice-Chancellor of the County Palatine of Lancashire who gave judgment for the defendants. The plaintiff had for some time been negotiating to buy certain house property in Flamank Street, Birkenhead from the building society whom the defendants represent. On 7th July 1891 the secretary of the society, in the Liverpool office of the society, handed to the plaintiff a letter stating: 'I hereby give you the refusal of the Flamank Street property at £750 for fourteen days.' On 8th July a letter, written by the plaintiff's solicitor and accepting the offer, was posted in Birkenhead at 3.50 p.m. This letter was not received at the defendants' office until after working hours on the 8th. Earlier on that day, a letter was sent to the plaintiff by the secretary of the building society saying: 'Please take notice that my letter to you of the 7th inst. giving you the option of purchasing the property Flamank Street, Birkenhead, for £750, in fourteen days, is withdrawn and the offer cancelled.' This was posted in Liverpool shortly after mid-day and was received by the plaintiff at 5.30 p.m. The plaintiff, contending that a contract was made on 8th July, brought this action for specific performance. The Vice-Chancellor of the County Palatine of Lancashire gave judgment for the defendants. The plaintiff appealed.

HELD by LORD HERSCHELL and LINDLEY and KAY, L.JJ., that a contract was made when the plaintiff's letter of acceptance (written by his solicitor) was posted.

LORD HERSCHELL: Where the circumstances are such that it must have been within the contemplation of the parties that, according to the ordinary usages of mankind, the post might be used as a means of communicating the acceptance of an offer, the acceptance is complete as soon as it is posted ... The learned Vice Chancellor appears to have based his decision to some extent on the fact that before the acceptance was posted the defendants had sold the property to another person. The case of *Dickinson* v. *Dodds* was relied upon in support of that defence. In that case, however, the plaintiff knew of the subsequent sale before he accepted the offer, which, in my judgment, distinguishes it entirely from the present case. For the reasons I have given, I think the judgment must be reversed and the usual decree for specific performance made.

LINDLEY, L.J. I quite concur. I am not prepared to accede to the argument that because the offer was not made by post there was no authority to send an acceptance by post, and the Vice-Chancellor, in my opinion, fell into a mistake by acceding to it.

NOTE

The question whether it must have been 'within the contemplation' of the parties that the post might be used, is decided objectively. See, e.g., *Quenerduaine* v. *Cole* [1883], where the factual circumstances indicated that postal acceptance would not have been appropriate.

In *Holwell Securities* v. *Hughes* [1974] the offeror had stipulated for the actual communication of acceptance by written notice. The general rule in *Henthorn* v. *Fraser* was, therefore, not applicable even though the acceptance had been posted. In Holwell, therefore, the posting of the notice which went astray did not constitute a valid exercise of the option and there was no contract for the sale of the land.

The Household Fire and Carriage Accident Insurance Company Ltd. v. Grant

[1879] 4 Ex.D. 216; [1874–80] All E.R. Rep. 919
Court of Appeal

The defendant applied for 100 shares in the plaintiff company. The company allotted the shares to him and duly addresed to him and posted a notice of allotment, but this never reached the defendant. The company claimed the sum due on the shares allotted and the defendant disclaimed liability, contending that he was not a shareholder, *i.e.* that his offer to buy the shares had not been accepted.

HELD BY BAGGALLAY and THESIGER, L.JJ. (BRAMWELL, L.J., dissenting), that there was a contract between the company and the defendant from the time of posting of the allotment notice and that, accordingly, the defendant was liable as a shareholder.

THESIGER, L.J. To me it appears that in practice a contract complete upon the acceptance of an offer being posted, but liable to be put an end to by an accident in the post, would be more mischievous than a contract only binding upon the parties to it upon the acceptance actually reaching the offeror, and I can see no principle of law from which such an anomalous contract can be deduced. There is no doubt that the implication of a complete, final and absolutely binding contract being formed as soon as the acceptance of an offer is posted, may in some cases lead to inconvenience and hardship. But such there must be at times in any view of the law. It is impossible in transactions which pass between parties at a distance, and have to be carried on through the medium of correspondence, to adjust conflicting rights between innocent parties so as to make the consequences of mistake on the part of a mutual agent fall equally upon the shoulders of both. At the same time I am not prepared to admit that the implication in question will lead to any great or general inconvenience or hardship. An offeror, if he choose, may always make the formation of the contract which he proposes dependent upon the actual communication to himself of the acceptance. If he trusts to the post, he trusts to a means of communication which as a rule does not fail, and if no answer to his offer is received by him, and the matter is of importance to him, he can make inquiries of the person to whom this offer was addressed. On the other hand, if the contract is not finally concluded except in the event of the acceptance actually reaching the offeror, the door would be opened to the perpetration of much fraud, and, putting aside this consideration, considerable delay in commercial transactions, in which dispatch is, as a rule, of the greatest consequence, would be occasioned, for the acceptor would never be entirely safe in acting upon his acceptance until he had received notice that his letter of acceptance had reached its destination.

NOTE

Although this case was decided before *Henthorn* v. *Fraser* [1892], it harmonises with the principle enunciated by Lord Herschell in that case.

Hyde v. Wrench

[1840] 3 Beav. 334

Rolls Court

On 6th June the defendant made a written offer to sell his farm to the plaintiff for £1,000. The plaintiff's agent then called on the defendant and made a counter-offer of £950, which the defendant said he wished to have a few days to consider. On 27th June the defendant wrote to say that he did not feel disposed to accept the offer of £950 for his farm. On receipt of this letter the plaintiff's agent replied as follows: 'I beg to acknowledge the receipt of your letter of the 27th instant, informing me that your are not disposed to accept the sum of £950 for your farm at Luddenham. This being the case, I at once agree to the terms on which you offered the farm, *viz.*, £1,000 through your tenant Mr Kent, by your letter of the 6th instant.' The plaintiff claimed specific performance of the sale for £1,000.

HELD by LORD LANGDALE, M.R., that there was no contract. The counter-offer of £950 operated as a rejection of the offer to sell at £1,000 which could not subsequently be accepted.

LORD LANGDALE, M.R. under the circumstances stated in this bill, I think there exists no valid binding contract between the parties for the purchase of the property. The defendant offered to sell it for £1,000, and if that had been at once unconditionally accepted, there would undoubtedly have been a perfect binding contract; instead of that, the plaintiff made an offer of his own to purchase the property for £950, and he thereby rejected the offer previously made by the defendant. I think that it was not afterwards competent for him to revive the proposal of the defendant, by tendering an accetance of it; and that, therefore, there exists no obligation of any sort between the parties.

NOTE
Where a counter-offer is accepted, then the terms of the counter-offer become the terms of the contract: *Davies & Co.* v. *William Old* [1969].

Boulton v. Jones
[1857] 2 H. & N. 564
Passage Court of Liverpool
The plaintiff had been manager for one Brocklehurst, with whom the defendant had a running account. The plaintiff bought and paid for Brocklehurst's business and immediately afterwards, a written order was received from the defendant, addressed to Brocklehurst. The goods were supplied to the defendant and the plaintiff's book-keeper struck out Brocklehurst's name on the order, inserting the plaintiff's. When the plaintiff sent an invoice to the defendant, he said that he knew nothing of him and refused to pay him. The plaintiff brought this action for the price of goods sold.
HELD, by POLLOCK C.B., MARTIN, BRAMWELL and CHANNELL. BB, that there was no contract because the offer made by the defendant was not addressed to the plaintiff who, therefore could not accept it.

POLLOCK, C.B. The point raised is, whether the facts proved did not show an intention on the part of the defendants to deal with Brocklehurst. The plaintiff, who succeeded Brocklehurst in business, executed the order without any intimation of the change that had taken place, and brought this action to recover the price of the goods supplied. It is a rule of law, that if a person intends to contract with A, B cannot give himself any right under it. Here the order in writing was given to Brocklehurst. Possibly Brocklehurst might have adopted the act of the plaintiff in supplying the goods, and maintained an action for their price. But since the plaintiff has chosen to sue, the only course these defendants could take was to plead that there was no contract with him.

NOTE

Only the offeree can make a valid acceptance. Any purported acceptance by any person other than the offeree will not bring about the formation of a contract. In *Powell* v. *Lee* [1980] the plaintiff had applied to a commitee of school managers for the post of headmaster. The commitee met and decided to appoint the plaintiff, but did not inform him of the decision. A member of the committee, without authorisation, informed him that he had been selected. The committee then had a change of mind and selected another person for the post. The plaintiff contended that this was a breach of contract. HELD: there was no contract because the committee had not communicated an acceptance of the plaintiff's offer to take the post. The purported acceptance made without authority was not binding on the committee.

An offer made generally to the whole world may be accepted by any person with notice of the offer: *Carlill* v. *Carbolic Smoke Ball Co.* [1892].

Holwell Securities v. Hughes

[1974] 1 W.L.R. 155; [1974] 1 All E.R. 161
Court of Appeal, Civil Division
By clause 1 of an agreement between the plaintiffs and the defendant dated 19th October, 1971, the plaintiffs were granted an option to purchase certain freehold property from the defendant. Clause 2 provided: 'The said option shall be exercisable by notice in writing to the [defendant] at any time within six months from the date hereof . . . ' The plaintiffs' solicitors wrote on 14th April 1972, giving notice of the exercise of the option. This letter was posted, properly addressed and prepaid, on 14th April, but it was never delivered. The option was due to expire on 19th April. The plaintiff brought this action for specific performance of the option agreement contending that the option had been validly exercised when the letter of 14th April was posted and that a binding contract came into force on that date. TEMPLEMAN, J., gave judgment for the defendant. The plaintiff appealed.

HELD, by RUSSELL, BUCKLEY and LAWTON, L.J.J., that the option had not been validly exercised. The requirement of clause 2 of 'notice in writing to' the defendant meant that the document had to be communicated to the defendant. This requirement was inconsistent with the application of the rule that the mere posting of the document was sufficient. Furthermore, since the option agreement was an 'instrument affecting property' within s. 196 (5) of the *Law of Property Act,* 1925, the provision of s.196 (4) were incorporated into the agreement and those provisions contemplated that a notice would be effective only upon its delivery.

RUSSELL, L.J. It is the law in the first place that prima facie acceptance of an offer must be communicated to the offeror. On this principle the law has engrafted a doctrine that, if in any given case the true view is that the parties contemplated that the postal service might be used for the purpose of forwarding an acceptance of the offer, committal of the acceptance in a regular manner to the postal service will be acceptance of the offer so as to constitute a contract, even if the letter goes astray and is lost. Nor, as was once suggested, are such cases limited to cases in which the offer has been made by post. it suffices I think at this stage to refer to *Henthorn* v. *Fraser.* In the present case, as I read a passage in the judgment below, TEMPLEMAN, J. concluded that the parties here contemplated that the postal service might be used to communicate acceptance of the offer (by exercise of the option); and I agree with that.

But that is not and cannot be the end of the matter. In any case, before one can find that the basic principle of the need for communication of acceptance to the offeror is displaced by this artificial concept of communication by the act of posting, it is necessary that the offer is in its terms consistent with such displacement and not one which by its terms points rather in the direction of actual communication. We were referred to *Henthorn* v. *Fraser* and to the obiter dicta of FAREWELL J. in *Bruner* v. *Moore,* which latter was a case of an option to purchase patent rights. But in neither of those cases was there apparently any language in the offer directed to the manner of acceptance of the offer or exercise of the option.

The relevant language here is, 'The said option shall be exercisable by notice in writing to the Intending Vendor . . .,' a very common phrase in an option agreement. There is, of course, nothing in that phrase to suggest that the notification to the defendant could not be made by post. But the requirement of 'notice . . . to,' in my judgment, is language which should be taken expressly to assert the ordinary situation in law that acceptance requires to be communicated or notified to the offeror, and is inconsistent with the theory that acceptance can be constituted by the act of posting, referred to by Anson (23rd ed., p.47) as 'acceptance *without notification.*'

NOTE

The rule in *Henthorn* v. *Fraser* is an exception to the general rule that acceptance must be actually communicated to the offeror. In *Holwell Securities* v. *Hughes* the offeror, by requiring written notice, was simply stipulating for the application of the general rule, thus rendering the 'postal rule' inapplicable.

In general, the offeree may decide for himself the manner of communication of acceptance, e.g. by telex, telephone or post, etc. But as the manner is prescribed by the offeror or by the circumstances of the case, the question may arise whether communication of acceptance in any other manner will suffice. In *Manchester Diocesan Council for Education* v. *Commercial and General Investments* [1969] Buckley J. said: 'It may be that an offeror, who by the terms of his offer insists on acceptance in a particular manner, is entitled to insist that he is not bound unless acceptance is effected or communicated in that precise way, although it seems probable that, even so, if the other party communicates his acceptance in some other way, the offeror may by conduct or otherwise waive his right to insist on the prescribed method of acceptance. Where, however, the offeror has prescribed a particular method of acceptance, but not in terms insisting that only acceptance in that mode shall be binding, I am of opinion that acceptance communicated to the offeror by any other mode which is no less advantageous to him will conclude the contract. In *Tinn* v. *Hoffman & Co.* [1837], where acceptance was requested by return of post, Honeyman J. said: 'That does not mean exclusively a reply by return of post, but you may reply by telegram or by verbal message, or by any means not later than a letter written and sent by return of post'. If an offeror intends that he shall be bound only if his offer is accepted in some particular manner, it must be for him to make this clear.'

Wettern Electric v. *Welsh Development Agency* [1983] provides a further example of the power of the offeror to control the manner of acceptance. The Agency offered a manufacturing company a licence to occupy a factory unit for twelve months on stated terms. The offer contained the following passage: 'If you accept this licence on the above terms, will you please complete acknowledgement and acceptance at the foot of the enclosed copy and return it to us at your earliest convenience'. The company did not accept the offer in the required manner but instead went into occupation of the unit. It was held that there was no acceptance of the Agency's offer, but the occupation constituted an offer to enter a contractual licence on the terms already communicated by the Agency.

Quenerduaine v. Cole

[1883] 32 W.R. 185
Queen's Bench Division
The defendant, a Bristol merchant, made an offer through B, the plaintiff's agent, to buy a cargo of potatoes from the plaintiff, who was resident in France. B telegraphed the offer to the plaintiff on 30th December. There being no answer from the plaintiff by 31st December, the defendant went to B's office on that date and withdrew his offer. The plaintiff had answered the telegram by letter dated 30th December, which arrived after the withdrawal of the offer on 31st December. The defendant refused to accept delivery of the cargo of potatoes and the plaintiff brought this action for damages.
HELD, by GROVE and MATTHEW, JJ., that the plaintiff's acceptance was not made in a reasonable time. No contract was made.

GROVE, J. The plaintiff knew that the offer was only to be kept open till the 31st December and that the answer could not be received by letter till after that. The fact of receiving the offer by telegram imposing a new condition implied the expectation of a prompt reply, and the acceptance by letter was not, therefore, made in a reasonable time.

NOTE
A further example of the lapse of an offer by passage of time is to be found in *Ramsgate Victoria Hotel Co.* v. *Montefiore* [1866]. in this

case, M offered in June to buy shares from the hotel company. In November, the company alloted shares to M, who refused to take them, contending that his offer had lapsed. It was held that the offer had lapsed through passage of time as acceptance had not been made within a reasonable period from the date of the offer. The procedure for the allotment of shares is now governed by the Companies Act 1985.

Byrne & Co v. Leon Van Tienhoven & Co.

[1880] 5 C.P.D. 344

Common Pleas Division

The defendants carried on business in Cardiff and the plaintiffs in New York. The defendants wrote to the plaintiffs on 1st October 1879 offering to sell 'Hensol' brand tinplates, the 'offer of 1000 boxes of this brand 14 x 20 at 15*s*. 6*d*. per box f.o.b. here with 1 per cent for our commission; terms, four months' bankers' acceptance on London or Liverpool against shipping documents, but subject to your cable on or before the 15th inst. here.' This letter was received in New York by the plaintiffs on 11th October and on that day a telegram was sent to the defendants: 'Accept thousand Hensols.' The telegram was followed by a letter, posted on 15th October saying: 'We have to thank you for your valued letter under date 1st inst., which we had on Saturday p.m., and immediately cabled acceptance of the 1000 boxes 'Hensol' lc. 14/20 as offered. Against this transaction we have pleasure in handing you herewith the Canadian Bank of Commerce letter of credit No. 78, October 13th, on Messrs A. R. McMaster & Brothers, London, for £1000.' In the meantime the defendants had, on 8th October, posted a letter to the plaintiffs stating that the offer of 1st October was withdrawn because of a sudden rise in prices on the tinplate market. This letter reached the plaintiffs on 20th October. The plaintiffs brought this action for damages for non-delivery and the defendants contended that there was no contract, the offer of 1st October being validly withdrawn by the letter of 8th October.

HELD, by LINDLEY, J., That the withdrawal was not effective because it did not reach the plaintiffs until after 11th October on which date the offer was accepted, resulting in a binding contract.

LINDLEY, J. It may be taken as now settled that where an offer is made and accepted by letters sent through the post, the contract is completed the moment the letter accepting the offer is posted, even although it never reaches its destination. When, however, these authorities are looked at, it will be seen that they are based upon the principle that the writer of the offer has expressly or impliedly assented to treat an answer to him by a letter duly posted as a sufficient acceptance and notification to himself, or, in other words, he has made the post office his agent to receive the acceptance and notification of it. But this principle appears to me to be inapplicable to the case of the withdrawal of an offer. In this particular case I can find no evidence of any authority in fact given by the plaintiffs to the defendants to notify a withdrawal of their offer by merely posting a letter; and there is no legal principle or decision which compels me to hold, contrary to the fact, that the letter of the 8th October is to be treated as communicated to the plaintiff on that day or on any day before 20th, when the letter reaches them. But before that letter had reached the plaintiff they had accepted the offer, both by telegram and by post; and they had themselves resold the tin plates at a profit. In my opinion the withdrawal by the defendants on the 8th October of their offer of the 1st was inoperative; and a complete contract binding on both parties was entered into on the 11th of October, when the plaintiffs accepted the offer of the 1st, which they had no reason to suppose had been withdrawn.

NOTE

In *Payne* v. *Cave* [1789] it was decided that, in a sale by auction, the fall of the hammer constituted acceptance of the highest bid. It follows that a bid may be withdrawn at any time before the fall of the hammer.

The rule in *Payne* v. *Cave* is codified by s.57(2) of the Sale of Goods Act 1979 which provides that: 'A sale by auction is complete when the auctioneer announces its completion by the fall of the hammer, or in other customary manner; and until the announcement is made any bidder may retract his bid'.

Dickinson v. Dodds

[1876] 2Ch.D. 463
Court of Appeal
On Wednesday, 10th June 1874, the defendant, Dodds, delivered to

the plaintiff a signed offer to sell a house for £800, 'This offer to be left over until Friday, 9 o'clock a.m., 12th June, 1874.' On the following afternoon the plaintiff was informed by a Mr. Berry that the defendant had been offering or agreeing to sell the house to another. The plaintiff then went immediately to the house where the defendant was staying, leaving there a formal acceptance in writing. but this, in fact, was never delivered to the defendant. On the next morning (Friday), Berry, acting as the plaintiff's agent, handed to the defendant a copy of the acceptance, to which the defendant responded that he had sold the property. On Thursday, 11th June, the defendant had entered a formal contract to sell the property. The plaintiff brought this action for specific performance. HELD, by JAMES and MELLISH, L.JJ., and BAGGALLAY, J.A., that the defendant's offer was effectively withdrawn when it came to the notice of the offeree that there had been a sale to a third person.

JAMES, L.J. It appears to me that there is neither principle nor authority for the proposition that there must be an express and actual withdrawal of the offer, or what is called a retraction. It must, to constitute a contract, appear that the two minds were at one, at the same moment of time, that is, that there was an offer continuing up to the time of acceptance. If there was not such a continuing offer, then the acceptance comes to nothing. Of course it may well be that the one man is bound in some way or other to let the other man know that his mind with regard to the offer had been changed; but in this case, beyond all question, the plaintiff knew that Dodds was no longer minded to sell the property to him as plainly and clearly as if Dodds had told him in so many words, 'I withdraw the offer'.

Sale of Goods Act 1979

57. Auction sales

(1) Where goods are put up for sale by auction in lots, each lot is prima facie deemed to be the subject of a separate contract of sale.

(2) A sale by auction is complete when the auctioneer announces its completion by the fall of the hammer, or in other customary manner; and until the announcement is made any bidder may retract his bid.

(3) A sale by auction may be notified to be subject to a reserve or upset price, and a right to bid may also be reserved expressly by or on behalf of the seller.

(4) Where a sale by auction is not notified to be subject to a right to bid by or on behalf of the seller, it is not lawful for the seller to bid himself or to employ any person to bid at the sale, or for the auctioneer knowingly to take any bid from the seller or any such person.

(5) A sale contravening subsection (4) above may be treated as fraudulent by the buyer.

(6) Where, in respect of a sale by auction, a right to bid is expressly reserved (but not otherwise) the seller or any one person on his behalf may bid at the auction.

2. Intention to create legal relations

> *There is, I think, no doubt that it is essential to the creation of a contract, using that word in its legal sense, that the parties to an agreement shall not only be* ad idem *as to the terms of their agreement, but that they shall have intended that it shall have legal consequences and be legally enforceable*: Rose and Frank v. Crompton, per BANKES, L.J.

Summary

1. The essential intention

An agreement does not became a binding contract unless the parties have shown, expressly or by implication, that they intended to create legal relations: *Rose and Frank* v. *Crompton Bros.* [1923].

2. The presumptions

In professional and business agreements there is a rebuttable presumption that the parties intended to create legal relations: *Rose and Frank Co.* v. *Crompton* [1923]; *Edwards* v. *Skyways* [1964].

In domestic and social agreements there is a rebuttable presumption that the parties did not intend to create legal relations: *Balfour* v. *Balfour* [1919]; *Merritt* v. *Merritt* [1970]; *Jones* v. *Padavatton* [1969].

3. The objective test

Where there is any doubt as to the intention of the parties it is not discovered by looking into the minds of the parties, but rather by the application of an objective test. The court looks at the facts and asks: 'Would reasonable people regard the agreement as intended to be binding?': see particularly the judgment of Lord Denning in *Merritt* v. *Merritt* [1970].

Rose and Frank Co. v. Crompton & Bros. Ltd.

[1923] 2 K.B. 261; [1924] All E.R. Rep. 245

Court of Appeal

The plaintiffs and defendants signed an agreement to the effect that the existing commercial arrangements between them should be continued for a specified period and that prices should be quoted for periods of six months. The document provided in detail for the course of business to be followed by the parties. The penultimate clause of the document provided that: 'This arrangement is not entered into, nor is this memorandum written, as a formal or legal agreement, and shall not be subject to legal jurisdiction in the law courts either of the United States or England, but it is only a definite expression and record of the purpose and intention of the three parties concerned, to which they each honourably pledge themselves with the fullest confidence based on past business with each other that it will be carried through by each of the three parties with mutual loyalty and friendly co-operation.' On the question whether the document expressed the terms of a binding contract:

HELD, by BANKES, SCRUTTON and ATKIN, L.JJ., that the agreement was not a binding contract because the parties had expressed an intention not to create legal relations.

BANKES, L.J. There is, I think, no doubt that it is essential to the creation of a contract, using the word in its legal sense, that the parties to an agreement shall not only be *ad idem* as to the terms of their agreement, but that they shall have intended that it shall have legal consequences and be legally enforceable. . . It no doubt sounds in the highest degree improbable that two firms in this country, arranging with a firm in the United States the terms upon which a very considerable business should be carried on between them over a term of years, should not have intended that their agreement as to those terms should be attended by legal consequences. It cannot, however, be denied that there is no reason in law why they should not so provide, if they desire to do so.

SCRUTTON, L.J. It is quite possible for parties to come to an agreement by accepting a proposal with the result that the agreement concluded does not give rise to legal relations. The reason of this is that the parties do not intend that their agreement shall give rise to legal relations. This intention may be implied from the subject-matter of the agreement, but it may also be expressed by the parties. In social and family relations such an intention is readily implied, while in business matters the opposite result would ordinarily follow. But I can see no reason why, even in business matters, the parties should not intend to rely on each other's good faith and honour, and to exclude all idea of settling disputes by any outside intervention with the accompanying necessity of expressing themselves so precisely that outsiders may have no difficulty in understanding what they mean. If they clearly express such an intention I can see no reason in public policy why effect should not be given to their intention.

ATKIN, L.J. To create a contract there must be a common intention of the parties to enter into legal obligations, mutually communicated expressly or impliedly. Such an intention ordinarily will be inferred when parties enter into an agreement which in other respects conforms to the rules of law as to the formation of contract. It may be negatived impliedly by the nature of the agreed promise or promises, as in the case of offer and acceptance of hospitality, or of some arrangements made in the course of family life between members of a family as in *Balfour* v. *Balfour*. If the intention may be negatived impliedly it may be negatived expressly. In this document, construed as a whole, I find myself driven to the conclusion that the clause in question expresses in clear terms the mutual intention of the parties not to enter into legal obligations in respect of the matters upon which they are recording their agreement.

NOTE

The decision of the Court of Appeal on this point was affirmed by the House of Lords, [1925] A.C. 445; [1924] All E.R. Rep. 255.

In this case, the words 'not subject to legal jurisdiction in the law courts' were sufficient to rebut the presumption of contractual intention. In *Appleson* v. *Littlewood* [1939], a football pools coupon contained a condition that it 'shall not be attended by or give rise to any legal relationship, rights, duties, consequences'. It was held by the Court of Appeal that the condition was valid and the agreement was not binding. In *Edwards* v. *Skyways* [1964] it was held that the

use of the words *ex gratia* did not show that there was no intention
to create legal relations.

Esso Petroleum Co. v. *Commissioners of Customs and Excise*
[1976] is a case for comparison. The presumption of contractual
intention was rebutted not by any words used by the parties but
rather by the factual circumstances of the case, namely, the offer of
a free coin to each purchaser of four gallons of petrol. The coins
were specially produced and distributed by Esso to their dealers,
who made the offer to their customers. It was held by the House of
Lords that, in these circumstances, the offer of a gift in return for
the purchase of petrol was not intended to be legally binding.

Edwards v. Skyways, Ltd.

[1964] 1 W.L.R. 349; [1964] 1 All E.R. 494
Queen's Bench Division

The plaintiff was employed by the defendant company as an air
pilot. He was a member of the defendant company's contributory
pension fund and entitled under its rules to choose between two
options in the event of his leaving the company's employment
before reaching retirement age. Option one: to withdraw the sum
of his own contributions to the fund. Option two: to take the right
to a pension payable at retirement age. The plaintiff was one of a
number of pilots declared redundant, and he was given three
months notice to terminate his employment. At a meeting between
representatives of the company and of BALPA (British Airline
Pilot's Association), there was a recorded agreement that 'pilots
declared redundant and leaving the company would be given an *ex
gratia* payment equivalent to the company's contribution to the
Pension Fund' where they elect to withdraw the sum of their own
contributions. The plaintiff was informed of this agreement in a
publication called 'Newsletter' issued by BALPA. After leaving the
service of the defendant company, the plaintiff elected to withdraw
the sum of his own contributions and to receive the *ex gratia*
payment. The company paid the sum of the employee's
contributions, but failed to make the *ex gratia* payment. The
plaintiff brought this action to recover the sum of the contributions
made to the pension fund by the company in respect of himself.
The company contended that the agreement was not intended to
create legal relations: that the agreement was, consequently, not

legally binding. The company further contended that the agreement
was too vague to be enforceable on the grounds that the recorded
agreement was incorrect in the use of the word 'equivalent', the
word 'approximating' being the word actually used by the
representative of the company.

HELD, by MEGAW, J., that, as the agreement related to business
affairs, the onus of establishing that it was not intended to create
legal relations was on the party setting up that defence, and that the
use of the words *ex gratia* did not show that there was no intention
to create legal relations. The defendant company had failed to
establish that the parties – both of them – affirmatively intended
not to enter into legal relations in respect of the company's promise
to pay. It was also held that the agreement was not too vaguely
expressed to be binding, the words 'approximating to' connoting a
rounding off of a few pounds to a round figure.

MEGAW, J. In the present case, the subject-matter of the
agreement is business relations, not social or domestic matters.
There was a meeting of minds – an intention to agree. There was,
admittedly, consideration for the defendant company's promise. I
accept the propositions of counsel for the plaintiff that in a case of
this nature the onus is on the party who asserts that no legal effect
was intended, and the onus is a heavy one. Counsel for the
plaintiffs also submitted, with the support of the well-known
textbooks on the law of contract (ANSON, and CHESHIRE AND
FIFOOT), that the test of intention to create or not to create
relations is 'objective', I am not sure that I know what that means in
this context. I do, however, think that there are grave difficulties in
trying to apply a test as to the actual intention or understanding or
knowledge of the parties; especially where the alleged agreement is
arrived at between a limited liability company and a trade
association; and especially where it is arrived at at a meeting
attended by five or six representatives on each side. Whose
knowledge, understanding or intention is relevant? But if it be the
'objective' test of the reasonable man, what background knowledge
is to be imputed to the reasonable man, when the background
knowledge of the ten or twelve persons who took part in arriving at
the decision no doubt varied greatly between one another?
However that may be, the defendant company say, first, as I
understand it, that the mere use of the phrase 'ex gratia' by itself, as
a part of the promise to pay, shows that the parties contemplated

that the promise, when accepted, should have no binding force in law. They say, secondly, that even if their first proposition is not correct as a general proposition, nevertheless here there was certain background knowledge, present in the minds of everyone, which gave unambiguous significance to *ex gratia* as excluding legal relationship.

As to the first proposition, the words *ex gratia* do not, in my judgment, carry a necessary, or even a probable, implication that the agreement is to be without legal effect. It is, I think, common experience amongst practitioners of the law that litigation or threatened litigation is frequently compromised on the terms that one party shall make to the other a payment described in express terms as *ex gratia* or 'without admission of liability'. The two phrases are, I think synonymous. No one would imagine that a settlement, so made, is unenforceable at law. The words *ex gratia* or 'without admission of liability' are used simply to indicate – it may be as a matter of amour propre, or it may be to avoid a precedent in subsequent cases – that the party agreeing to pay does not admit any pre-existing liability on his part; but he is certainly not seeking to preclude the legal enforceability of the settlement itself by describing the contemplated payment as *ex gratia*. So here, there are obvious reasons why the phrase might have been used by the defendant company in just such a way. They might have desired to avoid conceding that any such payment was due under the employers' contract of service. They might have wished – perhaps ironically in the event – to show, by using the phrase, their generosity in making a payment beyond what was required by the contract of service. I see nothing in the mere use of the words *ex gratia*, unless in the circumstances some very special meaning has to be given to them, to warrant the conclusion that this promise, duly made and accepted, for valid consideration, was not intended by the parties to be enforceable in law.

Balfour v. Balfour

[1919] 2 K.B. 571; [1918–19] All E.R. Rep. 860
Court of Appeal
The defendant was a civil engineer employed in Ceylon. In November 1915 he came to England on leave with the plaintiff, his wife, remaining until August 1916, the end of his leave. The

plaintiff, on her doctor's advice, did not return to Ceylon with her husband. Before leaving England, the defendant orally promised to give the plaintiff £30 a month until she returned to Ceylon. The marriage subsequently broke down and the plaintiff sued for the £30 a month. The defendant contended that when the promise to pay £30 a month was made, there was no agreement for a separation, the promise related only to what was expected to be a temporary separation; that this was only a temporary domestic arrangement and was not intended to operate as a binding contract.

HELD, by WARRINGTON, DUKE and ATKIN, L.JJ., that there was no contract because the parties did not intend to create legal relations.

ATKIN, L.J. The defence to this action on the alleged contract is that the defendant, the husband, entered into no contract with his wife, and for the determination of that it is necessary to remember that there are agreements between parties which do not result in contracts within the meaning of that term in our law. The ordinary example is where two parties agree to take a walk together, or where there is an offer and an acceptance of hospitality. Nobody would suggest in ordinary circumstances that those agreements result in what we know as a contract, and one of the most usual forms of agreement which does not constitute a contract appears to me to be the arrangements which are made between husband and wife. It is quite common, and it is the natural and inevitable result of the relationship of husband and wife, that the two spouses should make arrangements between themselves – agreements such as are in dispute in this action – agreements for allowances, by which the husband agrees that he will pay to his wife a certain sum of money, per week, or per month, or per year, to cover either her own expenses or the necessary expenses of the household and of the children of the marriage, and in which the wife promises either expressly or impliedly to apply the allowance for the purpose for which it is given. To my mind those agreements, or many of them, do not result in contracts at all, and they do not result in contracts even though there may be what as between other parties would constitute consideration for the agreement. The consideration, as we know, may consist either in some right, interest, profit or benefit accruing to one party, or some forbearance, detriment, loss or responsibility given, suffered or undertaken by the other. That is a well-known definition and it constantly happens, I think, that such arrangements made between husband and wife are arrangements in which there are mutual promises, or in which there is consideration in form within the definition that I have mentioned. Nevertheless they are not contracts, and they are not contracts because the parties did not intend that they should be attended by legal consequences.

NOTE

The circumstances of this husband and wife agreement should be compared with those in *Merritt* v. *Merritt* [1970]. In *Balfour*, the circumstances were not sufficient to rebut the presumption of no legal relations, whereas in *Merritt* the circumstances were sufficient for the rebuttal and the agreement was, therefore, binding. Consider also *Simpkins* v. *Pays* [1955], in which a lodger and the family with whom he lived agreed to go shares in a newspaper competition. Their entry won a large sum of prize money and it was held that, in the circumstances, the agreement to go shares was intended to be legally binding.

Merritt v. Merritt

[1970] 1 W.L.R. 1211; [1970] 2 All E.R. 760
Court of Appeal, Civil Division
This case concerned an agreement between husband and wife. They were married in 1941 and had three children. In 1966 the husband left home to live with another woman. The matrimonial home, a freehold house, was in the joint names of the husband and wife and was subject to an outstanding mortgage of some £180. In order to make arrangements for the future, the wife met the husband and they talked the matter over in his car. He said that he would pay her £40 a month out of which she would have to pay off the outstanding mortgage. He gave her the building society mortgage book. Before leaving the car, the wife insisted that he put into writing the following further agreement: 'In consideration of the fact that you will pay all charges in connection with the house. . .until such time as the mortgage repayment has been completed, when the mortgage has been completed I will agree to transfer the property into your sole ownership.' The husband signed and dated the agreement and the wife took and kept the piece of paper on which it was written. When the mortgage was paid off the husband

refused to transfer ownership of the house to her. The trial judge held that the wife was entitled to a declaration that she was now sole beneficial owner of the house and he ordered the husband to join with wife in transferring the property to her. The husband appealed.

HELD, by LORD DENNING, M.R., WIDGERY and KARMINSKY, L.JJ., that the written agreement was intended to create legal relations because the presumption of fact against such an intention where arrangements were made by a husband and wife living in amity did not apply to arrangements made when they were not living in amity but were separated or about to separate, when it might safely be presumed that they intended to create legal relations; the surrounding circumstances of the present case showed that the parties did so intend; accordingly, the wife was entitled to sue on the agreement, and it being sufficiently certain and there being good consideration by the wife paying off the mortgage, she was entitled to a declaration that she was the sole owner of the house and to an order that the husband join in transferring it to her.

LORD DENNING, M.R. The first point taken on his behalf by counsel for the husband was that the agreement was not intended to create legal relations. It was, he says, a family arrangement such as was considered by the court in *Balfour* v. *Balfour* and in *Jones* v. *Padavatton*. So the wife could not sue on it. I do not think the those cases have any application here. The parties there were living together in amity. In such cases their domestic arrangements are ordinarily not intended to create legal relations. It is altogether different when the parties are not living in amity but are separated, or about to separate. They then bargain keenly. They do not rely on honourable understandings. They want everything cut and dried. It may safely be presumed that they intend to create legal relations.

Counsel for the husband then relied on the recent case of *Gould* v. *Gould*, when the parties had separated, and the husband agreed to pay the wife £12 a week 'so long as he could manage it.' The majority of the court thought that those words introduced such an element of uncertainty that the agreement was not intended to create legal relations. But for that element of uncertainty, I am sure that the majority would have held the agreement to be binding. They did not differ from the general proposition which I stated:

'When . . . husband and wife, at arm's length, decide to separate and the husband promises to pay a sum as maintenance to the wife during the separation, the court does, as a rule, impute to them an intention to create legal relations.'

In all these cases the court does not try to discover the intention by looking into the minds of the parties. It looks at the situation in which they were placed and asks itself: would reasonable people regard the agreement as intended to be binding?

Jones v. Padavatton

[1969] 1 W.L.R. 328; [1969] 2 All E.R. 616
Court of Appeal
In this action the plaintiff and defendant were mother and daughter, respectively. There was an agreement between the parties to the effect that if the daughter gave up her very satisfactory pensionable job in the USA and came to London to read for the Bar with the intention of practising law in Trinidad (where the mother lived), the mother would pay an allowance of 200 dollars a month to maintain the daughter and her small son while in England. According to this agreement, the daughter began her legal studies in November 1962, continuing up to the time this action was brought. At the time of the agreement, the mother meant 200 West Indian dollars a month and the daughter understood it to be 200 US dollars. But once arrived, the daughter accepted the allowance in West Indian dollars without dispute. In 1964, because the daughter was finding it difficult to live on her allowance, a house was found and the purchase price of £6,000 was provided by the mother, to whom the property was conveyed. The varied arrangement was that the daughter should live in part of the house and let the rest furnished, using the rent to cover expenses and the daughter's maintenance in place of the 200 dollars a month. In 1967 the parties quarrelled and the mother, complaining that she could not get any accounts, brought this action for possession of the house, on the grounds that the agreement between the parties was not made with the intention to create legal relations.
HELD, by DANCKWERTS, SALMON and FENTON ATKINSON, L.JJ., that the arrangement of 1964 by which the

daughter had the use of the house was lacking in contractual intent. The mother was entitled to possession.

DANCKWERTS, L.J. I have reached a conclusion that the present case is one of those family arrangements which depend on the good faith of the promises which are made and are not intended to be rigid, binding agreements. *Balfour* v. *Balfour* was a case of husband and wife, but there is no doubt that the same principles apply to dealings between other relations, such as father and son and daughter and mother. . . The operation about the house was, in my view, not a completely fresh arrangement, but an adaptation of the mother's financial assistance to her daughter due to the situation which was found to exist in England. It was not a still contractual operation any more than the original arrangement.

FENTON ATKINSON, L.J. At the time when the first arrangement was made, mother and daughter were, and always had been to use the daughter's own words, 'very close' I am satisfied that neither party at that time intended to enter into a legally binding contract, either then or later when the house was bought. The daughter was prepared to trust her mother to honour her promise of support, just as the mother no doubt trusted her daughter to study for the Bar with diligence, and to get through her examinations as early as she could.

3. Consideration

> '*A valuable consideration, in the sense of the law, may consist either in some right, interest, or benefit accruing to the one party, or some forbearance, detriment, loss or responsibility, given, suffered, or undertaken by the other*'. Definition given by the Court of Exchequer Chamber in Currie *v*. Misa.
>
> *I am content to adopt from a work of Sir Frederick POLLOCK (POLLOCK ON CONTRACTS (8th Edn.)), to which I have often been under obligation, the following words as to consideration: 'An act or forbearance of one party, or the promise thereof, is the price for which the promise of the other is bought, and the promise thus given for value is enforceable*': Dunlop *v*. Selfridge, per LORD DUNEDIN.

Summary

1. Definitions

A promise must be supported by consideration: if a promise is given for no consideration it will not be binding even though there may have been some good moral reason for the making of the promise: *Eastwood* v. *Kenyon* [1840].

The two authoritative definitions of consideration are those given by the Court of Exchequer Chamber and the House of Lords, respectively, in *Currie* v. *Misa* [1875] and *Dunlop* v. *Selfridge* [1915]: see head text above.

2. The rules

(*a*) Consideration must be real, that is to say, it must have some value, no matter how small. It follows that the discharge of a pre-existing obligation cannot amount to consideration. This rule applies equally whether the pre-existing obligation arose:

(*i*)   under a previous contract between the same parties: *Stilk* v. *Myrick* [1809]; *Hartley* v. *Ponsonby* [1857], or

(*ii*)   under a pre-existing contract with a third party: *Scotson* v. *Pegg* [1861]; *New Zealand Shipping Co.* v. *Satterthwaithe* [1975]; or

(*iii*)   under the public law: *Glasbrook Bros* v. *Glamorgan County Council* [1925]; *Ward* v. *Byham* [1956].

The question running through these cases is whether the party claiming to have given consideration did more than he was already bound to do. Where the answer is affirmative there is consideration. Where the answer is negative there is no consideration.

(b)   Consideration need not be adequate: *Bainbridge* v. *Firmstone* [1838]

(c)   Consideration must not be past: Roscorla v. Thomas [1842]; Re McArdle [1951]. Exception to the rule: s.27(1) of the Bills of Exchange Act 1882.

(d)   Consideration must move from the promisee: Dunlop v. Selfridge [1915]; Beswick v. Beswick [1967]. This aspect of consideration must be seen in relation to the doctrine of privity of contract: see Chapter 7.

Eastwood v. Kenyon

[1840] 11 Ad. & El. 438; [1835–42] All E.R. Rep. 133
Court of Queen's Bench
The plaintiff was the executor of John Sutcliffe, who had died
intestate as to his real property leaving as his heir-at-law his only
child, Sarah, an infant at the time of his death. The plaintiff spent
his own money on the improvement of the realty. To reimburse
himself, the plaintiff borrowed £140 from one Blackburn, giving a
promissory note. When Sarah reached full age she promised the
plaintiff that she would pay the amount of the note. After Sarah's
marriage, her husband promised the plaintiff that he would pay to
the plaintiff the amount of the note. The plaintiff sued Sarah's
husband on this promise and was met with the defence that there
was no consideration given for the promise.
HELD, by LORD DENMAN, C.J., PATTESON, WILLIAMS and
COLERIDGE, JJ., the benefit conferred on the defendant
(through his wife) by the plaintiff was not consideration to support
the defendant's subsequent promise to pay the plaintiff.

LORD DENMAN, C.J., delivered the judgment of the court:
Taking then the promise of the defendant, as stated on this record,
to have been an express promise, we find that the consideration for
it was past and executed long before; and yet it is not laid to have
been at the request of the defendant nor even of his wife while sole
. . . and the declaration really discloses nothing but a benefit
voluntarily conferred by the plaintiff and received by the defendant
with an express promise by the defendant to pay money. . .
   In holding this declaration bad because it states no consideration
but a past benefit not conferred at the request of the defendant, we
conceive that we are justified by the old common law of England.
Lampleigh v. *Braithwaite* is selected by Mr. Smith [1 SMITH'S
LEADING CASES] as the leading case on this subject which was
there fully discussed, though not necessary to the decision.
HOBART, C.J., lays it down that 'a mere voluntary courtesy will
not have a consideration to uphold an assumpsit. But if that
courtesy were moved by a suit or request of the party that gives the
assumpsit, it will bind; for the promise, though it follows, yet it is
not naked, but couples itself with the suit before, and the merits of
the party procured by that suit; which is the difference.'
   That difference is brought fully out by *Hunt* v. *Bate*, where a
promise to indemnify the plaintiff against the consequences of

having bailed the defendant's servant, which the plaintiff had done without request of the defendant, was held to be made without consideration; but a promise to pay £20 to the plaintiff who had married the defendant's cousin, but at the defendant's special instance, was held binding . . . the principle of moral obligation does not make its appearance till the days of LORD MANSFIELD, and then under circumstances not inconsistent with this ancient doctrine when properly explained.

Stilk v. Myrick

[1809] 2 Camp. 317
Court of Common Pleas
In the course of a voyage from London to the Baltic and back, two seamen deserted and the captain, being unable to replace them, promised the plaintiff and eight other crew members that they should have the wages of the two deserters divided equally among them. The plaintiff brought this action for wages including the share promised to him. The defendant contended that the agreement to pay extra wages was contrary to public policy and void, and that the plaintiff was entitled only to the £5 a month provided for by the ship's articles, executed before the commencement of the voyage.
HELD, by LORD ELLENBOROUGH, C.J., the promise to pay extra money to the plaintiff was void for want of consideration.

LORD ELLENBOROUGH, C.J. There was no consideration for the ulterior pay promised to the mariners who remained with the ship. Before they sailed from London they had undertaken to do all that they could under all the emergencies of the voyage. They had sold all their services till the voyage should be completed. If they had been at liberty to quit the vessel at Cronstadt, the case would have been quite different; or if the captain had capriciously discharged the two men who were wanting, the others might not have been compellable to take the whole duty upon themselves, and their agreeing to do so might have been sufficient consideration for the promise of an advance of wages. But the desertion of part of the crew is to be considered an emergency of the voyage as much as their death; and those who remain are bound by the terms of their original contract to exert themselves to the utmost to bring the ship in safety to her destined port. Therefore, without looking at the policy of this agreement, I think it is void for want of consideration, and that the plaintiff can only recover at the rate of £5 a month.

Hartley v. Ponsonby

[1857] 7 El. & Bl. 872
Queen's Bench
The plaintiff was a seaman who had signed articles to serve on a voyage from Liverpool to Port Philip (Australia) and thence to other ports and places in the Pacific and Indian Oceans. While the ship was at Port Philip, seventeen of the complement of thirty-six refused to work and were sent to prison. The remaining nineteen men included only four or five able seamen. To induce this diminished crew to sail the vessel to Bombay, the master promised the plaintiff and eight others an additional payment. It was unreasonable or unsafe to attempt the voyage with such a depleted crew. The plaintiff brought this action against the master to recover the promised payment.
HELD, by LORD CAMPBELL, C.J., COLERIDGE, J., ERLE, J. and CROMPTON, J., that the plaintiff was not bound by his original contract to undertake an unsafe voyage with such a seriously diminished crew. His undertaking to make the voyage was, accordingly, a good consideration to support the master's promise of additional payment.

LORD CAMPBELL, C.J. The answer given by the jury to the third question imports to my mind that for the ship to go to sea with so few hands was dangerous to life. If so, it was not incumbent on the plaintiff to perform the work; and he was in the condition of a free man. There was therefore a consideration for the contract; and the captain made it without coercion.

COLERIDGE, J. If they were not bound to go, they were free to make a new contract: and the master was justified in hiring them on the best terms he could make. It may be that the plaintiff took advantage of his position to make a hard bargain; but there was no duress.

NOTE

Hartley v. *Ponsonby* should be compared with *Stilk* v. *Myrick*. An important part of the distinction is that, in *Hartley*, the plaintiff was discharged from liability under his original contract and thus free to contract under new terms, whereas, in *Stilk*, the opposite was the case.

Scotson v. Pegg

[1861] 6 H & N 295; 158 E.R. 121
Court of Exchequer

By a previous contract with a third party, X, the plaintiffs had undertaken to deliver a cargo of coal to X or to the order of X. X, having sold the coal to the defendants, directed the plaintiffs to deliver it to the defendants. The defendants promised the plaintiffs that they would unload this cargo at a stated rate. The plaintiffs sued for breach of this promise. The defendants contended that the promise was not binding for lack of consideration. It was argued that the plaintiffs were already bound under the previous contract with X to deliver the cargo and that, therefore, no consideration moved from the plaintiffs to the defendants.

HELD, by MARTIN and WILDE, BB., the delivery of the coal was a benefit to the defendants and was consideration. The defendants' promise was binding.

MARTIN B. I am of opinion that the plea is bad, both on principle and in law. It is bad in law because the ordinary rule is, that any act done whereby the contracting party receives a benefit is a good consideration for a promise by him. Here the benefit is the delivery of the coals to the defendant. It is consistent with the declaration that there may have been some dispute as to the defendant's right to have the coals, or it may be that the plaintiffs detained them for demurrage; in either case there would be good consideration that the plaintiffs, who were in possession of the coals, would allow the defendant to take them out of the ship. Then is it any answer that the plaintiffs had entered into a prior contract with other persons to deliver the coals to their order upon the same terms, and that the defendant was a stranger to the contract? In my opinion it is not.

We must deal with this case as if no prior contract had been entered into. Suppose the plaintiffs had no chance of getting their money from the other persons who might perhaps have become bankrupt. The defendant gets a benefit by the delivery of the coals to him, and it is immaterial that the plaintiffs had previously contracted with third parties to deliver to their order.

WILDE B. I am also of opinion that the plaintiffs are entitled to judgment. The plaintiffs say, that in consideration that they would deliver to the defendant a cargo of coals from their ship, the defendant promised to discharge the cargo in a certain way. The defendant, in answer, says, 'You made a previous contract with other persons that they should discharge the cargo in the same way, and therefore there is no consideration for my promise.' But why is there no consideration? It is said, because the plaintiffs in delivering the coals are only performing that which they were already bound to do. But to say that there is no consideration is to say that it is not possible for one man to have an interest in the performance of a contract made by another. But if a person chooses to promise to pay a sum of money in order to induce another to perform that which he has already contracted with a third person to do, I confess I cannot see why such a promise should not be binding. Here the defendant, who was a stranger to the original contract, induced the plaintiffs to part with the cargo, which they might not otherwise have been willing to do, and the delivery of it to the defendant was a benefit to him. I accede to the proposition that if a person contracts with another to do a certain thing, he cannot make the performance of it a consideration for a new promise to the same individual. But there is no authority for the proposition that where there has been a promise to one person to do a certain thing, it is not possible to make a valid promise to another to do the same thing. Therefore, deciding this matter on principle, it is plain to my mind that the delivery of the coals to the defendant was a good consideration for his promise, although the plaintiffs had made a previous contract to deliver them to the order of other persons.

NOTE
It is clear from *Scotson* v. *Pegg* [1861] that performance of a contractual duty owed to a third party may be good consideration for a promise. This principle was applied by the Privy Council in

New Zealand Shipping Co. v. *Satterthwaite* [1975]. In this case it was said that 'An agreement to do an act which the promisor is under an existing obligation to do may quite well amount to valid consideration and does so in the present case: the promisee obtains the benefit of a direct obligation which he can enforce. This proposition is illustrated and supported by *Scotson v. Pegg* which their Lordships consider to be good law.'

The next question to consider is whether a promise to perform a contractual duty to a third party could constitute consideration. The view expressed by the Privy Council in *Pao On* v. *Lau Yiu Long* [1980] was that: 'A promise to perform, or the performance of, a pre-existing contractual obligation to a third party can be valid consideration'.

Glasbrook Bros. Ltd v. Glamorgan County Council

[1925] A.C. 270; [1924] All E.R. Rep. 579
House of Lords
During a strike at the appellant company's mine, the colliery manager requested the police authority to provide a standing garrison in the colliery premises to protect the safety men, without whom the mine would be flooded. The police authority took the view that adequate protection could be given by the use of mobile patrols. The police authority agreed, however, to garrison the colliery in return for payment at specified rates. The manager, having the necessary authority from his directors, signed the police requisition form setting out the terms of the agreement. When the strike was over, the appellant company refused to pay, contending that there was no binding contract, the police authority having given no consideration, it being their public duty to protect property. The police authority brought this action to recover payment according to the agreed rates.
HELD, by VISCOUNT CAVE, L.C., VISCOUNT FINLAY and LORD SHAW (LORD CARSON and LORD BLANESBURGH dissenting), that the police authority gave consideration to support the promise to pay for the maintenance of the garrison, for this measure was more than the police authority considered necessary for the adequate protection of the colliery.

VISCOUNT FINLAY. It appears to me that there in nothing in the first point made for the colliery owners that there was no consideration for the promise. It is clear that there was abundant consideration. The police authorities thought that it would be best to give protection by means of a flying column of police, but the colliery owners wanted the 'garrison' and promised to pay for it if it was sent.

NOTE
In *Harris* v. *Sheffield United Football Club* [1987] it became necessary to have a substantial police presence at football matches in order to maintain law and order and to protect life and property. The Court of Appeal decided that the extent of police services provided was beyond that which the club could expect to be provided without payment. In *Glasbrook*, the problem was very different from that in *Harris* v. *Sheffield United*. In the former, it arose out of an industrial dispute: in the latter, it arose because the defendant club had voluntarily chosen to invite a large number of people to watch football matches.

Ward v. Byham
[1956] 1 W.L.R. 496; [1956] 2 All E.R. 318
Court of Appeal
An unmarried man and woman who lived together between 1949 and 1956 were the parents of a girl born in 1950. In 1954 the man turned the woman out of the house and put the child into the care of a neighbour, paying the neighbour £1 a week. The woman subsequently obtained a post as housekeeper to a man who was prepared to take the child into his house. The woman then wrote to the child's father, asking for the child and £1 a week for her maintenance. He replied, 'I am prepared to let you have (the child) and pay you up to £1 per week allowance for her providing you can prove that she will be well looked after and happy and also that she is allowed to decide for herself whether or not she wishes to come and live with you.' The child was then taken to live with her mother and the father paid the agreed allowance until seven months later, when the woman married the man whose housekeeper she had

become. The father refused to make further payments after the woman had married and the woman brought this action, contending that the father was bound by his promise to pay £1 a week for the child's maintenance. She was met with the defence that she had given no consideration for the father's promise: that as the mother of an illegitimate child, she is bound to maintain it.

HELD, by DENNING, MORRIS and PARKER, L.JJ., there was consideration moving from the mother to support the father's promise.

DENNING, L.J. I approach this case on the footing that, in looking after the child, the mother is only doing what she is legally bound to do. Even so, I think that there was sufficient consideration to support the promise. I have always thought that a promise to perform an existing duty, or the performance of it, should be regarded as good consideration, because it is a benefit to the person to whom it is given. Take this very case. It is as much a benefit for the father to have the child looked after by the mother as by a neighbour. If he gets the benefit for which he stipulated he ought to honour his promise, and he ought not to avoid it by saying that the mother was herself under a duty to maintain the child.

I regard the father's promise in this case as what is sometimes called a unilateral contract, a promise in return for an act, a promise by the father to pay £1 a week in return for the mother's looking after the child. Once the mother embarked on the task of looking after the child, there was a binding contract. So long as she looked after the child, she would be entitled to £1 a week.

MORRIS, L.J. It seems to me that the father was saying, in effect: Irrespective of what may be the strict legal position, what I am asking is that you shall prove that the child will be well looked after and happy, and also that you must agree that the child is to be allowed to decide for herself whether or not she wishes to come and live with you. If those conditions were fulfilled the father was agreeable to pay. On those terms, which in fact became operative, the father agreed to pay £1 a week. In my judgment, there was ample consideration there to be found for his promise, which I think was binding.

Bainbridge v. Firmstone

[1838] 8 Ad. & El. 743
Court of Queen's Bench

Assumpsit. The plaintiff, at the request of the defendant, consented to allow the defendant to weigh his (the plaintiff's) two valuable boilers, taking a promise from the defendant that he would, within a reasonable time, return the plaintiff's boilers in the same perfect and complete condition. The defendant took the boilers to pieces and refused to put them together again. The plaintiff sued in assumpsit and the defendant contended that the plaintiff had given no consideration to support the promise to return the boilers in complete condition.

HELD, by LORD DENMAN, C.J., PATTESON, WILLIAMS and COLERIDGE, JJ., that the plaintiff's consent given at the defendant's request amounted to consideration. The defendant's promise was binding.

LORD DENMAN, C.J. The defendant had some reason for wishing to weigh the boilers; and he could do so only by obtaining permission from the plaintiff, which he did obtain by promising to return them in good condition. We need not enquire what benefit he expected to derive. The plaintiff might have given or refused leave.

PATTESON, J. The consideration is, that the plaintiff, at the defendant's request, had consented to allow the defendant to weigh the boilers. I suppose the defendant thought he had some benefit; at any rate, there is a detriment to the plaintiff from his parting with the possession for even so short a time.

NOTE
Consideration need not be adequate. Provided that there is no allegation of fraud, the courts will not interfere with a bargain freely struck merely because the consideration moving from one party appears to be of lesser value than that moving from the other.

Roscorla v. Thomas

[1842] 3 Q.B. 234

Court of Queen's Bench

The defendant sold a horse to the plaintiff and then promised the plaintiff that the horse was sound and free from vice. The plaintiff brought this action in assumpsit for the breach of warranty of the soundness of the horse, contending that an executed consideration with a request, express or implied, will support a promise. The defendant contended that the warranty, being given after the sale, was made without consideration.

HELD, by LORD DENMAN, C.J., PATTESON, WILLIAMS and WIGHTMAN JJ., the plaintiff gave no consideration for the defendant's warranty which was, accordingly, not binding.

LORD DENMAN, C.J., delivered the judgment of the court: It may be taken as a general rule, subject to exceptions not applicable to this case, that the promise must be co-extensive with the consideration. In the present case, the only promise that would result from the consideration, as stated, and be co-extensive with it, would be to deliver the horse upon request. The precedent sale, without warranty, though at the request of the defendant imposes no other duty or obligation upon him. It is clear, therefore, that the consideration stated would not raise an implied promise by the defendant that the horse was sound or free from vice.

But the promise in the present case must be taken to be, as in fact it was, express: and the question is, whether that fact will warrant the extension of the promise beyond that which would be implied by law; and whether the consideration, though unsufficient to raise an implied promise will nevertheless support an express one. And we think it will not.

NOTE

Consideration must not be past. Thus, where one party has already performed an act before the other party's promise was made, that act cannot constitute consideration to support that promise.

In *Re McArdle* [1951] M and his wife (Mrs M) lived in a house which was part of the estate of M's father, in which M and his brothers and sister were beneficially interested expectant on the death of their mother, who was tenant for life. Mrs M paid £488 for improvements and decoration of the house. The then beneficiaries all signed a document addressed to Mrs M which provided that: 'In consideration of your carrying out certain alterations and improvements to the house, we the beneficiaries hereby agree that the executors shall repay you from the said estate when so distributed the sum of £488 in settlement of the amount spent on such improvements.' The tenant for life died and Mrs M claimed payment of £488. She failed in her claim before the Court of Appeal because the work was done before the promise to pay was made. The consideration for the promise was past and the promise was, therefore, not binding.

Section 27(1) of the Bills of Exchange Act 1882 provides that 'Valuable consideration for a bill may be constituted by: (a) Any consideration to support a simple contract; (b) An antecedent debt or liability. Such debt or liability is deemed valuable consideration whether the bill is payable on demand or at a future time.'

This is the only exception to the common law rule of past consideration. There are, however, two apparent exceptions as follows: First, where the plaintiff performs a service at the request of the defendant and the defendant subsequently makes a promise to pay. In this case an action will be allowed on the defendant's promise. In *Re Casey's Patents* [1892] Bowen, L.J. said, 'The fact of a past service raises an implication that at the time it was rendered it was to be paid for, and, if it was a service which was to be paid for, when you get in a subsequent document a promise to pay, that promise may be treated either as an admission which evidences or as a positive bargain which fixes the amount of that reasonable remuneration on the faith of which the service was originally rendered'. This dictum was applied by the Privy Council in *Pao On* v. *Lau Yiu Long* [1980]. The second apparent exception to the rule of past consideration is provided by the Limitation Act 1980. Section 29(5) of the Act provides that where any right of action has accrued to recover any debt or other liquidated pecuniary claim and the person liable or accountable for the claim acknowledges the claim or makes any payment in respect of it the right shall be treated as having accrued on and not before the date of the acknowledgement or payment. If this provision is applied to a statute-barred debt, the debtor's subsequent promise to pay would be actionable because of the fresh accrual of the creditor's right of action.

4. Express terms of contract

> *It was said* by HOLT, C.J., *and repeated in* Heilbut, Symons & Co. v. Buckleton: *'An affirmation at the time of the sale is a warranty, provided it appear on evidence to be so intended.'* But that word 'intended' has given rise to difficulties. I endeavoured to explain in Oscar Chess, Ltd. v. Williams *that the question whether a warranty was intended depends on the conduct of the parties, on their words and behaviour, rather than on their thoughts. If an intelligent bystander would reasonably infer that a warranty was intended, that will suffice:* Dick Bentley Productions v. Harold Smith, per LORD DENNING, M.R.

Summary

1. The objective test of intention

The express terms of a contract comprise those statements made by the parties to one another during negotiations leading to a contract and by which they intended to be bound. To discover intention, the court will apply an objective test. The court will seek an answer to the question, 'What would a reasonable man understand to be the intention of the parties, having regard to all the circumstances': see, e.g., *Dick Bentley Productions* v. *Harold Smith* [1965].

2. The parol evidence rule

The general rule is that, where the parties have entered into a written contract, parol evidence or other extrinsic evidence, cannot be admitted to add to or to vary the written instrument. This general rule is subject to many exceptions; see, e.g., *Evans* v. *Merzario* [1976}.

3. Conditions and warranties

If a promisor breaks a condition in any respect, the other party may elect to treat himself as discharged from future obligations and to sue immediately for damages. If a promisor breaks a warranty in any respect, the promisee's remedy will be in damages only. For a discussion of the question whether a term is a condition or a warranty, see *Hong Kong Fir Shipping Co.* v. *Kawasaki Kisen Kaisha* [1962] in 18, and *The Mihalis Angelos* [1970]. For conditions and warranties in sale of goods contracts, see Sale of Goods Act 1979, ss. 11 and 61.

4. Express terms

The question whether a warranty was intended depends on the conduct of the parties, on their words and behaviour, rather than on their thoughts: *Dick Bentley Production* v. *Harold Smith* [1965].

Where, after oral negotiations, a contract is put into writing, and some previous oral statement is not included in the instrument, it tends to show that the oral statement is not a term of the contract: *Routledge* v. *McKay* [1954] in 8. But, when other factors are taken into account, the result may be different, for example, in *Evans* v. *Merzario* [1976], a previous oral statement was held to be binding even though it was not included in the written document.

Where any condition was particularly onerous or unusual and would not be generally known to the other party, that condition will not be enforceable unless it can be shown that it had been fairly and reasonably brought to the other party's attention: *Interfoto Picture Library* v. *Stiletto Visual Programmes* [1988]. See also *Davies & Co.* v. *William Old* [1969].

Where it is claimed that the terms of a principal contract are added to or varied by a collateral contract, any such collateral contract will be viewed with suspicion and must be strictly proved: *Heilbut, Symons* v. *Buckleton* [1913].

Dick Bentley Productions, Ltd v. Harold Smith (Motors), Ltd.

[1965] W.L.R. 623; [1965] 2 All E.R. 65
Court of Appeal

The second plaintiff, Mr. Bentley, told Mr. Smith of the defendant company that he was on the look-out for a well vetted Bentley car. Mr. Smith subsequently obtained a Bentley car and Mr. Bentley went to see it. Mr. Smith told Mr. Bentley that the car had done twenty thousand miles only since the fitting of a new engine and gear box. (The speedometer showed twenty thousand miles.) later that day Mr. Bentley took his wife to see the car and Mr. Smith repeated his statement. Mr. Bentley took the car out for a run and then bought it for £1,850, paying by cheque. The car was a disappointment to Mr. Bentley and it soon became clear that the car had done more than twenty thousand miles since the change of engine and gear box. The action for £400 damages was brought against the defendant company in the county court, the plaintiffs alleging fraud. The defendants counterclaimed for £190 for work carried out on the car. His Honour JUDGE HERBERT held that there was a breach of warranty, awarding £400 damages to the plaintiffs and £77 to the defendants on their counterclaim. The defendants appealed, contending that their representation did not amount to a warranty.

HELD, by LORD DENNING, M.R., DANCKWERTS and SOLOMON, L.JJ., that the representation was a warranty.

LORD DENNING, M.R. The first point is whether this representation, namely that the car had done twenty thousand miles only since it had been fitted with a replacement engine and gearbox, was an innocent misrepresentation (which does not give rise to damages), or whether it was a warranty. It was said by HOLT, C.J., and repeated in *Heilbut, Symons & Co.* v. *Buckleton*: 'An affirmation at the time of the sale is a warranty, provided it appear on evidence to be so intended.' But that word 'intended' has given rise to difficulties. I endeavoured to explain in *Oscar Chess, Ltd.* v. *Williams* that the question whether a warranty was intended depends on the conduct of the parties, on their words and behaviour, rather than on their thoughts. If an intelligent bystander, would reasonably infer that a warranty was intended, that will suffice. What conduct, then? What words and behaviour, lead to the inference of a warranty?

Looking at the cases once more, as we have done so often, it seems to me that if a representation is made in the course of dealings for a contract for the very purpose of inducing the other party to act on it, and it actually induces him to act on it by entering into the contract, that is prima facie ground for inferring that the representation was intended as a warranty. It is not necessary to speak of it as being collateral. Suffice it that the representation was intended to be acted on and was in fact acted on. But the maker of the representation can rebut this inference if he can show that it really was an innocent misrepresentation, in that he was in fact innocent of fault in making it, and that it would not be reasonable in the circumstances for him to be bound by it. In the *Oscar Chess* case the inference was rebutted. There a man had bought a secondhand car and received with it a log-book, which stated the year of the car, 1948. He afterwards resold the car. When he resold it he simply repeated what was in the log-book and passed it onto the buyer. He honestly believed on reasonable grounds that it was true. He was completely innocent of any fault. There was no warranty by him but only an innocent misrepresentation. Whereas in the present case it is very different. The inference is not rebutted. Here we have a dealer, Mr. Smith, who was in a position to know, or at least to find out, the history of the car. He could get it by writing to the makers. He did not do so. Indeed it was done later. When the history of this car was examined, his statement turned out to be quite wrong. He ought to have known better. There was no reasonable foundation for it.

(HIS LORDSHIP summarised the history of the car, and continued:) The county court judge found that the representations were not dishonest. Mr. Smith was not found guilty of fraud. But he made the statement as to twenty thousand miles without any foundation. And the judge was well justified in finding that there was a warranty. He said: 'I have no hesitation that as a matter of law the statement was a warranty. Mr. Smith stated a fact that should be within his own knowledge. He had jumped to a conclusion and stated it as a fact. A fact that a buyer would act on.' That is ample foundation for the inference of a warranty.

J Evans & Son (Portsmouth) Ltd. v. Andrea Merzario Ltd.

[1976] 2 All E.R. 930
Court of Appeal, Civil Division

The plaintiffs were importers of machines from Italy. Since 1959 they had contracted under standard form conditions with the defendants to make arrangements for the carriage of the machines to England. The defendant forwarding agents proposed in 1967 to change to container transportation. The defendants gave an oral assurance to the plaintiffs that their machines to be transported in containers would be shipped under deck. On the faith of this assurance the plaintiffs accepted the defendant's new quotations for container transportation of their machines. Owing to an oversight on the part of the defendants, a container with one of the plaintiff's machines inside was shipped on deck and the machine was lost overboard. By the standard form conditions of contract between the parties, (*a*) the defendants were free in respect of the means and procedures to be followed in the transportation and (*b*) they were exempted from liability for loss or damage to the goods in certain circumstances. The plaintiffs claimed damages for loss of the machine, alleging that the carriage of the container on deck was a breach of contract. KERR, J. dismissed the action on the grounds that the oral statement made by the defendants as to carriage below deck did not constitute a binding collateral warranty and therefore did not prevail over the standard form conditions The plaintiffs appealed.

HELD, by LORD DENNING, M.R. ROSKILL and GEOFFREY LANE, L.JJ., that the oral statement made by the defendants was a binding warranty which was to be treated as overriding the printed conditions and the plaintiffs were entitled to damages for its breach. The statement was (*per* LORD DENNING, M.R.) binding as a collateral warranty because it induced the plaintiff to enter the contract. Alternatively (*per* ROSKILL and GEOFFREY LANE, L.JJ.) the oral statement constituted an express term of the contract of carriage which overrode the printed conditions because these would have made the oral assurance illusory.

LORD DENNING, M.R. So, after these containers fell off the deck into the water, the English importers, through their insurers, claimed damages against the forwarding agents. In reply the forwarding agent said there was no contractual promise that the goods would be carried under deck. Alternatively, if there was, they relied on the printed terms and conditions. The judge held there was no contractual promise that these containers should be carried under deck. He thought that, in order to be binding, the initial conversation ought to be contemporaneous, and that here it was too remote in point of time from the actual transport; furthermore that, viewed objectively, it should not be considered binding. The judge quoted largely from the well-known case of *Heilbut, Symons & Co* v. *Buckleton* in which it was held that a person is not liable in damages for an innocent misrepresentation; and that the courts should be slow to hold that there was a collateral contract. I must say that much of what was said in that case is entirely out of date. We now have the Misrepresentation Act 1967 under which damages can be obtained for innocent misrepresentation of fact. This Act does not apply here because we are concerned with an assurance as to the future, we have a different approach nowadays to collateral contracts. When a person gives a promise, or an assurance to another, intending that he should act on it by entering into a contract, and he does act on it by entering into the contract, we hold that it is binding: see *Dick Bentley Productions* v. *Harold Smith (Motors) Ltd.* That case was concerned with a representation of fact, but it applies also to promises as to the future. Following this approach it seems to me plain that Mr Spano gave an oral promise or assurance that the goods in this new container traffic would be carried under deck. He made the promise in order to induce Mr. Leonard to agree to the goods being carried in containers. On the faith of it, Mr Leonard accepted the quotations and gave orders for transport. In those circumstances the promise was binding. There was a breach of that promise and the forwarding agents are liable – unless they can rely on the printed conditions.

It is common ground that the course of dealing was on the standard conditions of the forwarding trade. Those conditions were relied on. Condition 4 which gives the company complete freedom in respect of means, route and procedure in the transportation of goods. Condition 11 which says that the company will not be liable for loss or damage unless it occurs whilst in their actual custody and then only if they are guilty of wilful neglect or default. Condition 13 which says that their liability shall not exceed the value of the goods or a sum at the rate of £50 per ton of 20cwt. The question is whether the company can rely on those exemptions. I do not think so. The cases are numerous in which oral promises have been held binding in spite of written exempting conditions; such as *Couchman* v. *Hill, Harling* v. *Eddy, City & Westminster Properties (1934) Ltd* v. *Mudd*.

ROSKILL, L.J. I unreservedly accept counsel for the defendants' submission that one must not look alone or two isolated answers given in evidence; one should look at the totality of the evidence. When one does that, one finds first, as I have already mentioned, that these parties had been doing business in transporting goods from Milan to England for some time before; secondly, that transportation of goods from Milan to England was always done on trailers which were always under deck; thirdly, that the defendants wanted a change in the practice – they wanted containers used instead of trailers; fourthly, that the plaintiffs were only willing to agree to that change if they were promised by the defendant that those containers would be shipped under deck, and would not have agreed to the change but for that promise. The defendants gave such a promise which to my mind against this background plainly amounted to an enforceable contractual promise. In those circumstances it seems to me that the contract was this: 'if we continue to give you our business, you will ensure that those goods in containers are shipped under deck', and the defendants agreed that this would be so. Thus there was a breach of that contract by the defendants when this container was shipped on deck; and it seems to me to be plain that the damage which the plaintiffs suffered resulted from that breach. That being the position, I think that counsel for the defendant's first argument fails.

Maredelanto Compania Naviera S.A. v. Bergbau-Handel G.m.b.H. The Mihalis Angelos

[1970] 1 Q.B. 164; [1970] 3 All E.R. 125
Court of Appeal, Civil Division
Clause 1 of a charterparty dated 25th May 1965, provided that the vessel Mihalis Angelos 'now trading and expected ready to load under this charter about 1st July 1965' (the expected readiness clause) would proceed to Haiphong and there load a cargo of apatite. Clause II provided that 'Should the vessel not be ready to

load . . . on or before 20th July 1965 Charterers have the option of cancelling this contract . . .' The vessel arrived at Hong Kong on 23rd June but did not complete discharging until 23rd July. The ship needed a special survey which took two days. It would have taken a further two days to sail to Haiphong. Meanwhile, events for which the charterers were not responsible prevented the transport of apatite to Haiphong. On 17th July, the charterers informed the owners that they cancelled the charter on the grounds of *force majeure*. The owners accepted that information as a repudiation of contract and on 29th July contracted to sell the vessel in Hong Kong. It was found in arbitration that the charter was not frustated before 17th July, but that, at the date of the charter, the owners could not reasonably have estimated that the vessel would arrive at Haiphong 'about 1st July 1965'. It was further found that, had the vessel ultimately proceeded to Haiphong, the charterers would have cancelled in any event on the grounds of delay.

HELD, by LORD DENNING, M.R., EDMUND DAVIES and MEGAW, L.JJ. (*i*) The expected readiness clause was properly to be described as a condition of the charterparty and an assurance by the owners that they honestly expected on reasonable grounds that the vessel would be ready to load on 1st July; accordingly, when the charterers discovered the falsity of the owners' assurance, they were entitled to terminate the charter forthwith. (*ii*) LORD DENNING dissenting: The charterers could not have relied on cl. 11 to justify cancellation of the charterparty on 17th July because on a strict construction of the clause, the option to cancel was not exercisable before 20th July although it had become apparent before that date that the vessel would not be ready to load on 20th July. (*iii*) Even if the charterers had not been entitled by virtue of cl. 1 to terminate the charter on 17th July, the owners would have been awarded nominal damages only for the repudiation by the charterers, because the charterers would later have become entitled under cl. 11 to cancel, and would have cancelled, for delay, which contingency had to be taken into account as reducing the owners' loss.

MEGAW, L.J. It is not disputed that when charter includes the words: 'expected ready to load . . . ' a contractual obligation on the part of the shipowner is involved. It is not an obligation that the vessel will be ready to load on the stated date, nor about the stated date, if the date is qualified, as here, by 'about.' The owner is not in breach merely because the vessel arrives much later, or indeed does not arrive at all. The owner is not undertaking that there will be no unexpected delay, but he is undertaking that he honestly and on reasonable grounds believes, at the time of the contract, that the date named is the date when the vessel will be ready to load. Therefore in order to establish a breach of that obligation the charterer has the burden of showing that the owner's contractually expressed expectation was not his honest expectation or, at the least, that the owner did not have reasonable grounds for it.

In my judgment such a term in a charterparty ought to be regarded as being a condition of the contract, in the old sense of the word 'condition', *i.e.* that when it has been broken, the other party can, if he wishes, by intimation to the party in breach, elect to be released from performance of his further obligations under the contract; and that he can validly do so without having to establish that, on the facts of the particular case, the breach has produced serious consequences which can be treated as 'going to the root of the contract' or as being 'fundamental', or whatever other metaphor may be thought appropriate for a frustration case.

Interfoto Picture Library Ltd. v. Stiletto Visual Programmes Ltd.

[1988] 1 All E.R. 348
Court of Appeal, Civil Division

The defendants were an advertising agency and the plaintiffs ran a library of photographic transparencies. They had not dealt with each other before. The defendants needed period photographs of the 1950's for a presentation. On 5 March 1984, they telephoned the plaintiffs, enquiring whether they had any photographs of that period which might be suitable. On the same day, the plaintiffs dispatched to the defendants 47 transparencies packed in a jiffy bag together with a delivery note. At the top right hand corner of the delivery note the date for return was clearly stated as 19 March. Across the bottom of this document, under the heading 'Conditions' fairly prominently printed in capitals, there were nine conditions, printed in four colums. Condition no. 2 in the first column read as follows: 'All transparencies must be returned to us within 14 days from the date of delivery. A holding fee of £5.00

plus VAT per day will be charged for each transparency which is retained by you longer than the said period of 14 days save where a copyright licence is granted or we agree a longer period in writing with you.' The defendants accepted delivery of the transparencies but did not use them for their presentation. They put the transparencies aside and forgot them. They were not returned until 2 April. The plaintiffs sent an invoice for the holding charge calculated at £5 per transparency per day from 19 March to 2 April, total £3,783.50. The defendants refused to pay and the plaintiffs sued for the amount invoiced. Judgment was given for the plaintiffs and the defendants appealed to the Court of Appeal.

HELD, by DILLON and BINGHAM, L.J.J., that, where a condition in a contract was particularly onerous or unusual, and would not be generally known to the other party, the party seeking to enforce that condition had to show that it had been fairly and reasonably brought to the attention of the other party. Condition 2 was an unreasonable and extortionate clause which the plaintiffs had not bought to the attention of the defendants and therefore it did not become part of the contract. The defendants were ordered to pay a sum which the trial judge would have awarded on a *quantum meruit* on his alternative findings, i.e., the reasonaable charge of £3.50 per transparency per week for the retention of the transparencies beyond a reasonable period fixed as 14 days from the date of their receipt by the defendants.

DILLON, L.J., There was never any oral discussion of terms between the parties before the contract was made. In particular there was no discussion whatever of terms in the original telephone conversation when Mr Beeching made his preliminary inquiry. The question is therefore whether condition 2 was sufficiently brought to the defendant's attention to make it a term of the contract which was only concluded after the defendants had received, and must have known that they had received the transparencies *and* the delivery note.

This sort of question was posed, in relation to printed conditions, in the ticket cases, such as *Parker* v. *South Eastern Rly. Co.* in the last century. At that stage the printed conditions were looked at as a whole and the question considered by the courts was whether the printed conditions as a whole had been sufficiently drawn to a customer's attention to make the whole set of conditions part of the contract; if so the customer was bound by the printed conditions even though he never read them.

More recently the question has been discussed whether it is enough to look at a set of printed conditions as a whole. When for instance one condition in a set is particularly onerous does something special need to be done to draw customers' attention to that particular condition? In an obiter dictum in *J. Spurling Ltd.* v. *Bradshaw* Denning, L.J. stated:

'Some clauses which I have seen would need to be printed in red ink on the face of the document with a red hand pointing to it before the notice could be held to be sufficient.'

Then in *Thornton* v. *Shoe Lane Parking Ltd.* both Lord Denning, M.R. and Megaw, L.J. held as one of their grounds of decision, as I read their judgments, that where a condition is particularly onerous or unusual the party seeking to enforce it must show that the condition, or an unusual condition of that particular nature, was fairly brought to the notice of the other party. Lord Denning restated and applied what he had said in the *Spurling* case, and held that the court should not hold any man bound by such condition unless it was drawn to his attention in the most explicit way.

NOTE
In the *Interfoto* case, the Court of Appeal applied *Parker* v. *South Eastern Rly. Co.* and *Thornton* v. *Shoe Lane Parking*. These were both exclusion clause cases. In *Interfoto*, counsel for the plaintiffs failed in his submission that what was said in *Thornton* must be limited to exemption clauses and, in particular, to exemption clauses which would deprive the part on whom they are imposed of statutory rights.

Davies & Co. (Shopfitters) Ltd. v. William Old, Ltd.

[1969] Sol. Jo. 262
Queen's Bench Division
In April 1964 the defendants entered into a building contract with employers (not parties to this action) in the R.I.B.A. standard

main form. In May 1965 the architect, as agent for the employers, invited the plaintiffs to tender for certain sub-contract works and the plaintiffs tendered. The architect, as agent for the employers, gave written instructions to the defendants to enter into a sub-contract with the nominated sub-contractors, *i.e.* the plaintiffs, for the shopfitting works. The defendants thereupon sent to the plaintiffs their own standard form of order, instructing them to carry out the sub-contract works according to their tender. At the bottom of the order form it was stated that the order was subject to the conditions overleaf. On the other side of the form were certain conditions, number 8 of which provided that the contractor (*i.e.* the defendants) should from time to time apply under the main contract for certificates of payment to include the amount for the sub-contract work, but that the main contractor would be under no liability to pay the sub-contractor for this work until it had been approved and paid for by the employer under the main contract. The plaintiffs accepted the order by letter dated 15th June and work was done for which the plaintiffs brought this action against the main contractor contending that the failure to pay the sum certified was a breach of the sub-contract.

HELD, by BLAIN, J., that the conditions on the back of the order form were binding and that the main contractor was under no liability to pay the sub-contractor until he (the main contractor) was paid by the employers.

BLAIN, J. The problem is to define the sub-contract itself. The architect was not the agent of the defendants in nominating the sub-contractors. The tender when received by the architect constituted an offer by the plaintiffs. The defendants had done what was reasonable to bring the conditions or the existence of the conditions to the notice of the plaintiffs. The general principle is that in case of doubt and where words in a contract are in conflict, greater force is to be given to words selected by the parties to express their intent than to general words of a pro forma nature, but for that doctrine to apply the words selected by the parties had to be selected to show a mutual intent. The conditions in the order varied or modified the terms of the tender, and so the order was not an unqualified acceptance of the offer comprised in the tender but was a counter-offer. That was accepted by the plaintiffs' letter dated 15 June either by itself or together with the carrying out of the work. The conditions were incorporated in the sub-contract and since the defendants had not received from the employer the sums claimed, they were not liable to pay them to the plaintiffs.

Heilbut, Symons & Co. v. Buckleton

[1913] A.C. 30; [1911–13] All E.R. Rep 83
House of Lords
The defendants underwrote a large number of shares in Filisola Rubber and Produce Estates, Ltd. The defendants instructed one Johnston, their Liverpool manager, to obtain applications for shares. The plaintiff telephoned Johnston, saying, 'I understand that you are bringing out a rubber company'. To which Johnston replied, 'We are'. The plaintiff then asked Johnston whether he had any prospectuses, and he replied that he had not. The plaintiff then asked 'if it was all right', to which Johnston replied, 'We are bringing it out'. The plaintiff then said 'That is good enough for me'. As a result of this telephone conversation a large number of shares were allotted to the plaintiff. At this time there was a rubber boom and the Filisola shares were at a premium. Shortly afterwards, the shares fell in value. The plaintiff brought this action for fraudulent misrepresentation by the defendants through their agent Johnston, and, alternatively, damages for breach of warranty that the Filisola company was a rubber company whose main object was to produce rubber. At Liverpool Assizes before LUSH, J., and a special jury, the jury found that there was no fraud: but that the company could not properly be described as a rubber company and that the defendants or Johnston or both had warranted that the company was a rubber company. The jury based its findings as to warranty on the telephone conversation, there being no other evidence, The defendants appealed without success to the Court of Appeal. The defendants then appealed to the House of Lords.
HELD, by VISCOUNT HALDANE, L.C., LORD ATKINSON and LORD MOULTON, that Johnston's telephone statements did not amount to a warranty. There was, accordingly, no breach of contract.

LORD MOULTON. It is not contested that the only company referred to was the Filisola Rubber and Produce Estates, Limited, or that the reply of Mr. Johnston to the plaintiff's question over the telephone was a representation by the defendants that the company was a 'rubber company,' whatever may be the meaning of that phrase; nor is there any controversy as to the legal nature of that which the plaintiff must establish. He must show a warranty, *i.e.*, a contract collateral to the main contract to take the shares, whereby the defendants in consideration of the plaintiffs taking the shares promised that the company itself was a rubber company. The question in issue is whether there was any evidence that such a contract was made between the parties.

It is evident, both on principle and on authority, that there may be a contract the consideration for which is the making of some other contract. 'If you will make such and such a contract I will give you one hundred pounds,' is in every sense of the word a complete legal contract. It is collateral to the main contract, but each has an independent existence, and they do not differ in respect of their possessing to the full the character and status of a contract. But such collateral contracts must from their very nature be rare. The effect of a collateral contract such as that which I have instanced would be to increase the consideration of the main contract by £100, and the more natural and usual way of carrying this out would be by so modifying the main contract and not by executing a concurrent and collateral contract. Such collateral contracts, the sole effect of which is to vary or add to the terms of the principal contract, are therefore viewed with suspicion by the law. They must be proved strictly. Not only the terms of such contracts but the existence of an *animus contrahendi* on the part of the parties to them must be clearly shewn. Any laxity on these points would enable parties to escape from the full performance of the obligations of contracts unquestionably entered into by them and more especially would have the effect of lessening the authority of written contracts by making it possible to vary them by suggesting the existence of verbal collateral agreements relating to the same subject-matter

There is in the present case an entire absence of any evidence to support the existence of such a collateral contract. The statement of Mr. Johnston in answer to plaintiff's question was beyond controversy a mere statement of fact, for it was in reply to a question for information and nothing more. No doubt it was a representation as to fact, and indeed it was the actual representation upon which the main case of the plaintiff rested. It was this representation which he alleged to have been false and fraudulent and which he alleged induced him to enter into the contracts and to take the shares. There is no suggestion throughout the whole of his evidence that he regarded it as anything but a representation. Neither the plaintiff nor the defendants were asked any question or gave any evidence tending to shew the existence of any *animus contrahendi* other than as regards the main contracts. The whole case for the existence of a collateral contract therefore rests on the mere fact that the statement was made as to the character of the company, and if this is to be treated as evidence sufficient to establish the existence of a collateral contract of the kind alleged the same result must follow with regard to any other statement relating to the subject-matter of a contract made by a contracting party prior to its execution. This would negative entirely the firmly established rule that an innocent representation gives no right to damages.

Sale Of Goods Act 1979

11. When condition to be treated as warranty.
(1) Subsection (2) to (4) and (7) below do not apply to Scotland and subsection (5) below applies only to Scotland.

(2) Where a contract of sale is subject to a condition to be fulfilled by the seller, the buyer may waive the condition, or may elect to treat the breach of the condition as a breach of warranty and not as a ground for treating the contract as repudiated.

(3) Whether a stipulation in a contract of sale is a condition, the breach of which may give rise to a right to treat the contract as repudiated, or a warranty, the breach of which may give rise to a claim for damages but not to a right to reject the goods and treat the contract as repudiated, depends in each case on the construction of the contract; and a stipulation may be a condition, though called a warranty in the contract.

(4) Where a contract of sale is not severable and the buyer has accepted the goods or part of them, the breach of a condition to be fulfilled by the seller can only be treated as a breach of warranty, and not as a ground for rejecting the goods and treating the

contract as repudiated, unless there is an express or implied term of the contract to that effect.

(5) In Scotland, failure by the seller to perform any material part of a contract of sale is a breach of contract, which entitles the buyer either within a reasonable time after delivery to reject the goods and treat the contract as repudiated, or to retain the goods and treat the failure to perform such material part as a breach which may give rise to a claim for compensation or damages.

(6) Nothing in this section affects a condition or warranty whose fulfilment is excused by law by reason of impossibility or otherwise.

(7) Paragraph 2 of Schedule 1 below applies in relation to a contract made before 22 April 1967 or (in the application of this Act to Northern Ireland) 28 July 1967.

60. Rights etc. enforceable by action
Where a right, duty or liability is declared by this Act, it may (unless otherwise provided by this Act) be enforced by action.

61. Interpretation
(1)   In this Act, unless the context or subject matter otherwise requires, —
  "delivery" means voluntary transfer of possession from one person to another;
  "buyer" means a person who buys or agrees to buy goods;
  "contract of sale" includes an agreement to sell as well as a sale;
  "goods" includes all personal chattels other than things in action and money, and in Scotland all corporeal moveables except money; and in particular "goods" includes emblements, industrial growing crops, and things attached to or forming part of the land which are agreed to be severed before sale or under the contract of sale;
  "quality", in relation to goods, includes their state or condition;
  "sale" includes a bargain and sale as well as a sale and delivery;
  "seller" means a person who sells or agrees to sell goods;
  "specific goods" means goods identified and agreed on at the time a contract of sale is made;
  "warranty" (as regards England and Wales and Northern Ireland) means an agreement with reference to goods which are the subject of a contract of sale, but collateral to the main purpose of

such contract, the breach of which gives rise to a claim for damages, but not to a right to reject the goods and treat the contract as repudiated.

5. Implied terms of contract

> *An implied warranty, . . . as distinguished from an express contract or express warranty, really is in every instance founded on the presumed intention of the parties and upon reason:* The Moorcock, per BOWEN, L.J.

Summary

There are two kinds of implied contract term, namely, terms implied in fact and terms implied in law.

1. Terms implied in fact

A term may be implied to give effect to the presumed but unexpressed intentions of the parties. It is presumed, e.g., that contracting parties intended to contract with reference to custom and usage. The intention of the parties may sometimes be gathered from their conduct. Where the parties have not expressed some term which is necessary in order to give the contract business efficacy, that term may be implied: *The Moorcock* [1889]; *Gardner* v. *Coutts & Co.* [1967]; *Liverpool City Council* v. *Irwin* [1976]. A term will not be implied on the basis of reasonableness.

2. Terms implied in law

Certain terms have long been implied at common law in contracts of employment, sale of goods and contracts for work and materials. Many of these implied terms are now given statutory force, the best-known example being the implied terms provided for in ss. 12 to 15 of the Sale of Goods Act 1979.

The Moorcock

[1889] P.D. 64; [1886–90] All E.R. Rep. 530
Court of Appeal
There was a contract between the defendants, who owned a Thames side wharf and jetty, and the plaintiffs that the plaintiffs' vessel *Moorcock* should be unloaded and reloaded at the defendants' wharf. The *Moorcock* was, accordingly, moored alongside the wharf but, as the tide fell, she took to the ground and sustained damage on account of the unevenness of the river bed at that place. The plaintiffs brought this action for damages for breach of contract.
HELD, by LORD ESHER, M.R., BOWEN and FRY, L.JJ., that there was an implied term in the contract that the defendants would take reasonable care to see that the berth was safe: that both parties must have known at the time of the agreement that if the ground were not safe the ship would be endangered when the tide ebbed: that there was a breach of the implied term.

LORD ESHER, M.R. A vessel like the *Moorcock* cannot be moored to this wharf without being obliged to take the ground at low water on every tide. That is a necessary part of the transaction. Therefore, we have got this, that, in order that the defendants' wharf may be used so that they may earn profit, a vessel like the *Moorcock* must be moored to their wharf under such circumstances that she must take the ground at every tide. The defendants are always on the spot, and if anything happens in front of their wharf they know or have the means of finding out. They, in making such agreements as they made with the *Moorcock*, may be doing so with foreign vessels, or with British vessels coming from abroad or other parts of the United Kingdom. A ship's officers have no reasonable means of discovering what the bottom of the river is until they are moored at the wharf and their ship has taken the ground.

What, then, is the reasonable implication from such a contract for such a purpose among people of this class? In my opinion honest business could not be carried on between people in the position of the plaintiffs and the defendants unless you imply that the defendants have undertaken some duty to the plaintiffs with regard to the bottom of the river at this place. . . . .

Whether they can see the actual bottom of the river or not at low water is not, to my mind, the least material. Supposing at low water there were two feet of water always over the mud; it makes no difference that they cannot see the bottom. They can feel for the bottom by sounding, or in some similar way, and find out its condition with as much accuracy, nay, with a great deal more accuracy, than if they could see it with their own eyes. When it is so easy to do this, and when, in order to earn money, business requires a ship to be brought alongside their wharf, in my opinion honesty of business requires, and we are bound to imply it, that the defendants have undertaken to see that the bottom of the river is reasonably fit for the purpose, or that they ought, at all events, to take reasonable care to find out whether the bottom of the river is reasonably fit for the purpose for which they agree that their jetty should be used, and then, if not either procure it to be made reasonably fit for the purpose, or inform the persons with whom they have contracted that it is not so. That, I think, is the least that can be implied as the defendants' duty, . . .I myself have not the least doubt in making this implication as part of the contract.

BOWEN, L.J. An implied warranty, as distinguished from an express contract or express warranty, really is in every instance founded on the presumed intention of the parties and upon reason. It is the implication which the law draws from what must obviously have been the intention of the parties, an implication which the law draws with the object of giving efficacy to the transaction and preventing such a failure of consideration as cannot have been within the contemplation of either of the parties. I believe that if one were to take all the instances, which are many, of implied warranties and covenants in law which occur in the earlier cases which deal with real property, passing through the instances which relate to the warranties of title and of quality, and the cases of executory contracts of sale and other classes of implied warranties like the implied authority of an agent to make contracts, it will be seen that in all these cases the law is raising an implication from the presumed intentions of the parties with the object of giving the transaction such efficacy as both parties must have intended it should have. If that is so, the reasonable implication which the law draws must differ according to the circumstances of the various transactions, and in business transactions what the law desires to effect by the implication is to give such business efficacy to the transaction as must have been intended by both parties; not to impose on one side all the perils of the transaction, or to emancipate one side from all the burdens, but to make each party promise in law as much, at all events, as it must have been in the contemplation of both parties that he should be responsible for.

NOTE

The principle in *The Moorcock* that the implication must be necessary to give the contract business efficacy has been re-inforced by subsequent cases in which the strictness of application has been emphasised. In particular, see *Reigate* v. *Union Manufacturing Co. Ltd* [1918], in which Scrutton L.J. said: 'The first thing is to see what the parties have expressed in the contract; and then an implied term is not to be added because the court thinks it would have been reasonable to have inserted it in the contract. A term can only be implied if it is necessary in the business sense to give efficacy to the contract; that is, it is such a term that it can be confidently said that if at the time the contract was being negotiated someone had said to the parties, 'What will happen in such a case', they would both have replied, 'Of course, so and so will happen; we did not trouble to say that; it is too clear'. Unless the court comes to some such conclusion as that, it ought not to imply a term which the parties themselves have not expressed.' In *Shirlaw* v. *Southern Foundries* [1939], MacKinnon L.J. said: 'Prima facie that which in any contract is left to be implied and need not be expressed is something so obvious that it goes without saying. Thus, if, while the parties were making their bargain, an officious bystander were to suggest some express provision for it in their agreement, they would testily suppress him with a common: 'Oh, of course!' At least it is true, I think, that, if a term were never to be implied by a judge unless it could pass that test, he could not be held to be wrong.' The presumption against the implication of unexpressed terms was further emphasised by the House of Lords in *Luxor* v. *Cooper* [1941].

Gardner v. Coutts & Co.

[1968] 1 W.L.R. 173; [1967] 2 All E.R. 1064
Chancery Division
One Jekyll owned two adjoining properties, known respectively as Munstead Wood and Munstead Hut. In July 1948 he conveyed Munstead Wood and, on the day following the conveyance, he entered into a written agreement giving the purchaser and her successors the first refusal of the fee simple of the adjoining

property 'In the event of Mr Jekyll at any time during his lifetime desiring to sell his freehold property known as Munstead Hut. . .' In January 1963 Jekyll conveyed Munstead Hut to his sister for no consideration by way of gift, without previously offering the property to the plaintiff, who was the successor of the purchaser from him of Munstead Wood. In March 1965 Jekyll died and probate was granted to the defendants who were named his executors. The plaintiff brought this action for damages for breach of the agreement of July 1948.

HELD, by CROSS, J., that there was an implied term in the agreement giving first refusal to the original purchaser of Munstead Wood that Jekyll would not give the property away without offering it first to the plaintiff. The plaintiff was entitled to damages against Jekyll's estate.

CROSS, J. In *Reigate* v. *Union Manufacturing Co. (Ramsbottom), Ltd.,* SCRUTTON, L.J., said: 'The first thing is to see what the parties have expressed in the contract; and then an implied term is not to be added because the court thinks it would have been reasonable to have inserted it in the contract. A term can only be implied if it is necessary in the business sense to give efficacy to the contract; that is, if it is such a term that it can confidently be said that if at the time the contract was being negotiated someone had said to the parties, "What will happen in such a case", they would both have replied, "Of course, so and so will happen; we did not trouble to say that; it is too clear". Unless the court comes to some such conclusion as that, it ought not to imply a term which the parties themselves have not expressed.'

In the case of *Shirlaw* v. *Southern Foundries (1926), Ltd. and Federated Foundries, Ltd.,* MACKINNON, L.J., said: 'I recognise that the right or duty of a court to find the existence of an implied term or implied terms in a written contract is a matter to be exercised with care, and a court is too often invited to do so upon vague and uncertain grounds. Too often, also, such an invitation is backed by the citation of a sentence or two from the judgment of BOWEN, L.J., in *The Moorcock*. They are sentences from an extempore judgment as sound and sensible as are all the utterances of that great judge, but I fancy that he would have been rather surprised if he could have foreseen that these general remarks of his would come to be a favourite citation of a supposed principle of law, and I even think that he might sympathise with the occasional impatience of his successors when *The Moorcock* is so often flashed before them in that guise. For my part, I think that there is a test that may be at least as useful as such generalities. If I may quote from an essay which I wrote some years ago, I then said: 'Prima facie that which in any contract is left to be implied and need not be expressed is something so obvious that it goes without saying.' Thus, if, while the parties were making their bargain, an officious bystander were to suggest some express provision for it in their agreement, they would testily suppress him with a common: 'Oh, of course!'

Liverpool City Council v. Irwin

[1977] A.C. 235; [1976] 2 W.L.R. 562; [1976] 2 All E.R. 39
House of Lords

The City Council was owner of a tower block containing some 70 units. Access was provided by a common staircase and two electrically controlled lifts. Tenants were provided with an internal rubbish chute. In July 1966 the defendants (husband and wife) became tenants of a maisonette in the block. There was no formal lease or tenancy agreement. There was, however, a document described as 'Conditions of Tenancy' consisting entirely of obligations on the tenants: there was no mention of any obligations on the Council. In the course of time, the condition of the block deteriorated badly, partly because of vandalism and partly because of the lack of co-operation on the part of tenants. The defects included the following: (*a*) continual failure of the lifts, (*b*) lack of proper lighting on the stairs and (*c*) blockage of the rubbish chutes. The defendants protested by refusing to pay rent to the Council. The Council sought an order for possession of the defendants' maisonette and the defendants counterclaimed alleging a breach on the part of the Council of its implied covenant for the defendants' quiet enjoyment of the property. The trial judge granted an order for possession to the Council but awarded £10 damages against it for breach of the implied covenant to repair the common parts. The Council appealed to the Court of Appeal where it was held that there was no implied covenant on the part of the council to repair the common parts. The defendants appealed to the House of Lords, contending that there was an implied obligation on the Council to keep the staircase and corridors of the block in repair and the lights in working order, and that the Coucil was in breach of it.

HELD, by LORD WILBERFORCE, LORD CROSS, LORD SALMON, LORD EDMUND-DAVIES and LORD FRASER, that, since it was necessary for the tenants occupying the block to use the stairs, lifts and rubbish chutes, the appropriate easements (or rights in the nature of easements) would be implied into the tenancy agreements. Further, the subject-matter of the agreement, and the nature of the relationship of landlord and tenant of necessity required the implication of a contractual obligation on the part of the Council with regard to those easements. But the obligation was not absolute, being subject to the tenants' own responsibilities, and was related to what reasonable tenants should do for themselves. The obligation to be implied was, therefore, to take reasonable care to maintain the common parts in a state of reasonable repair and efficiency. It had not been shown that the Council had not taken such reasonable care and, accordingly, the appeal should be dismissed.

LORD WILBERFORCE. There can be no doubt that there must be implied (*i*) an easement for the tenants and their licensees to use the stairs, (*ii*) a right in the nature of an easement to use the lifts and (*iii*) an easement to use the rubbish chutes.

But are these easements to be accompanied by any obligation on the landlord, and what obligation? There seem to be two alternatives. The first, for which the corporation contends, is for an easement coupled with no legal obligation, except such as may arise under the Occupiers' Liability Act 1957 as regards the safety of those using the facilities, and possibly such other liability as might exist under the ordinary law of tort. The alternative is for easements coupled with some obligation on the part of the landlords as regards the maintenance of the subject of them, so that they are available for use.

My Lords, in order to be able to choose between these, it is necessary to define what test is to be applied, and I do not find this difficult. In my opinion such obligation should be read into the contract as the nature of the contract itself implicitly requires, no more, no less; a test in other words of necessity. The relationship accepted by the corporation is that of landlord and tenant; the tenant accepts obligations accordingly, in relation, inter alia, to the stairs, the lifts and the chutes. All these are not just facilities, or

conveniences provided at discretion; they are essentials of the
tenancy without which life in the dwellings, as a tenant, is not
possible. To leave the landlord free of contractual obligation as
regards these matters, and subject only to administrative or
political pressure, is, in my opinion, totally inconsistent with the
nature of this relationship. The subject-matter of the lease
(high-rise blocks) and the relationship created by the tenancy
demands, or its nature, some contractual obligation on the
landlord.

NOTE
The principle in *Liverpool C.C.* v. *Irwin* was applied in *Sim* v.
Rotherham Metropolitan Borough Council [1986], in which it was
decided that there was an implied term in teachers' contracts of
employment that teachers were bound to cover for absent col-
leagues when requested to do so by the head teacher.

Sale of Goods Act 1979
Sections 12, 13, 14, 15 and 55

12.   Implied terms about title etc.
(1) In a contract of sale, other than one to which subsection (3)
below applies, there is an implied condition on the part of the
seller that in the case of a sale he has a right to sell the goods, and
in the case of an agreement to sell he will have a right at the time
when the property is to pass.

(2) In a contract of sale, other than one to which subsection (3)
below applies, there is also an implied warranty that—

   (*a*) the goods are free, and will remain free until the time when
the property is to pass, from any charge or encumbrance not
disclosed or known to the buyer before the contract is made, and
   (*b*) the buyer will enjoy quiet possession of the goods except so
far as it may be disturbed by the owner or other person entitled to
the benefit of any charge or encumbrance so disclosed or known.

(3) This subsection applies to a contract of sale in the case of
which there appears from the contract or is to be inferred from its

circumstances an intention that the seller should transfer only such title as he or a third person may have.

(4) In a contract to which subsection (3) above applies there is an implied warranty that all charges or encumbrances known to the seller and not known to the buyer have been disclosed to the buyer before the contract is made.

(5) In a contract to which subsection (3) above applies there is also an implied warranty that none of the following will disturb the buyer's quiet possession of the goods, namely—

(*a*) the seller;

(*b*) in a case where the parties to the contract intend that the seller should transfer only such title as a third person may have, that person;

(*c*) anyone claiming through or under the seller or that third person otherwise than under a charge or encumbrance disclosed or known to the buyer before the contract is made.

(6) Paragraph 3 of Schedule 1 below applies in relation to a contract made before 18 May 1973.

13. Sale by description

(1) Where there is a contract for the sale of goods by description, there is an implied condition that the goods will correspond with the description.

(2) If the sale is by sample as well as by description it is not sufficient that the bulk of the goods corresponds with the sample if the goods do not also correspond with the description.

(3) A sale of goods is not prevented from being a sale by description by reason only that, being exposed for sale or hire, they are selected by the buyer.

(4) Paragraph 4 of Schedule 1 below applies in relation to a contract made before 18 May 1973.

14. Implied terms about quality or fitness

(1) Except as provided by this section and section 15 below and subject to any other enactment, there is no implied condition or warranty about the quality or fitness for any particular purpose of goods supplied under a contract of sale.

(2) Where the seller sells goods in the course of a business, there is an implied condition that the goods supplied under the contract are of merchantable quality, except that there is no such condition—

(*a*) as regards defects specifically drawn to the buyer's attention before the contract is made; or

(*b*) if the buyer examines the goods before the contract is made, as regards defects which that examination ought to reveal.

(3) Where the seller sells goods in the course of a business and the buyer, expressly or by implication, makes known—

(*a*) to the seller, or

(*b*) where the purchase price or part of it is payable by instalments and the goods were previously sold by a credit-broker to the seller, to that credit-broker,

any particular purpose for which the goods are being bought, there is an implied condition that the goods supplied under the contract are reasonably fit for that purpose, whether or not that is a purpose for which such goods are commonly supplied, except where the circumstances show that the buyer does not rely, or that it is unreasonable for him to rely, on the skill or judgment of the seller or credit-broker.

(4) An implied condition or warranty about quality or fitness for a particular purpose may be annexed to a contract of sale by usage.

(5) The preceding provisions of this section apply to a sale by a person who in the course of a business is acting as agent for another as they apply to a sale by a principal in the course of a business, except where that other is not selling in the course of a business and either the buyer knows that fact or reasonable steps

are taken to bring it to the notice of the buyer before the contract is made.

(6) Goods of any kind are of merchantable quality within the meaning of subsection (2) above if they are as fit for the purpose or purposes for which goods of that kind are commonly bought as it is reasonable to expect having regard to any description applied to them, the price (if relevant) and all the other relevant circumstances.

(7) Paragraph 5 of Schedule 1 below applies in relation to a contract made on or after 18 May 1973 and before the appointed day, and paragraph 6 in relation to one made before 18 May 1973.

(8) In subsection (7) above and paragraph 5 of Schedule 1 below references to the appointed day are to the day appointed for the purposes of those provisions by an order of the Secretary of State made by statutory instrument.

15. Sale by sample
(1) A contract of sale is a contract for sale by sample where there is an express or implied term to that effect in the contract.

(2) In the case of a contract for sale by sample there is an implied condition –

(a) that the bulk will correspond with the sample in quality;

(b) that the buyer will have a reasonable opportunity of comparing the bulk with the sample;

(c) that the goods will be free from any defect, rendering them unmerchantable, which would not be apparent on reasonable examination of the sample.

(3) In subsection (2)(c) above 'unmerchantable' is to be construed in accordance with section 14(6) above.

Supplementary

55. Exclusion of implied terms. 1977 c. 50.
(1) Where a right, duty or liability would arise under a contract of

sale of goods by implication of law, it may (subject to the Unfair Contract Terms Act 1977) by negatived or varied by express agreement, or by the course of dealing between the parties, or by such usage as binds both parties to the contract.

(2) An express condition or warranty does not negative a condition or warranty implied by this Act unless inconsistent with it.

6. Exclusion Clauses

> *All I say is that [the exempting condition] is so wide and so
> destructive of rights that the court should not rule any man
> bound by it unless it is drawn to his attention in the most
> explicit way. It is an instance of what I had in mind in*
> Spurling v. Bradshaw. *In order to give sufficient notice, it
> would need to be printed in red ink with a red hand
> pointing to it, or something equally startling:* Thornton v.
> Shoe Lane Parking, per LORD DENNING, M.R.
>
> *Whether a clause limiting liability is effective or not is a
> question of construction of that clause in the context of the
> contract as a whole:* Ailsa Craig Fishing Co. v. Malvern
> Fishing Co., per LORD WILBERFORCE.

Summary

1. Definition

An exclusion clause is one which excludes or modifies an
obligation, whether primary, general secondary or anticipatory
secondary, that would otherwise arise under the contract by
implication of law: *Photo Production Ltd* v. *Securicor Transport Ltd.*
[1980] *per* Lord Diplock.

2. Is the exclusion clause a term of the contract?

The party seeking to enforce the exclusion must be able to show
that the exclusion was fairly and reasonably brought to the

attention of the other party: *Parker* v. *South Eastern Rail Co.* [1877]; *Thornton* v. *Shoe Lane Parking* [1971]; *McCutcheon* v. *MacBrayne Ltd* [1964].

Where an overriding oral assurance has been given in conflict with printed clauses, breach of that oral assurance will disentitle the contract-breaker from reliance on any of those printed clauses: *Evans Ltd* v. *Merzario Ltd* [1976]. (*See* Chapter 4.)

3. Construction of an exclusion clause

The question whether, and to what extent, an exclusion clause is to be applied to *any* breach of contract, is a matter of construction of the contract as a whole: *Suisse Atlantique* case.

A clause which purports to exclude liability totally is likely to be construed more restrictively than one which seeks merely to modify or limit the secondary obligation to pay damages: *Ailsa Craig Fishing Co.* v. *Malvern Fishing Co.* [1983].

Where an exclusion is unclear or ambiguous the court will construe the clause so as to give effect to what must have been the intention of the parties at the time of the contract. This will often result in the construction of the clause contra proferentem: *Ailsa Craig Fishing Co.* v. *Malvern Fishing Co.* [1983]; *Photo Production Ltd.* v. *Securicor Transport Ltd.* [1980].

The court is not entitled to reject an exclusion clause, however unreasonable the court itself may think it is, if the words are clear and fairly susceptible of one meaning only: the *Photo Production* case.

4. The effect of the Unfair Contract Terms Act 1977

The 1977 Act imposes limits on the extent to which liability for breach of contract or negligence can be avoided by means of exclusion clauses. To this end the Act provides that certain specified kinds of exclusion are to have no effect and that certain other specified kinds of exclusion are effective only in so far as they satisfy the requirements of reasonableness: *Thompson* v. *Lohan* [1987]; *Phillips Products* v. *Hyland* [1987], decided 1974. Part I of the Unfair Contract Terms Act 1977 is set out below.

5. Disclaimers and the requirement of reasonableness

Where a disclaimer is effective to prevent a duty of care arising, the disclaimer is subject to the requirement of reasonableness under s. 2(2) of the 1977 Act: Harris v. Wyre Forest District Council [1988]; *Smith* v. *Eric S. Bush* [1989].

Parker v. South Eastern Rail Co.

[1877] 2 C.P.D. 416; [1874–80] All E.R. Rep. 166
Court of Appeal

The plaintiff handed a parcel into a cloakroom at a railway station. The plaintiff paid 2*d.* and received a ticket on whose face appeared the words: 'See back.' On the back of the ticket was a condition in the following words: 'This company will not be responsible for articles left by passengers at the station, unless the same be duly registered, for which a charge of 2*d.* per article will be made, and a ticket given in exchange; and no article will be given up without the production of the ticket, or satisfactory evidence of the ownership being adduced. A charge of 1*d.* per diem in addition will be made on all articles left in the cloakroom for a longer period than twenty-four hours. The company will not be responsible for any package exceeding the value of £10.' The parcel handed in by the plaintiff exceeded £10 in value. The plaintiff did not know that the ticket contained any conditions; he thought it was merely a receipt for the money he had paid. The plaintiff's parcel was lost because of the carelessness of the servants of the railway company and the plaintiff brought this action claiming damages. The railway company contended that the plaintiff was bound by the condition contained in the ticket and that, accordingly, the company was not responsible for the loss of the package, its value being above £10.

HELD, by MELLISH and BAGGALLAY, L.JJ., that the jury's attention had not been directed at the trial to the question whether the defendants had done what was reasonably sufficient to give the plaintiff notice of the condition on the back of the ticket.

MELLISH, L.J. I am of opinion that the proper direction to the jury in these cases is that, if the person receiving the ticket did not see or know that there was any writing on the ticket, he is not bound by the conditions; that if he knew there was writing, and knew or believed that the writing contained conditions, then he is bound by the conditions; that if he knew there was writing on the ticket, but did not know or believe that the writing contained conditions, nevertheless he would be bound if the delivering of the ticket to him in such a manner that he could see there was writing on it, was, in the opinion of the jury, reasonable notice that the writing contained conditions.

NOTE

In *Thornton* v. *Shoe Lane Parking* [1971] Lord Denning summarised the principle in the judgment of Mellish. L.J., in the *Parker* case as follows: 'The customer is bound by the exempting condition if he knows that the ticket is issued subject to it; or, if the company did what was reasonably sufficient to give him notice of it'.

Thornton v. Shoe Lane Parking Ltd

[1971] 2 Q.B. 163; [1971] 1 All E.R. 686
Court of Appeal, Civil Division

The plaintiff drove his car to a multi-storey automatic car park which he had never used before. On the outside of the park there was a notice under the heading 'Shoe Lane Parking.' The notice contained the parking charges and other information. At the end of the notice were the following words. 'ALL CARS PARKED AT OWNERS RISK.' When the plaintiff reached the entrance there was no one in attendance. A traffic light turned from red to green and a ticket was pushed out from a machine. The plaintiff took the ticket and drove into the car park. He left his car there and returned for it several hours later. As he attempted to put his belongings into his car the plaintiff was severely injured. The trial judge held that the accident was half the fault of Shoe Lane Parking Ltd., and half the fault of the plaintiff himself. The defendants claimed that they were exempted from liability by certain conditions which had become part of the contract. The defendants claimed that the ticket was a contractual document and that it incorporated a condition exempting them from liability. On the ticket appeared the words: 'This ticket is issued subject to the conditions of issue as displayed on the premises.' The plaintiff, who had looked at the ticket to see the time printed on it, had not read the other printing on the ticket. He did not read the words which provided that the ticket was issued subject to conditions. Nor did he read the conditions which were set out on a pillar opposite the ticket machine. One of these conditions provided that the defendants would not be responsible or liable for injury to the customer occurring when the customer's motor vehicle was in the parking building. It was this condition which the defendants relied upon.

HELD, by LORD DENNING, M.R., MEGAW, L.J., and SIR

GORDON WILLMER, that the exempting condition did not bind the plaintiff because he did not know of it and the defendants did not do what was reasonably sufficient to give him notice of it.

LORD DENNING, M.R. Assuming that an automatic machine is a booking clerk in disguise, so that the old-fashioned ticket cases still apply to it, we then have to go back to the three questions put by MELLISH, L.J. in *Parker* v. *South Eastern Railway Co.,* subject to this qualification: MELLISH, L.J., used the word 'conditions' in the plural, whereas it would be more apt to use the word 'condition' in the singular, as indeed MELLISH, L.J., himself did at the end of his judgment. After all, the only condition that matters for this purpose is the exempting condition. It is no use telling the customer that the ticket is issued subject to some 'conditions' or other, without more; for he may reasonably regard 'conditions' in general as merely regulatory, and not as taking away his rights, unless the exempting condition is drawn specifically to his attention. Telescoping the three questions, they come to this: the customer is bound by the exempting condition if he knows that the ticket is issued subject to it; or, if the company did what was reasonably sufficient to give him notice of it. Counsel for the defendants admitted here that the defendants did not do what was reasonably sufficient to give the plaintiff notice of the exempting condition. That admission was properly made. I do not pause to enquire whether the exempting condition is void for unreasonableness. All I say is that it is so wide and so destructive of rights that the court should not rule any man bound by it unless it is drawn to his attention in the most explicit way. It is an instance of what I had in mind in *Spurling* v. *Bradshaw*. In order to give sufficient notice, it would need to be printed in red ink with a red hand pointing to it, or something equally startling.

However, although reasonable notice of it was not given, counsel for the defendants said that this case came within the second question propounded by MELLISH, L.J., namely that the plaintiff 'knew or believed that the writing contained conditions.' There was no finding to that effect. The burden was on the defendants to prove and they did not do so. Certainly there was no evidence that the plaintiff knew of this exempting condition. He is not, therefore, bound by it.

MEGAW, L.J. I agree with Lord Denning, M.R., that the question here is of the particular condition on which the defendants seek to rely, and not of the conditions in general. When the conditions sought to be attached all constitute, in Lord Dunedin's words in *Hood* v. *Anchor Line (Henderson Bros.) Ltd.*, 'the sort of restriction ... that is usual', it may not be necessary for a defendant to prove more than that the intention to attach *some* conditions has been fairly brought to the notice of the other party. But at least where the particular condition relied on involves a sort of restriction that is not shown to be usual in that class of contract, a defendant must show that his intention to attach an unusual condition *of that particular nature* was fairly brought to the notice of the other party. How much is required as being, in the words of Mellish, L.J. [in *Parker* v. *South Eastern Rly. Co.*, 'reasonably sufficient to give the plaintiff notice of the condition', depends on the nature of the restrictive condition.

In the present case what has to be sought in answer to the third question is whether the defendant company did what was reasonable fairly to bring to the notice of the plaintiff, at or before the time when the contract was made, the existence of this particular condition. This condition is that part of the clause – a few words embedded in a lengthy clause – which Lord Denning, M.R. has read, by which, in the midst of provisions as to damage to property, the defendants sought to exempt themselves from liability for any personal injury suffered by the customer while he was on their premises. Be it noted that such a condition is one which involves the abrogation of the right given to a person such as the plaintiff by statute, the Occupiers' Liability Act 1957. True, it is open under that Act for the occupier of property by a contractual term to exclude that liability. In my view, however, before it can be said that a condition of that sort, restrictive of statutory rights, has been fairly brought to the notice of a party to a contract there must be some clear indication which would lead an ordinary sensible person to realise, at or before the time of making the contract, that a term of that sort, relating to personal injury, was sought to be included. I certainly would not accept that the position has been reached today in which it is to be assumed as a matter of general knowledge, custom, practice, or whatever is the phrase that is chosen to describe it, that when one is invited to go on the property of another for such purposes as garaging a car, a contractual term is normally included that if one suffers any injury on those premises as a result of negligence on the part of the occupiers of the premises they shall not be liable.

McCutcheon v. David MacBrayne Ltd.

[1964] 1 W.L.R. 125; [1964] 1 All E.R. 304

House of Lords

McCutcheon asked his brother-in-law, one McSporran, to have his car sent by the MacBrayne shipping company from the Isle of Islay to the Scottish mainland. McSporran went to the company where he was quoted the freight for the return journey of the car. He paid the money, for which he was given a receipt, and he delivered the car. The car was then shipped on a vessel which subsequently sank owing to the negligent navigation of the company's employees. The car was lost. Now the company's practice was to require consignors to sign risk notes which included elaborate printed conditions, one of which excluded liability for negligence. On the occasion in question, McSporran was not asked to sign such a document. McSporran had previously consigned goods to the mainland and had sometimes signed a risk note and sometimes not. He had never read the printed conditions on the risk note. McCutcheon had consigned goods on four previous occasions and each time he had signed a risk note, but he had never read the conditions and did not know what they contained. The company contended that McCutcheon was bound by the conditions in the risk note by reason of the previous transactions of McCutcheon and his agent, McSporran. McCutcheon contended that he was not bound by the conditions. He sought to recover the value of the car on the ground of the negligence of the company's employees. The trial judge found in his favour but this decision was reversed by Scottish Court of Session. On appeal to the House of Lords on the question whether the exclusion clause in the conditions was part of the contract:

HELD, by LORD REID, LORD HODSON, LORD GUEST, LORD DEVLIN and LORD PEARCE, that the contract of carriage was an oral contract, not incorporating the conditions and that, accordingly, the exclusion clause did not operate to exclude the company's liability in negligence.

LORD REID. The respondents contend that, by reason of the

knowledge thus gained by the appellant and his agent in these previous transactions, the appellant is bound by their conditions. But this case differs essentially from the ticket cases. There, the carrier in making the contract hands over a document containing or referring to conditions which he intends to be part of the contract. So if the consignor or passenger, when accepting the document, knows or ought as a reasonable man to know that that is the carrier's intention, he can hardly deny that the conditions are part of the contract, or claim, in the absence of special circumstances, to be in a better position than he would be if he had read the document. But here, in making the contract neither party referred to, or indeed had in mind, any additional terms, and the contract was complete and fully effective without any additional terms. If it could be said that when making the contract Mr McSporran knew that the respondents always required a risk note to be signed and knew that the purser was simply forgetting to put it before him for signature, then it might be said that neither he nor his principal could take advantage of the error of the other party of which he was aware. But counsel frankly admitted that he could not put his case as high as that. The only other ground on which it would seem possible to import these conditions is that based on a course of dealing. If two parties have made a series of similar contracts each containing certain conditions, and then they make another without expressly referring to those conditions it may be that those conditions ought to be implied. If the officious bystander had asked them whether they had intended to leave out the conditions this time, both must, as honest men, have said 'of course not.' But again the facts here will not support that ground. According to Mr. McSporran, there had been no consistent course of dealing; sometimes he was asked to sign and sometimes not. And, moreover, he did not know what the conditions were. This time he was offered an oral contract without any reference to conditions, and he accepted the offer in good faith.

Suisse Atlantique Société D'Armament Maritime S.A. v. N.V. Rotterdamsche Kolen Centrale

[1967] 1 A.C. 361; [1966] 2 All E.R. 61

House of Lords

The plaintiffs agreed by a charterparty dated December 1956 to charter their ship to the defendants for carrying coal from the U.S.A. to Europe. The charter was expressed to remain in force for two years' consecutive voyages between U.S.A. and Europe. By the charter, if the vessel was delayed beyond the agreed loading time, the defendants were to pay $1,000 a day demurrage. Similarly, demurrage was payable if the vessel was delayed beyond the agreed unloading time. In September 1957 the plaintiffs regarded themselves as being entitled to treat the charterparty as repudiated by reason of the defendants' delays in loading and unloading the vessel. The defendants did not accept this intention, and it was agreed (without prejudice to this dispute) that the charterparty should be continued. From October 1957 the vessel made eight round voyages under the charter. It was contended by the plaintiffs that each round voyage ought reasonably to have been completed in thirty to thirty-seven days, including loading and unloading. On this basis, the eight voyages which took 511 days should have been completed in 240 or 296 days. From this the plaintiffs argued that they had lost the freights which they would have earned on nine or, alternatively, six voyages. The plaintiffs claimed damages of $773,000 or alternatively, $476,000. The basis of the plaintiff's contention was that the charterparty gave them a contractual right to the number of voyages which would be made in the event of both parties carrying out their contractual obligations, and that their claim was not limited to their entitlement to demurrage. The plaintiffs (who failed before MOCATTA, J., and before the Court of Appeal) appealed to the House of Lords. An argument, not advanced in the courts below, was put forward, namely, that if the delays were such as to entitle the appellants to treat the charterparty as repudiated, the demurrage clauses did not apply, and that the appellants would then be entitled to recover their full loss on basis they claimed.

HELD, by VISCOUNT DILHORNE, LORD REID, LORD HODSON, LORD UPJOHN and LORD WILBERFORCE, that the appellants, having elected in 1957 to affirm the charterparty, were bound by its provisions, including the demurrage clauses, which operated as agreed damages. The appellants were not entitled to damages for loss of freight, nor would they be so entitled if the respondent's breaches were deliberate. The question whether an exceptions clause was applicable where there was a fundamental breach was one of the true construction of the contract.

VISCOUNT DILHORNE. I think that the legal position was most clearly and accurately stated by PEARSON, L.J. in *U.G.S. Finance Ltd.* v. *National Mortgage Bank of Greece and National Bank of Greece, S.A.* He said: 'As to the question of "fundamental breach", I think there is a rule of construction that normally an exception or exclusion clause or similar provision in a contract should be construed as not applying to a situation created by a fundamental breach of contract. This is not an independent rule of law imposed by the court on the parties willy-nilly in disregard of their contractual intention. On the contrary it is a rule of construction based on the presumed intention of the contracting parties. It involves the implication of a term to give to the contract that business efficacy which the parties as reasonable men must have intended it to have. This rule of construction is not new in principle but it has become prominent in recent years in consequence of the tendency to have standard forms of contract containing exceptions clauses drawn in extravagantly wide terms, which would produce absurd results if applied literally.' Although the terms are sometimes used as if their meaning was the same, a fundamental breach differs from a breach of a fundamental term. In *Smeaton Hanscomb & Co., Ltd.* v. *Sasso*
on I. Setty, Son & Co. (No. 1), DEVLIN, J., said that he thought a fundamental term was 'something which underlies the whole contract so that, if it is not complied with, the performance becomes something totally different from that which the contract contemplates.'

In this case, the appellants contend that the totality of the delays in loading and unloading constituted a fundamental breach entitling them to treat the contract as repudiated and the demurrage provisions as not applying. They do not suggest that, at any particular time between Oct. 16, 1957, and the end of the charter, the delays were such as to constitute a fundamental breach. If there was a time after Oct. 16, 1957, and before the end of the charterparty when they could have said that it had been repudiated by the respondents, they did not do so. They had full knowledge of the delays as they occurred, and, if there was a time when they could have elected to treat the charterparty as at an end, they must, in my view, be taken to have elected to waive the repudiation and to have affirmed the charterparty. If they affirmed the charterparty, then they were bound by its provisions in respect of events occurring after the affirmation, but waiver of the breach does not mean waiver of the right to damages for that breach: *Hain S.S. Co., Ltd.* v. *Tate & Lyle Ltd.*: *Chandris* v. *Isbrandtsen Moller Co., Inc.*, per

DEVLIN, J. In this connexion there are, I think, certain passages in *Charterhouse Credit Co., Ltd.* v. *Tolly* which require reconsideration. If the appellants were entitled to treat the charterparty as repudiated, the demurrage provisions could be held not to apply only if they were provisions limiting the respondents' liability and, on construction of the contract as a whole, they were held not to apply in relation to the fundamental breach.

In my view, the demurrage provisions are not to be regarded as limiting the respondents' liability. In the circumstances of this case, it may be that the amount of the demurrage payments bears little relation to the loss which the appellants claim to have suffered. In *Chandris* v. *Isbrandtsen Moller Co., Inc.,* DEVLIN, J., said that the sum produced by demurrage 'is generally less than damages for detention' and that a demurrage clause is merely a clause providing for liquidated damages for a certain type of breach. While it may be that a demurrage clause in a particular case is so drawn that, on its proper construction, it is to be treated as imposing a limitation on liability, in this case the demurrage provisions are, in my opinion, clearly provisions for the payment of agreed damages. If the clauses imposed a limit on liability, then the appellants would have to prove the actual loss they sustained and if it was less than the amount stated they would recover only the loss which they proved. Here the parties agreed that demurrage at a daily rate should be paid in respect of the detention of the vessel and, on proof of breach of the charterparty by detention, the appellants are entitled to the demurrage payments without having to prove the loss which they suffered in consequence. In my view, the appellants cannot avoid the operation of these provisions and cannot recover more than the agreed damages for the detention of their vessel: see *Cellulose Acetate Silk Co., Ltd.* v. *Widnes Foundry (1925), Ltd.*

NOTE
The question whether an exclusion clause would apply when there was fundamental breach, or any other breach, depends on the construction of the contract as a whole. This is the principle in the *Suisse Atlantique* case but which the Court of Appeal declined to apply, thus causing the House of Lords to reaffirm the principle in *Photo Production* v. *Securicor Transport* [1980]. In *Photo Production*, the Court of Appeal held that fundamental breach on

the part of Securicor precluded their relying on the exclusion clause. This decision was reversed on appeal to the House of Lords.

Photo Production Ltd. v. Securicor Transport Ltd.

[1980] A.C. 827; [1980] 1 All E.R. 556

House of Lords

The plaintiffs owned a factory. They contracted with Securicor, the defendants, for the provision of security services including night patrols. While carrying out a night patrol at the factory, a Securicor employee deliberately lit a small fire which then got out of control. The plaintiff's factory and stock were completely destroyed. The total value was £615,000. The plaintiffs brought this action, contending that Securicor were vicariously liable for the act of their employee. Securicor pleaded an exclusion clause in the contract which provided as follows: 'under no circumstances' were Securicor to be 'responsible for any injurious act or default by any employee ... unless such act or default could have been foreseen and avoided by the exercise of due diligence on the part of [Securicor] as his employer; nor, in any event, [were Securicor to] be held responsible for . . . any loss suffered by the [plaintiffs] through . . . fire or any cause except so far as such loss [was] solely attributable to the negligence of [Securicor] employees acting within the course of their employment . . .' Negligence was not alleged against Securicor for employing the employee in question. At first instance it was held that Securicor could rely on the exclusion clause. The Court of Appeal reversed this decision on the ground that there had been a fundamental breach of contract by Securicor which precluded reliance on the clause. Securicor appealed to the House of Lords.

HELD, by LORD WILBERFORCE, LORD DIPLOCK, LORD SALMON, LORD KEITH of KINKEL and LORD SCARMAN, that there was no rule of law by which an exclusion clause could be eliminated from consideration when there was a breach of contract (fundamental or otherwise) or by which an exclusion could be deprived of effect regardless of the terms of the contract, because the parties were free to agree to whatever exclusion or modification of their obligation as they chose. The question whether an exclusion clause applied when there was any breach of contract (fundamental or otherwise) turned on the construction of the whole contract, including the exclusion clause. The exclusion clause was clear and unambiguous and protected Securicor from liability.

LORD DIPLOCK. Leaving aside those comparatively rare cases in which the court is able to enforce a primary obligation by decreeing specific performance of it, breaches of primary obligations give rise to substituted secondary obligations on the part of the party in default, and, in some cases, may entitle the other party to be relieved from further performance of his own primary obligations. These secondary obligations of the contract breaker and any concomitant relief of the other party from his own primary obligations also arise by implication of law, generally common law, but sometimes statute, as in the case of codifying statutes passed at the turn of the century, notably the *Sale of Goods Act,* 1893. The contract, however, is just as much the source of secondary obligations as it is of primary obligations; and like primary obligations that are implied by law secondary obligations too can be modified by agreement between the parties, although, for reasons to be mentioned later, they cannot, in my view, be totally excluded. In the instant case, the only secondary obligations and concomittant reliefs that are applicable arise by implication of the common law as modified by the express words of the contract.

Every failure to perform a primary obligation is a breach of contract. The secondary obligation on the part of the contract breaker to which it gives rise by implication of the common law is to pay monetary compensation to the other party for the loss sustained by him in consequence of the breach; but, with two exceptions, the primary obligations of both parties so far as they have not yet been fully performed remain unchanged. This secondary obligation to pay compensation (damages) for non-performance of primary obligations I will call the 'general secondary obligation'. It applies in the cases of the two exceptions as well.

The exceptions are: (1) where the event resulting from the failure by one party to perform a primary obligation has the effect of depriving the other party of substantially the whole benefit which it was the intention of the parties that he should obtain from the contract, the party not in default may elect to put an end to all primary obligations of both parties remaining unperformed (if the expression 'fundamental breach' is to be retained, it should in the interests of clarity, be confined to this exception); (2) where the contracting parties have agreed, whether by express words or by implication of law, that *any* failure by one party to perform a particular primary obligation ('condition' in the nomenclature of the *Sale of Goods Act*, 1893), irrespective of the gravity of the event that has in fact resulted from the breach, shall entitle the other party to elect to put an end to all primary obligation of both parties remaining unperformed (in the interests of clarity, the nomenclature of the *Sale of Goods Act*, 1893, 'breach of condition', should be reserved for this exception).

Where such an election is made (a) there is substituted by implication of law for the primary obligations of the party in default which remain unperformed a secondary obligation to pay monetary compensation to the other party for the loss sustained by him in consequence of their non-performance in the future and (b) the unperformed primary obligations of that other party are discharged. This secondary obligation is additional to the general secondary obligation; I will call it 'the anticipatory secondary obligation.'

In cases falling within the first exception, fundamental breach, the anticipatory secondary obligation arises under contracts of all kinds by implication of the common law, except to the extent that it is excluded or modified by the express words of the contract. In cases falling within the second exception, breach of condition, the anticipatory secondary obligation generally arises under particular kinds of contracts by implication of statute law; though in the case of 'deviation' from the contract voyage under a contract of carriage of goods by sea it arises by implication of the common law. The anticipatory secondary obligation in these cases too can be excluded or modified by express words.

When there has been a fundamental breach or breach of condition, the coming to an end of the primary obligations of both parties to the contract at the election of the party not in default is often referred to as the 'determination' or 'rescission' of the contract or, as in the *Sale of Goods Act,* 1893, 'treating the contract as repudiated.' The first two of these expressions, however, are misleading unless it is borne in mind that for the unperformed primary obligations of the party in default there are substituted by operation of law what I have called the secondary obligations.

NOTE

The *Photo Production* case gave the House of Lords the opportunity to affirm the principle applied in *Suisse Atlantique*, namely, that the question whether an exclusion clause applied when there was a breach of contract (fundamental or otherwise) turned on the construction of the whole contract, including the exclusion clause. At common law, the parties are free to agree to whatever exclusion or modification they please within the limits that the agreement must retain the legal characteristics of a contract and must not offend against the equitable rule against penalties. At common law, an exclusion clause is enforceable if the wording is clear and fairly susceptible of one meaning only.

Ailsa Craig Fishing Co. Ltd. v. Malvern Fishing Co. Ltd.

[1983] 1 All E.R. 101; 1982 S.L.T. 377
House of Lords

The Appellants owned a vessel (Strathallan) which sank while berthed in Aberdeen harbour on 31st December 1971. At this time, the Aberdeen Fishing Vessels Owners' Association was party to a contract with Securicor who had thereby undertaken to provide security cover in the harbour. The gallows of the Strathallan had fouled a neighbouring vessel and they had both sunk together when Strathallan's bows had been caught under the deck of the quay on a rising tide. The sinkings would not have occurred if the Securicor employee had not been negligent in carrying out his duties in the harbour on that night. The issue in the case was whether Securicor had succeeded in limiting their liability under the contract between themselves and the Owners' Association. The contract in question was headed 'Temporary Contract or Contract Ltd. to carry out the services detailed below subject to the Special Conditions printed overleaf.' The form requested 'continuous security cover for your vessels from 19.00 hours on 31/12/71 until 07.00 hours on 5/1/72' stating that the area covered the Fish Market area. This area contained the open quay where the sinkings occurred. The relevant paragraph of the Special Conditions was 2(f) which provided as follows: 'If, pursuant to the provisions set out herein, any liability on the part of the Company shall arise (whether under the express or implied terms of this Contract or at Common Law, or in any other way) to the customer for any loss or damage of whatever nature arising out of or connected with the provision of, or purported provision of, or failure in provision of, the services covered by this Contract, such liability shall be limited to the payment by the Company by way of damages of a sum:

(i) in the case of all services other than the Special Delivery Service:

(a) Not exceeding £1,000 in respect of any one claim arising from any duty assumed by the Company which involves the operation, testing, examination, or inspection of the operational condition of any machine, plant or equipment in or about the customer's premises, or which involves the provision of any service not solely related to the prevention or detection of fire or theft:
(b) Not exceeding a maximum of £10,000 for the consequences of any incident involving fire, theft or any other cause of liability in the Company under the terms hereof; and further provided that the total liability of the Company shall not in any circumstances exceed the sum of £10,000 in respect of all and any incidents arising during any consecutive period of twelve months.'

The Appellants argued that condition 2(f) applied only to liability which arose 'pursuant to' the provisions of the contract. This argument failed because clause (f), itself proclaims unambiguously that it applies to liability which shall arise under the 'express or implied' terms of the contract. It was also argued that sub-paragraph (f) was confused and uncertain in itself because the provisions of sub-paragraph (i) (a) and (b) did not make it clear whether the limit of liability in any particular case was £1,000 or £10,000. On appeal to the House of Lords:
HELD, by LORD WILBERFORCE, LORD ELWYN-JONES, LORD SALMON, LORD FRASER OF TULLYBELTON and LORD LOWRY that sub-clause (a) relates to any claim arising in any of the ways mentioned and it limits the liability of Securicor to £1,000 for each claim. Sub-paragraph (b) relates to any one incident and limits their liability to £10,000 in respect of each incident. The two provisions were held to overlap but not to be inconsistent. It was held by the House of Lords that the clause 2(f) was, in its context, sufficiently clear and unambiguous to receive effect in limiting the liability of Securicor for its own negligence or that of its employees.

LORD WILBERFORCE. Whether a clause limiting liability is effective or not is a question of construction of that clause in the context of the contract as a whole. If it is to exclude liability for negligence, it must be most clearly and unambiguously expressed, and in such a contract as this, must be construed *contra proferentem*. But I venture to add one further qualification, or at least clarification: one must not strive to create ambiguities by strained construction, as I think that the appellants have striven to do. The relevant words must be given, if possible, their natural plain meaning. Clauses of limitation are not regarded by the courts with the same hostility as clauses of exclusion: this is they must be related to other contractual terms, in particular to the risks to wi ich the defending party may be exposed, the remuneration which h:. receives, and possibly also the opportunity of the other party to insure.

LORD FRASER OF TULLYBELTON. (After referring to *Pollock & Co.* v. *Macrae* and *Mechans Ltd.* v. *Highland Marine Charters Ltd.*) There are later authorities which lay down very strict principles to be applied when considering the effect of clauses of exclusion or of indemnity — see particularly the Privy Council case of *Canada Steamship Lines Ltd.* v. *The King*, where Lord Moreton of Henryton, delivering the advice of the Board, summarised the principles in terms which have recently been applied by this House in *Smith* v. *U.M.B. Chrysler (Scotland) Ltd.* In my opinion these principles are not applicable in their full rigour when considering the effect of clauses merely limiting liability. Such clauses will of course be read *contra proferentem* and must be clearly expressed, but there is no reason why they should be judged by the specially exacting standards which are applied to exclusion and indemnity clauses. The reason for imposing such standards on these clauses is the inherent improbability that the other party to a contract including such a clause intended to release the proferens from a liability that would otherwise fall upon him. But there is no such high degree of improbability that we would agree to a limitation of the liability of the proferens, especially when, as explained in . . . the present contract, the potential losses that might be caused by the negligence of the proferens or its servants are so great in proportion to the sums that can be reasonably charged for the services contracted for. It is enough in the present case that the clause must be clear and unambiguous.

George Mitchell Ltd. v. Finney Lock Seeds Ltd.
[1983] 2 A.C. 803; [1983] 2 All E.R. 737
House of Lords

In December 1973 the plaintiffs ordered orally 30 lb. of Finney's Late Dutch Special cabbage seed from the defendants. In February 1974 the defendants delivered seeds with an invoice, on the back of which were many conditions including the following clause, 'All seeds, bulbs, corms, tubers, roots, shrubs, trees and plants (hereinafter referred to as "seeds or plants") offered for sale or sold by us to which the Seeds Act, 1920 or the Plant Varieties and Seeds Act, 1964 as the case may be and the Regulations thereunder apply have been tested in accordance with the provisions of the same. In the event of any seeds or plants sold or agreed to be sold by us not complying with the express terms of the contract of sale or with any representation made by us or by any duly authorised agent or representative on our behalf prior to, at the time of, or in any such contract, or any seeds or plants proving defective in varietal purity we will, at our option, replace the defective seeds or plants, free of charge to the buyer or will refund all payments made to us by the buyer in respect of the defective seeds or plants and this shall be the limit of our obligation. We hereby exclude all liability for any loss or damage arising from the use of any seeds or plants supplied by us and for any consequential loss or damage arising out of such use or any failure in the performance of or any defect in any seeds or plants supplied by us or for any other loss or damage whatsoever save for, at our option, liability for any such replacement or refund as aforesaid. In accordance with the established custom of the seed trade any express or implied condition, statement or warranty, statutory or otherwise, not stated in these conditions is hereby excluded. The price of any seeds or plants sold or offered for sale by us is based upon the foregoing limitations upon our liability. The price of such seeds or plants would be much greater if a more extensive liability were required to be undertaken by us.'

The seed supplied was not cabbage seed. It was planted over 60 acres by the plaintiffs and when it grew it was commercially useless and had to be ploughed in. The price of the seed was £192 and the loss suffered was £61,000. The plaintiffs claimed damages for breach of contract and were awarded £61,513 and interest. The defendant seed company appealed to the Court of Appeal, where it was held dismissing the appeal, that (*i*), as a matter of construction, there was nothing in the conditions of sale which protected the defendants against what amounted to negligence, and (*ii*) the exclusion clause was not 'fair or reasonable' within the meaning of s. 55(4) of the *Sale of Goods Act*, 1979 in para. 11 of Schedule 1 to that Act. The defendants appealed to the House of Lords.

HELD, by LORD DIPLOCK, LORD SCARMAN, LORD ROSKILL, LORD BRIDGE and LORD BRIGHTMAN, that (*i*) although a limitation clause was to be construed *contra proferentem* and should be clearly expressed, it was not subject to the very strict principles of construction applicable to clauses of complete exclusion of liability. Thus on its true construction the limitation clause was effective to limit the appellant's liability to the respondent of the seeds or the refund of the price paid, since the clause was concerned with 'seed' and the appellants had delivered seed, albeit of the wrong variety and of inferior quality. The clause was enforceable at common law: and (*ii*) applying s. 55 of the Sale of Goods Act 1979 as set out in para. 11 of Schedule 1, it would not be reasonable to permit the appellants to rely on the clause, because (*a*) in the past in other cases of seed failure the appellants had settled farmers' claims for damages rather than relying on the limitation clause, (*b*) the supply of the defective seed was due to the negligence of the appellant's associate company and (*c*) the appellants could have insured against such claims. The appeal should be dismissed.

LORD BRIDGE. The first issue is whether the condition is effective to limit liability – the common law issue. The judgments of the trial judge and Lord Justice Oliver on that issue come dangerously near to reintroducing by the back door the doctrine of 'fundamental breach' which has been so forcibly evicted by the front door in *Photo Production Ltd.* v. *Securicor Transport Ltd.* [1980] A.C. 827.

The clause in question unambiguously limits the appellant's liability and, that being the case, there is no principle of construction which can properly be applied to confine the effect of the limitation to breaches of contract arising without negligence. The common law issue should be decided in favour of the appellant in agreement with Lord Denning.

The statutory issue turned on the application of the modified section 55 of the Sale of Goods Act 1979. This Act re-enacted the relevant provisions of the Supply of Goods (Implied Terms) Act 1973. This is the first time the House of Lords had to consider a modern statutory provision giving the court the power to override contractual terms excluding or restricting liability, which depended on the court's view of what was 'fair and reasonable'.

The particular provision of section 55 was of limited and diminishing importance. But the several provisions of the Unfair Contract Terms Act 1977 which depend on the 'requirement of reasonableness', defined in section 11 by what is 'fair and reasonable', albeit in a different context, were likely to come before the courts with increasing frequency.

It would not be accurate to describe an original decision as to what is 'fair and reasonable' as an exercise of discretion. A court would entertain a whole range of considerations, put them in the scales on one side or the other, and decide on which side the balance came down.

There would probably be room for a legitimate difference of judicial opinion as to what the answer should be. An appellate court should treat the original decision with the utmost respect and refrain from interference unless it was satisfied that it is plainly and obviously wrong.

NOTE

The statement of Lord Bridge that, 'An appellate court should treat the original decision with the utmost respect and refrain from interference unless it was satisfied that it is plainly and obviously wrong', has been applied in subsequent cases: see, e.g., *Phillips Products* v. *Hyland*.

Mitchell v. *Finney Lock Seeds* required the application of the statutory reasonableness test. The Court of Appeal was unanimous in deciding that it would not be reasonable to allow the seed company to rely on the exclusion clause, giving the following reasons:

(*a*) the clause was not negotiated, but was imposed unilaterally as part of a set of trading conditions;
(*b*) as between the parties, all the fault lay on the defendants — in fact the damage could not have been incurred without their negligence, the buyers having no way of knowing or discovering that the seed was not cabbage seed;
(*c*) the buyers could not have insured against this kind of disaster, whereas there was some cover available to the suppliers; and

(*d*) to limit the suppliers' liability to the price of the seed as against the magnitude of the losses which farmers can incur in a disaster of this kind would be grossly disproportionate as an allocation of risk.

Thompson v. T. Lohan and another

[1987] All E.R. 631

Court of Appeal, Civil Division

The first defendants were a plant hire company. They hired an excavator together with driver to the third party for use at the third party's quarry. The first defendants had written to the third party stating that the hire would be under the terms and conditions of the Contractors' Plant Association (CPA) conditions. CPA condition 8 headed 'handling of plant' read as follows: 'When a driver or operator is supplied by the Owner with the plant, the Owner shall supply a person competent in operating the plant and such person shall be under the direction and control of the Hirer. Such drivers and operators shall be for all purposes in connection with their employment in the working of the plant be regarded as the servants or agents of the Hirer (but without prejudice to any of the provisions of Clause 13) who alone shall be responsible for all claims arising in connection with the operation of the plant by the said drivers and operators. The Hirer shall not allow any other person to operate such plant without the Owner's previous consent to be confirmed in writing'. Condition 13, headed 'Hirer's responsibility for loss and damage' read as follows: '(*a*) For the avoidance of doubt it is hereby declared and agreed that nothing in this Clause affects the operation of Clauses 5, 8 and 9 of this Agreement. (*b*) During the continuance of the hire period the Hirer shall subject to the provisions referred to in sub paragraph (*a*) make good to the Owner all loss or damage to the plant from whatever cause the same may arise, fair wear and tear excepted and except as provided in Clause 9 herein, and shall also fully and completely indemnify the Owner in respect of all claims by any person whatsoever for injury to person or property caused by or in connection with or arising out of the use of the plant and in respect of all costs and charges in connection therewith whether arising under statute or common law. In the event of loss of or damage to the plant, hire charges shall be continued at idle time rates until settlement has been effected . . .' There was an accident in the third party's quarry involving the excavator while driven by the driver supplied by the first defendants. The plaintiff's husband was killed in this accident. The plaintiff sued the first defendants for damages for negligence. The trial judge found that the driver had been negligent and awarded damages to the plaintiff against the first defendants. The first defendants sought to be indemnified by the third party by conditions 8 and 13 of the CPA conditions. The third party contended that (*i*) the CPA conditions were not expressly incorporated in the contract, that (*ii*) neither condition 8 nor 13 expressly excluded the first defendants' liability in negligence and, alternatively, that (*iii*) if condition 8 had validly and effectively excluded or restricted liability for negligence, it was, nevertheless, contrary to s. 2(1) of the Unfair Contract Terms Act 1977. The section provides that, 'A person cannot by reference to any contract term . . . exclude or restrict his liability for death or personal injury resulting from negligence'. The judge held that conditions 8 and 13 had the effect of transferring liability for the driver's negligence from the first defendants to the third party. The first defendants were entitled to be indemnified by the third party. The third party appealed to the Court of Appeal.

HELD, by FOX, DILLON and WOOLF, L.JJ., that where the parties showed a clear intention that, as between themselves, liability for negligence was to be transferred from one to the other, it was effective at common law as between the parties. The Unfair Contract Terms Act 1977, s. 2(1), was intended to prevent the restriction of exclusion of liability in relation to the victim of negligence. The section was not concerned with arrangements made by a wrongdoer with others for sharing or transferring the burden of compensating the victim. It followed that s. 2(1) did not apply to strike down condition 8, since the only relevant 'liability' for the purposes of s.2(1) was that owed to the plaintiff, who had obtained a judgment which she could enforce against the first defendants and which was not affected by the operation of condition 8. The condition was, therefore effective to transfer liability for the driver's negligence to the third party who was, accordingly, required to indemnify the first defendants under condition 13. Appeal dismissed.

FOX, L.J. It is said on behalf of the third party that, assuming cl. 8 to be otherwise valid and effective according to its tenor (as I have found), it operates to exclude or restrict a liability for death or personal injury resulting from negligence, and that therefore it offends in this case the provisions of s. 2(1) of the 1977 Act and is struck down.

We were referred to the decision of this court in *Phillips Products Ltd* v. *Hyland*. The case is concerned with the construction of the 1977 Act.

So far as material the facts were these. In 1980 Phillips were steel stockholders, were carrying out extensions to their factory. They arranged with a builder, Mr Pritchard, that he should do the building work, but they themselves were to be responsible for buying materials and arranging for the provision of plant, so far as necessary. However, they gave Mr Pritchard permission to place an order with the defendants, Hamstead Plant Hire Co. Ltd, for the hiring of a JCB excavator. Mr Pritchard made arrangements on the telephone for the hire of a JCB excavator with a driver. The first defendant, Mr Hyland, arrived at Phillips' premises with a JCB machine, of which he was the driver.

Kenneth Jones J found Mr Hyland had made it perfectly plain to Mr Pritchard that he would brook no interference in the way in which he operated the JCB. However, during the course of his operating the JCB excavator, Mr Hyland collided with a part of Phillips' building, doing a good deal of damage to it. In consequence, Phillips' issued a writ against Mr Hyland and Hamstead, and claimed damages against both defendants. It was conceded on behalf of the defendants that Mr Hyland had driven the JCB excavator with reasonable care and the cost of making good the damage was £3,000. Accordingly, the judge gave judgment for Phillips in that sum.

At the trial the argument centred on the liability or otherwise of Hamstead in tort. It was conceded on their behalf that, apart from any special terms in the contract of hire, they were liable for the negligence of Mr Hyland as their employee so as to entitle Phillips to judgment against them for such sum as was awarded Mr Hyland. However, it was contended on behalf of Hamstead that condition 8 of the terms of hire, which for all practical purposes are the same as condition 8 in the general terms and conditions in the present appeal, gave a complete defence to the claim. In giving the judgment of the Court of Appeal, Slade L.J. said: 'Certainly there is nothing which leads to the conclusion that a plant-owner who uses the general conditions is not *excluding* his liability for negligence in the relevant sense by reference to the contract term condition 8. We are unable to accept that, in the ordinary sensible meaning of words in the context of s. 2 of the 1977 Act as a whole, the provisions of condition 8 do not fall within the scope of s. 2(2). A transfer of liability from A to B necessarily and inevitably involves the exclusion of liability so far as A is concerned.' Slade L.J.'s emphasis.

It was held that, in the circumstances of that case, condition 8 could not operate, having regard to the provisions of s. 2(2), to give an indemnity as claimed.

Smith v. Eric S. Bush (a Firm) Harris and Another v. Wyre Forest District Council and Another

Times Law Report, April 24, 1989
House of Lords

A valuer instructed by a building society or a local authority to carry out a mortgage valuation of a modest house, with the knowledge that the purchaser would rely on his valuation without obtaining an independent survey, owed a duty of care to the purchaser to exercise reasonable skill and care in carrying out the valuation, unless an effective disclaimer excluding liability for negligence to the purchaser had been made by or on behalf of the valuer.

The Unfair Contract Terms Act 1977 applied to such a disclaimer which would be rendered ineffective by section 2(2) unless it satisfied the requirement of reasonableness provided by section 11(3).

Where the services of the valuer were paid for by the purchaser, who might or might not be supplied with a copy of the valuation report, it would not be fair or reasonable to allow the valuer, whether acting as an independent contractor of the building society or as an employee of the local authority, to rely on such a disclaimer to exclude his liability to the purchaser for the accuracy of the valuation.

The House of Lords so held in dismissing, in the first case, an appeal by a firm of surveyors and valuers, Eric S Bush, from the Court of Appeal (Lord Justice Dillon, Lord Justice Glidewell and Sir Edward Eveleigh) (*The Times* March 18, 1987; [1988] QB 743) who had dismissed their appeal from Mr Recorder Gerald

Draycott who gave judgment for the purchaser, Mrs Jean Patricia Smith, and awarded her damages of £4,379.99 including interest.

The House, in the second case, allowed an appeal by the purchasers, Mr and Mrs A.C. Harris, from the Court of Appeal (Lord Justice Kerr, Lord Justice Nourse and Mr Justice Caulfield) (*The Times* December 22, 1987; [1988] QB 835) who had allowed the appeal of the local authority, Wyre Forest District Council, and a valuer in their employment, Mr Trevor James Lee, from Mr Justice Schiemann who gave judgment for the purchasers and awarded them damages of £12,000.

In the first case, the purchaser applied for a mortgage to the Abbey National Building Society who instructed the valuers to carry out a mortgage valuation.

The valuer from the firm who carried out the inspection noticed that two chimney breasts had been removed but he failed to check whether the chimneys above had been left adequately supported. His report stated that no essential repairs were necessary.

The mortgage application form and the valuation report contained a disclaimer of liability for the accuracy of the report covering both the building society and the valuer.

The purchaser was also informed that the report was not a structural survey and she was advised to obtain independent professional advice. The building society, pursuant to an agreement with the purchaser who paid an inspection fee, supplied a copy of the report to her, and she relied on it and purchased the house without any further survey.

The chimneys were not adequately supported and they subsequently collapsed. The purchaser claimed damages from the valuers in negligence.

In the second case, the purchasers applied to the council for a mortgage. They filled in the council's standard mortgage application form and paid the inspection fee.

The form contained an acknowledgement that the valuation was confidential and solely for the benefit of the council who accepted no responsibility for the value or condition of the house by reason of the inspection report, and advised them to obtain their own survey.

The council instructed Mr Lee, a valuer in their employment, to carry out an inspection. He recommended a mortgage subject to certain minor repairs. The valuer's report was not shown to the purchasers but they were subsequently offered a mortgage by the council.

Three years later, when they tried to sell the property, Mr Lee inspected the property again for the council because a prospective purchaser had applied to them for a mortgage.

He recommended the mortgage to be held until a structural survey had been made and the recommended repairs carried out. The survey revealed the need for structural repairs which were estimated to cost thousands of pounds.

The property was regarded as uninhabitable and thus unsaleable. The purchasers claimed damages for the valuer's negligence as servant and agent of the council.

HELD by LORD KEITH OF KINKEL, LORD BRANDON OF OAKBROOK, LORD TEMPLEMAN, LORD GRIFFITHS and LORD JAUNCEY OF TULLICHETTLE, (i) that a valuer instructed by a building society or other mortgagee to value a house, knowing that his valuation would probably be relied on by the purchaser owed to the purchaser in tort a duty to exercise reasonable skill and care in carrying out the valuation unless the valuer disclaimed liability, (ii) that a disclaimer of liability made by or on behalf of a valuer constituted a notice which fell within the Unfair Contract Terms Act 1977 and must satisfy the requirement of reasonableness and (iii) that it would be unfair and unreasonable for a valuer to rely on an exclusion clause directed against a purchaser in the circumstances of the present appeals.

LORD TEMPLEMAN said that the appeals involved consideration of three questions.

First, whether a valuer instructed by a building society or other mortgagee to value a house, knowing that his valuation would probably be relied on by the purchaser owed to the purchaser in tort a duty to exercise reasonable skill and care in carrying out the valuation unless the valuer disclaimed liability.

If so, the second question was whether a disclaimer of liability by or on behalf of the valuer was a notice which purported to exclude liability for negligence within the Unfair Contract Terms Act 1977 and was ineffective unless it satisfied the requirements of reasonableness.

If so, the third question was whether in the absence of special circumstances, it was fair and reasonable for the valuer to rely on the notice excluding liability.

The two appeals were based on allegations of negligence in circumstances which were akin to contract. Mr and Mrs Harris paid £22 for a valuation to the council, who employed and paid Mr Lee for whose services as a valuer the council were vicariously liable.

Mrs Smith paid £36.89 for a report and valuation to the Abbey National who paid the valuers for the report and valuation.

In each case the valuer knew that the purchaser was providing the money for the valuation, that the purchaser would only contract to purchase the house if the valuation was satisfactory and that the purchaser might suffer injury or damage or both if the valuer did not exercise reasonable skill and care.

In those circumstances his Lordship would expect the law to impose on the valuer a duty owed to the purchaser to exercise reasonable skill and care in carrying out the valuation.

The considerations referred to by Lord Justice Denning in *Candler* v. *Crane, Christmas & Co.* ([1951] 2 KB 164, 176–181), whose dissenting judgment was subsequently approved by the House of Lords in *Hedley Byrne & Co. Ltd.* v. *Heller & Partners Ltd* ([1964] AC 465), applied to the valuers in the present appeals.

The statutory duty of the council to value the house did not prevent the council coming under a contractual or tortious duty to Mr and Mrs Harris who were informed of the valuation and relied on it.

The contractual duty of a valuer to value a house for the Abbey National did not prevent the valuer coming under a tortious duty to Mrs Smith who was furnished with a report of the valuation and relied on it.

In general, his Lordship was of the opinion that in the absence of a disclaimer of liability the valuer who valued a house for the purpose of a mortgage knowing that the mortgagee would, and the mortgagor would probably rely on the valuation, knowing that the purchaser mortgagor had in effect paid for the valuation, was under a duty to exercise reasonable skill and care, and that duty was owed to both parties to the mortgage for which the valuation was made.

Indeed, in both appeals the existence of such a dual duty was tacitly accepted and acknowledged because notices excluding liability for breach of the duty owed to the purchaser were drafted by the mortgagee and imposed on the purchaser.

In those circumstances it was necessary to consider the second question which arose in the appeals, namely, whether the disclaimers of liability were notices which fell within the Unfair Contract Terms Act 1977.

Section 11(3) provided that in considering whether it was fair and reasonable to allow reliance on a notice which excluded liability in tort account had to be taken of 'all the circumstances obtaining when the liability arose or (but for the notice) would have arisen'.

Section 13(1) prevented the exclusion of any right or remedy and (to that extent) section 2 also prevented the exclusion of liability 'by reference to . . . notices which exclude . . . the relevant obligation or duty'.

In his Lordship's opinion, both sections 11(3) and 13(1) supported the view that the 1977 Act required that all exclusion notices which would at common law provide a defence to an action for negligence must satisfy the requirement of reasonableness.

The answer to the second question was that the disclaimer of liability made by the council on its own behalf in the Harris case and by the Abbey National on behalf of the valuers in the Smith case constituted notices which fell within the 1977 Act and must satisfy the requirement of reasonableness.

The third question was whether each exclusion clause satisfied the requirement of reasonableness in section 11(3). Both present appeals involved typical house purchases.

In considering whether the exclusion clause might be relied on in each case, the general pattern of house purchases and the extent of the work and liability of the valuer had to be borne in mind.

The valuer was a professional man who offered his services for reward. He was paid for those services at the expense of the purchaser.

The valuer knew that 90 per cent of purchasers in fact relied on a mortgage valuation and did not commission their own survey. There was great pressure on a purchaser to rely on a mortgage valuation. Many purchasers could not afford a second valuation.

If a purchaser obtained a second valuation the sale might go off and then both valuations would be wasted. Moreover, he knew that mortgagees, such as building societies and local authorities, were trustworthy and that they appointed careful and competent valuers and he trusted the professional man so appointed.

Finally, the valuer knew that failure on his part to exercise reasonable skill and care might be disastrous to the purchaser. The evidence and findings of Mr Justice Park in *Yianni* v. *Edwin Evans & Sons*([1982] QB 438), supported the view that it was unfair and

unreasonable for a valuer to rely on an exclusion clause directed
against a purchaser in the circumstances of the present appeals.

LORD GRIFFITHS, concurring, said that it had to be
remembered that each of the appeals concerned a dwelling house
of modest value in which it was widely recognized by valuers that
purchasers were in fact relying on their care and skill. It would
obviously be of general application in broadly similar
circumstances.

But his Lordship expressly reserved his position in respect of
valuations of quite different types of property for mortgage
purposes, such as industrial property, large blocks of flats or very
expensive houses.

In such cases it might well be that the general expectation of the
behaviour of the purchaser was quite different.

With very large sums of money at stake prudence would demand
that the purchaser obtain his own structural survey to guide him in
his purchase and, in such circumstances, with such larger sums of
money at stake, it might be reasonable for the valuers acting on
behalf of the mortgagees to exclude or limit their liability to the
purchaser.

Lord Jauncey delivered a concurring judgement and Lord
Keith and Lord Brandon agreed.

© Times Newspapers Limited 1989

Unfair Contract Terms Act 1977

Part 1   Amendment of law for England and Wales
and Northern Ireland

Introductory

1.   Scope of Part I.
(1) For the purposes of this Part of this Act, 'negligence' means the
breach —

> (*a*) of any obligation, arising from the express or implied terms
>   of a contract, to take reasonable care or exercise
>   reasonable skill in the performance of the contract;
> (*b*) of any common law duty to take reasonable care or exercise
>   reasonable skill (but not any stricter duty);
> (*c*) of the common duty of care imposed by the Occupiers'

Liability Act 1957 or the Occupiers' Liability Act (Northern Ireland) 1957.

(2) This Part of this Act is subject to Part III; and in relation to contracts, the operation of sections 2 to 4 and 7 is subject to the exceptions made by Schedule 1.

(3) In the case of both contract and tort, sections 2 to 7 apply (except where the contrary is stated in section 6(4)) only to business liability, that is liability for breach of obligations or duties arising—

> (*a*) from things done or to be done by a person in the course of a business (whether his own business or another's); or
>
> (*b*) from the occupation of premises used for business purposes of the occupier;

and references to liability are to be read accordingly.

(4) In relation to any breach of duty or obligation, it is immaterial for any purpose of this Part of this Act whether the breach was inadvertent or intentional, or whether liability for it arises directly or vicariously.

Avoidance of liability for negligence, breach of contract, etc.

2. Negligence liability

(1) A person cannot by reference to any contract term or to a notice given to persons generally or to particular persons exclude or restrict his liability for death or personal injury resulting from negligence.

(2) In the case of other loss or damage, a person cannot so exclude or restrict his liability for negligence except in so far as the term or notice satisfies the requirement of reasonableness.

(3) Where a contract term or notice purports to exclude or restrict liability for negligence a person's agreement to or awareness of it is not of itself to be taken as indicating his voluntary acceptance of any risk.

3. Liability arising in contract.

(1) This section applies as between contracting parties where one of them deals as consumer or on the other's written standard terms of business.

(2) As against that party, the other cannot by reference to any contract term —

- (*a*) when himself in breach of contract, exclude or restrict any liability of his in respect of the breach; or
- (*b*) claim to be entitled —

  - (*i*) to render a contractual performance substantially different from that which was reasonably expected of him, or
  - (*ii*) in respect of the whole or any part of his contractual obligation, to render no performance at all,

except in so far as (in any of the cases mentioned above in this subsection) the contract term satisfies the requirement of reasonableness.

4. Unreasonable indemnity clauses.

(1) A person dealing as consumer cannot by reference to any contract term be made to indemnify another person (whether a party to the contract or not) in respect of liability that may be incurred by the other for negligence or breach of contract, except in so far as the contract term satisfies the requirement of reasonableness.

(2) This section applies whether the liability in question —

- (*a*) is directly that of the person to be indemnified or is incurred by him vicariously;
- (*b*) is to the person dealing as consumer or to someone else.

Liability arising from sale or supply of goods

5. 'Guarantee' of consumer goods

(1) In the case of goods of a type ordinarily supplied for private use or consumption, where loss or damage –

> (*a*) arises from the goods proving defective while in consumer use; and
>
> (*b*) results from the negligence of a person concerned in the manufacture or distribution of the goods.

liability for the loss or damage cannot be excluded or restricted by reference to any contract term or notice contained in or operating by reference to a guarantee of the goods.

(2) For these purposes –

> (*a*) goods are to be regarded as 'in consumer use' when a person is using them, or has them in his possession for use, otherwise than exclusively for the purposes of a business; and
>
> (*b*) anything in writing is a guarantee if it contains or purports to contain some promise of assurance (however worded or presented) that defects will be made good by complete or partial replacement, or by repair, monetary compensation or otherwise.

(3) This section does not apply as between the parties to a contract under or in pursuance of which possession or ownership of the goods passed.

6. Sale and hire-purchase. 1893 c. 71 (56 & 57 Vict.)

(1) Liability for breach of the obligations arising from –

> (*a*) section 12 of the Sale of Goods Act 1893 (seller's implied undertakings as to title, etc.);
>
> (*b*) section 8 of the Supply of Goods (Implied Terms) Act 1973 c. 13 (the corresponding thing in relation to hire-purchase),

cannot be excluded or restricted by reference to any contract term.

(2) As against a person dealing as consumer, liability for breach of the obligations arising from —

> (*a*) section 13, 14 or 15 of the 1893 Act (seller's implied undertakings as to conformity of goods with description or sample, or as to their quality or fitness for a particular purpose);
>
> (*b*) section 9, 10 or 11 of the 1973 Act (the corresponding things in relation to hire-purchase), cannot be excluded or restricted by reference to any contract term.

(3) As against a person dealing otherwise than as consumer, the liability specified in subsection (2) above can be excluded or restricted by reference to a contract term, but only in so far as the term satisfies the requirement of reasonableness.

(4) The liabilities referred to in this section are not only the business liabilities defined by section 1(3), but include those arising under any contract of sale of goods or hire-purchase agreement.

7. Miscellaneous contracts under which goods pass

(1) Where the possession or ownership of goods passes under or in pursuance of a contract not governed by the law of sale of goods or hire-purchase, subsections (2) to (4) below apply as regards the effect (if any) to be given to contract terms excluding or restricting liability for breach of obligation arising by implication of law from the nature of the contract.

(2) As against a person dealing as consumer, liability in respect of the goods' correspondence with description or sample, or their quality or fitness for any particular purpose, cannot be excluded or restricted by reference to any such term.

(3) As against a person dealing otherwise than a consumer, that liability can be excluded or restricted by reference to such a term, but only in so far as the term satisfies the requirement of reasonableness.

(4) Liability in respect of —

(*a*) the right to transfer ownership of the goods, or give possession; or

(*b*) the assurance of quiet possession to a person taking goods in pursuance of the contract,

cannot be excluded or restricted by reference to any such term except in so far as the term satisfies the requirement of reasonableness.

(5) This section does not apply in the case of goods passing on a redemption of trading stamps with the Trading Stamps Act 1964, c. 71 or the Trading Stamps Act (Northern Ireland) 1965, c. 6 (N.I.).

Other provisions about contracts

8. . . . .

9. Effect of breach.

(1) Where for reliance upon it a contract term has to satisfy the requirement of reasonableness, it may be found to do so and be given effect accordingly notwithstanding that the contract has been terminated either by breach or by a party electing to treat it as repudiated.

(2) Where on a breach the contract is nevertheless affirmed by a party entitled to treat it as repudiated, this does not Of itself exclude the requirement of reasonableness in relation to any contract term.

10. Evasion by means of secondary contract.

A person is not bound by any contract term prejudicing or taking away rights of his which arise under, or in connection with the performance of, another contract, so far as those rights extend to the enforcement of another's liability which this Part of this Act prevents that other from excluding or restricting.

Explanatory provisions

11. The 'reasonableness' test. 1967 c. 7. 1967 c. 14 (N.I.)

(1) In relation to a contract term, the requirement of reasonableness for the purposes of this Part of this Act, section 3 of the Misrepresentation Act 1967 and section 3 of the Misrepresentation Act (Northern Ireland) 1967 is that the term shall have been a fair and reasonable one to be included having regard to the circumstances which were, or ought reasonably to have been, known to or in the contemplation of the parties when the contract was made.

(2) In determining for the purposes of section 6 or 7 above whether a contract term satisfies the requirement of reasonableness, regard shall be had in particular to the matters specified in Schedule 2 to this Act; but this subsection does not prevent the court or arbitrator from holding, in accordance with any rule of law, that a term which purports to exclude or restrict any relevant liability is not a term of the contract.

(3) In relation to a notice (not being a notice having contractual effect), the requirement of reasonableness under this Act is that it should be fair and reasonable to allow reliance on it, having regard to all the circumstances, obtaining when the liability arose or (but for the notice) would have arisen.

(4) Where by reference to a contract term or notice a person seeks to restrict liability to a specified sum of money, and the question arises (under this or any other Act) whether the term or notice satisfies the requirement of reasonableness, regard shall be had in particular (but without prejudice to subsection (2) above in the case of contract terms) to —

> (*a*) the resources which he could expect to be available to him for the purpose of meeting the liability should it arise; and
> (*b*) how far it was open to him to cover himself by insurance.

(5) It is for those claiming that a contract term or notice satisfies the requirement of reasonableness to show that it does.

12. 'Dealing as consumer'

(1) A party to a contract 'deals as consumer' in relation to another party if —

(a) he neither makes the contract in the course of a business nor holds himself out as doing so; and

(b) the other party does make the contract in the course of a business; and

(c) in the case of a contract governed by the law of sale of goods or hire-purchase, or by section 7 of this Act, the goods passing under or in pursuance of the contract are of a type ordinarily supplied for private use or consumption.

(2) But on a sale by auction or by competitive tender the buyer is not in any circumstances to be regarded as dealing as consumer.

(3) Subject to this, it is for those claiming that a party does not deal as consumer to show that he does not.

13. Varieties of exemption clause

(1) To the extent that this Part of this Act prevents the exclusion or restriction of any liability it also prevents —

(a) making the liability or its enforcement subject to restrictive or onerous conditions;

(b) excluding or restricting any right or remedy in respect of the liability, or subjecting a person to any prejudice in consequence of his pursuing any such right or remedy;

(c) excluding or restricting rules of evidence or procedure;

and (to that extent) sections 2 and 5 to 7 also prevent excluding or restricting liability by reference to terms and notices which exclude or restrict the relevant obligation or duty.

(2) But an agreement in writing to submit present or future differences to arbitration is not to be treated under this Part of this Act as excluding or restricting any liability.

14. Interpretation of Part I

In this Part of this Act —

"business" includes a profession and the activities of any government department or local or public authority;

"goods" has the same meaning as in the Sale of Goods Act 1893 c. 71 (56 & 57 Vict.);

"hire-purchase agreement" has the same meaning as in the Consumer Credit Act 1974 c. 39;

"negligence" has the meaning given by section 1(1);

"notice" includes an announcement, whether or not in writing, and any other communication or pretended communication; and

"personal injury" includes any disease and any impairment of physical or mental condition.

Schedules

Schedule 1
Scope of sections 2 to 4 and 7

1. Sections 2 to 4 of this Act do not extend to —

    (*a*) any contract of insurance (including a contract to pay an annuity on human life);

    (*b*) any contract so far as it relates to the creation or transfer of an interest in land, or to the termination of such an interest, whether by extinction, merger, surrender, forfeiture or otherwise;

    (*c*) any contract so far as it relates to the creation or transfer of a right or interest in any patent, trade mark, copyright, registered design, technical or commercial information or other intellectual property, or relates to the termination of any such right or interest;

    (*d*) any contract so far as it relates —

        (*i*) to the formation or dissolution of a company (which means any body corporate or unincorporated association and includes a partnership), or (*ii*) to its constitution or the rights or obligations of its corporators or members;

(*e*) any contract so far as it relates to the creation or transfer of securities or of any right or interest in securities.

2. Section 2(1) extends to-

(*a*) any contract of marine salvage or towage;

(*b*) any charterparty of a ship or hovercraft; and

(*c*) any contract for the carriage of goods by ship or hovercraft;

but subject to this sections 2 to 4 and 7 do not extend to any such contract except in favour of a person dealing as consumer.

3. Where goods are carried by ship or hovercraft in pursuance of a contract which either —

(*a*) specifies that as the means of carriage over part of the journey to be covered, or

(*b*) makes no provision as to the means of carriage and does not exclude that means,

then sections 2(2), 3 and 4 do not, except in favour of a person dealing as consumer, extend to the contract as it operates for and in relation to the carriage of the goods by that means.

4. Section 2(1) and (2) do not extend to a contract of employment, except in favour of the employee.

5. Section 2(1) does not affect the validity of any discharge and indemnity given by a person, on or in connection with an award to him of compensation for pneumoconiosis attributable to employment in the coal industry, in respect of any further claim arising from his contracting that disease.

Schedule 2

'Guidelines' for application of reasonableness test

The matters to which regard is to be had in particular for the purposes of sections 6(3), 7(3) and (4), 20 and 21 are any of the following which appear to be relevant –

> (*a*) the strength of the bargaining positions of the parties relative to each other, taking into account (among other things) alternative means by which the customer's requirements could have been met;
> (*b*) whether the customer received an inducement to agree to the term, or in accepting it had an opportunity of entering into a similar contract with other persons, but without having to accept a similar term;
> (*c*) whether the customer knew or ought reasonably to have known of the existence and extent of the term (having regard, among other things, to any custom of the trade and any previous course of dealing between the parties);
> (*d*) where the term excludes or restricts any relevant liability if some condition is not complied with, whether it was reasonable at the time of the contract to expect that compliance with that condition would by practicable;
> (*e*) whether the goods were manufactured, processed or adapted to the special order of the customer.

Schedule 3

Amendments to the Unfair Contract Terms Act 1977

1. The Sale of Goods Act 1979.
Schedule 3, paras. 19–22 provides that:

> 19. In section 6 of the Unfair Contract Terms Act 1977 –
> (*a*) in subsection (1) (*a*) for 'section 12 of the Sale of Goods Act 1893' substitute 'section 12 of the Sale of Goods Act 1979';
> (*b*) in subsection (2) (*a*) for 'section 13, 14 or 15 of the 1893 Act' substitute 'section 13, 14 or 15 of the 1979 Act'.

20. In section 14 of the Unfair Contract Terms Act 1977, in the definition of 'goods', for 'the Sale of Goods Act 1893' substitute 'The Sale of Goods Act 1979'.

21. In section 20(1)(*a*) and (2)(*a*) of the Unfair Contract Terms Act 1977 for '1893' substitute (in each case) '1979'.

22. In section 25(1) of the Unfair Contract Terms Act 1977, in the definition of 'goods', for 'the Sale of Goods Act 1893' substitute 'the Sale of Goods Act 1979'.

2. The Supply of Goods and Services Act 1982
Section 17(2) provides that:

'(2) The following subsection shall be inserted after section 7(3) of the 1977 Act:

"(3A) Liability for breach of the obligations arising under section 2 of the Supply of Goods and Services Act 1982 (implied terms about title etc. in certain contracts for the transfer of the property in goods) cannot be excluded or restricted by reference to any such term."

(3) In consequence of subsection (2) above, in section 7(4) of the 1977 Act, after "cannot" there shall be inserted "(in a case to which subsection (3A) above does not apply".'

3. The Occupiers' Liability Act 1984.
Section 2 provides that:

'At the end of section 1(3) of the Unfair Contract Terms Act 1977 (which defines the liability, called "business liability", the exclusion or restriction of which is controlled by virtue of that Act) there is added —
"but liability of an occupier of premises for breach of an obligation or duty towards a person obtaining access to the premises for recreational or educational purposes, being liability for loss or damage suffered by reason of the dangerous state of the premises, is not a business liability of the occupier unless granting that person such access for the purposes concerned falls within the business purposes of the occupier".'

Misrepresentation Act 1967 (see particularly s. 3)

1. Removal of certain bars to rescission for innocent misrepresentation

Where a person has entered into a contract after a misrepresentation has been made to him, and —

(a) the misrepresentation has become a term of the contract; or

(b) the contract has been performed;

or both, then, if otherwise he would be entitled to rescind the contract without alleging fraud, he shall be so entitled, subject to the provisions of this Act, notwithstanding the matters mentioned in paragraphs (a) and (b) of this section.

2. Damages for mispresentation

(1) Where a person has entered into a contract after a misrepresentation has been made to him by another party thereto and as a result thereof he has suffered loss, then, if the person making the misrepresentation would be liable to damages in respect thereof had the misrepresentation been made fraudulently, that person shall be so liable notwithstanding that the misrepresentation was not made fraudulently, unless he proves that he had reasonable ground to believe and did believe up to the time the contract was made the facts represented were true.

(2) Where a person has entered into a contract after a misrepresentation has been made to him otherwise than fraudulently, and he would be entitled, by reason of the misrepresentation, to rescind the contract, then, if it is claimed, in any proceedings arising out of the contract, that the contract ought to be or has been rescinded, the court or arbitrator may declare the contract subsisting and award damages in lieu of rescission, if of opinion that it would be equitable to do so, having regard to the nature of the misrepresentation and the loss that would be caused by it if the contract were upheld, as well as to the loss that rescission would cause to the other party.

(3) Damages may be awarded against a person under subsection (2) of this section whether or not he is liable to damages under

subsection (1) thereof, but where he is so liable any award under the said subsection (2) shall be taken into account in assessing his liability under the said subsection (1).

3. Avoidance of provision excluding liability for misrepresentation
If a contract contains a term which would exclude or restrict —
- (a) any liability to which a party to a contract may be subject by reason of any misrepresentation made by him before the contract was made; or
- (b) any remedy available to another party to the contract by reason of such a misrepresentation,

that term shall be of no effect except in so far as it satisfies the requirement of reasonableness as stated in section 11(1) of the Unfair Contract Terms Act 1977; and it is for those claiming that the term satisfies that requirement to show that it does.

4. . . . .

5. Saving for past transactions
Nothing in this Act shall apply in relation to any misrepresentation or contract of sale which is made before the commencement of this Act.

6. Short title, commencement and extent
(1) This Act may be cited as the Misrepresentation Act 1967.

(2) This Act shall come into operation at the expiration of the period of one month beginning with the date on which it is passed.

(3) This Act, except section 4(2), does not extend to Scotland.

(4) This Act does not extend to Northern Ireland.

7. Privity of Contract

In the Law of England certain principles are fundamental. One is that only a person who is a party to a contract can sue on it: DUNLOP v. SELFRIDGE, per VISCOUNT HALDANE.

Summary

1. Definition

A contract creates rights and obligations only between the parties. Therefore, a contract cannot confer rights on a stranger, nor can it impose obligations on a stranger. In short, no one can sue or be sued on a contract unless he is a party to it: *Dunlop* v. *Selfridge* [1915].

2. Privity and consideration

The rule that consideration must move from the promisee should be set alongside the wider doctrine of privity of contract. The two principles combine to produce a rule that no one can sue on a simple contract unless *(a)* he is a party and *(b)* he gave consideration to the defendant.

3. Third party benefits

Where a contract purports to confer a benefit on a stranger, the question arises whether there are any circumstances in which the stranger could enforce the benefit. For example, if a contract between X and Y provides that X should pay £1,000 to Z; and if X fails to pay; can Z then enforce payment? See *Beswick* v. *Beswick* [1968].

Dunlop Pneumatic Tyre Co., Ltd. v. Selfridge & Co., Ltd.

[1915] A.C. 847; [1914–15] All E.R. Rep. 333

House of Lords

There was a contract dated 12th October 1911 by which Dew & Co., agreed to purchase a quantity of tyres and other goods from Dunlop. By this contract, Dew & Co., undertook not to sell at prices below the current list prices except to genuine trade customers, to whom they could sell at a discount. The contract provided that such discount would be substantially less than the discount that Dews themselves were to receive from Dunlop's. Where such sales took place, Dews undertook, as the agents of Dunlop, to obtain from the customer a written undertaking that he similarly would observe the terms so undertaken to be observed by themselves. On 2nd January 1912 Selfridges agreed to purchase goods made by Dunlop from Dew & Co., and gave the required undertaking to resell at the current list prices. Selfridge's broke this agreement and Dunlop sued for breach of contract.

HELD, by VISCOUNT HALDANE, L.C., LORD DUNEDIN, LORD ATKINSON, LORD PARKER OF WADDINGTON, LORD SUMNER and LORD PARMOOR, that the agreement of 2nd January 1912 was between Selfridge and Dew only and that Dunlop was not a party to that contract because no consideration moved from them to Selfridges.

VISCOUNT HALDANE, L.C. In the law of England certain principles are fundamental. One is that only a person who is a party to a contract can sue on it. Our law knows nothing of a *jus quaesitum tertio* arising by way of contract. Such a right may be conferred by way of property, as, for example, under a trust, but it cannot be conferred on a stranger to a contract as a right to enforce the contract *in personam*.

LORD DUNEDIN. I am content to adopt from a work of SIR FREDERICK POLLOCK (*Pollock on Contracts* (8th Edn)), to which I have often been under obligation, the following words as to consideration: 'An act or forbearance of one party, or the promise thereof, is the price for which the promise of the other is bought, and the promise thus given for value is enforceable.'

The agreement sued on is an agreement which on the face of it is an agreement between Dew and Selfridge. But speaking for myself, I should have no difficulty in the circumstances of this case in holding it proved that the agreement was truly made by Dew as agent for Dunlop or in other words that Dunlop was the undisclosed principal, and as such can sue on the agreement. None the less, in order to enforce he must show consideration, as above defined moving from Dunlop to Selfridge. In the circumstances, how can he do so? The agreement in question is not an agreement for sale. It is only collateral to an agreement for sale, but that agreement for sale is an agreement entirely between Dew and Selfridge. The tyres, the property in which upon the bargain are transferred to Selfridge, were the property of Dew, not of Dunlop, for Dew under his agreement with Dunlop, had sold these tyres as a proprietor, and not as agent. What then did Dunlop do, or forbear to do, in a question with Selfridge? The answer must be, Nothing. He did not do anything for Dew, having the right of property in the tyres, could give a good title to anyone he liked, subject, it might be, to an action of damages at the instance of Dunlop for breach of contract, which action, however, could never create a *vitium reale* in the property of the tyres. He did not forbear in anything, for he had no action against Dew which he gave up because Dew had fulfilled his contract with Dunlop in obtaining, on the occasion of the sale, a contract from Selfridge in the terms prescribed. To my mind, this ends the case.

NOTE

By the Resale Prices Act 1976, price maintenance agreements of the kind in *Dunlop* v. *Selfridge* are void. This does not, however diminish the authority of this important case with regard to the rules of consideration and privity of contract.

In this case, Viscount Haldane spoke of certain principles being fundamental in the law of England. He said that one such principle is that only a person who is party to a contract can sue on it. He went on to say that a second principle is that if a person with whom a contract not under seal has been made is to be able to enforce it consideration must have been given by him to the promisor or to some other person at the promisor's request.

The principle of privity is thus separate from that of consideration. In *Dunlop* v. *Selfridge*, only Lord Parmoor reached his decision by the application of the privity rule. The other judges applied the consideration rule. Nevertheless, in a subsequent

House of Lords case, *Scruttons* v. *Midland Silicones* [1962], it was said that, by the decision in the *Dunlop* case, the general rule was established that a 'stranger cannot in a question with either of the contracting parties take advantage of any of the provisions of the contract, even where it is clear from the contract that some provision in it was intended to benefit him'. But see Lord Denning's dissenting speech in the Scruttons case.

The privity doctrine was applied by the House of Lords in *Woodar Investment Developments* v. *Wimpey Construction* [1980] in which it was held that a party who had broken a promise to pay a sum of money to a third party was liable for nominal damages only.

Beswick v. Beswick
[1968] A.C. 58; [1967] 2 All E.R. 1197
House of Lords
In March 1962 a coal merchant, Peter Beswick, agreed to sell his business to his nephew John in return for the following undertakings: (*i*) that John should pay to Peter the weekly sum of £6 10*s*. during the rest of Peter's life: (*ii*) that, in the event of Peter's wife surviving him, John should pay her an annuity of £5 weekly. Peter died intestate in November 1963 and in 1964 his widow took out letters of administration. After Peter's death, John made one payment of £5 only to the widow, refusing to make any further payments. The widow, who brought this action as administratrix of her husband's estate and also in her personal capacity, claimed arrears of the annuity and specific performance of the contract between Peter and John. It was held by the Court of Appeal that she was entitled, as administratrix, to specific performance of the contract. And LORD DENNING and DANCKWERTS, L.J., held further that she could succeed under s. 56(1) of the Law of Property Act, 1925. (Section 56(1) provides that: 'A person may take an immediate or other interest in land or other property, or the benefit of any condition, right of entry, covenant or agreement over or respecting land or other property, although he may not be named as a party to the conveyance or other instrument.' The Act further provides, by s. 205, that: 'unless the context otherwise requires, the following expressions have the meaning hereby assigned to them respectively, that is to say . . . "Property includes any thing in action, and any interest in real or personal property." ') John appealed to the House of Lords.

HELD, by LORD REID, LORD HODSON, LORD GUEST, LORD PEARCE and LORD UPJOHN, that the widow, as administratrix, was entitled to specific performance of the agreement to which her deceased husband was a contracting party; but that the statute gave her no right of action against John in her personal capacity.

LORD HODSON. Section 56 had as long ago as 1937 received consideration by the Law Revision Committee presided over by LORD WRIGHT, then Master of the Rolls, and containing a number of illustrious lawyers. The committee was called on to report specially on consideration including the attitude of the common law towards the *jus quaesitum tertio*. It had available to it and considered the decision of LUXMOORE, J., in *Re Ecclesiastical Comrs. For England's Conveyance* which gave the orthodox view of the section. By its report (Cmd. 5449) it impliedly rejected the revolutionary view, for it recommended that 'Where a contract by its express terms purports to confer a benefit directly on a third party, it shall be enforceable by the third party in his own name.' Like my noble and learned friend, LORD REID, whose opinion I have had the opportunity of reading, I am of opinion that s. 56, one of twenty-five sections of the Act of 1925 appearing under the cross-heading 'Conveyances and other instruments', does not have the revolutionary effect claimed for it, appearing as it does in a consolidation Act. I think, as he does, that the context does otherwise require a limited meaning to be given to the word 'property' in the section

NOTE
When the Beswick case was before the Court of Appeal, Lord Denning M.R. said that, 'Where a contract is made for the benefit of a third person who has a legitimate interest to enforce it, it can be enforced by the third person in the name of the contracting party or jointly with him or, if he refuses to join, by adding him as a defendant'. When the case was before the House of Lords, their lordships declined to deal with the point as it was not essential to the decision.

8. Misrepresentation

> *There is a clear difference between a representation of fact and a representation that something will be done in the future. A representation that something will be done in the future cannot either be true or false at the moment it is made; and although you may call it a representation, if anything it is a contract or promise:* Beatty v. Ebury, per MELLISH, L.J.

Summary

1. Definitions

A representation is a statement of material fact, made by one party to another, during negotiations leading to a contract, which was intended to operate and did operate as an inducement to enter into the contract, but was not intended to be a binding contractual term. Where a statement of this class proves to be false, there is misrepresentation. See *Edgington* v. *Fitzmaurice* [1985]; *Bissett* v. *Wilkinson* [1927]; *Routledge* v. *Mackay* [1954].

A representation is, thus, an assertion of the truth that a fact does exist or did exist, as the case may be. A statement that something will be done in the future cannot be a representation of fact. *Beatty* v. *Ebury* [1872].

Fraudulent misrepresentation is a false statement which falls within the definition of fraud in *Derry* v. *Peek* [1889]. Where a misrepresentation falls outside of this definition, i.e., where it is made with an honest belief in its truth, it is innocent: *Derry* v. *Peek* [1989].

A negligent misstatement is any statement made carelessly and which breaches the common law duty of care owed to the person to whom the statement is made, and which causes that person loss or damage: *Hedley Byrne* v. *Heller & Partners* [1963].

2. Remedies

A party who has been deceived by a fraudulent misrepresentation may sue for rescission of the contract and/or damages for the tort of deceit: *Archer* v. *Brown* [1984]. Or he may sue for damages under s.2(1) of the Misrepresentation Act 1967 in the event of his failing to prove fraud.

A party who has been deceived by innocent misrepresentation may seek the equitable remedy of rescission or may sue for damages under s.2(1) of the Misrepresentation Act 1967: *Whittington* v. *Seale-Hayne* [1900]; *Howard Marine and Dredging Co.* v. *Ogden* [1978]. Where a party is entitled to rescission the court may declare the contract subsisting and award damages in lieu of rescission: s.2(92) of the 1967 Act.

Where a statement is negligently made, it may give rise to an action for damages for the tort of negligence: *Hedley Byrne* v. *Heller & Partners* [1963]; *Esso Petroleum* v. *Mardon* [1976]. Or an action might be more conveniently brought under the Misrepresentation Act 1967.

Edgington v. Fitzmaurice
[1885] 29 Ch.D. 459; [1881–5] All E.R. Rep. 856
Court of Appeal
The defendants, who were the directors of a company, issued a prospectus inviting members of the public to subscribe for debentures. The prospectus contained statements that the debentures were issued for the purpose of obtaining funds to purchase horses and vans, to complete alterations to the company's premises and to develop the company's business. In fact, the main purpose in raising money by the issue of debentures was to pay off debts. The plaintiff, who had advanced money to the company in reliance on the prospectus, brought this action for fraudulent misrepresentation.
HELD, by COTTON, BOWEN and FRY, L.JJ.; that the statements in the prospectus as to the objects of the issue were false in fact and were relied on by the plaintiff. The defendants were liable in deceit even though the plaintiff was influenced by matters other than those contained in the prospectus.

BOWEN, L.J. This is an action for deceit, in which the plaintiff complains that he was induced to take certain debentures by the misrepresentation of the defendants, and that he sustained damage thereby. The loss which the plaintiff sustained is not disputed. In order to sustain his action he must first prove that there was a statement as to facts which was false; and, secondly, that it was false to the knowledge of the defendants, or that they made it not caring whether it was true or false. For it is immaterial whether they made the statement knowing it to be untrue, or recklessly without caring whether it was true or not, because to make a statement recklessly for the purpose of influencing another person is dishonest. It is also clear that it is wholly immaterial with what object the lie is told.

Bowen, L.J., later referred to the statement of the objects for which the money was to be raised. He said: These were stated to be to complete the alterations and additions to the buildings, to purchase horses and vans, and to develop the supply of fish. A mere suggestion of possible purposes to which a portion of the money might be applied would not have formed the basis for an action of deceit. There must be a misstatement of an existing fact: But the state of a man's mind is as much a fact as the state of his digestion.

Bissett v. Wilkinson

[1927] A.C. 177; [1926] All E.R. Rep. 343
Privy Council

A vendor sold two blocks of land called 'Homestead' and 'Hogan's' to purchasers for the purpose of sheep farming. The purchasers failed in their enterprise and declined to pay the balance of the purchase moneys according to their agreement. When the vendor brought this action for the sum owed, the purchasers alleged by way of defence and counter-claim that the vendor had 'represented and warranted that the land which was the subject of the agreement had a carrying capacity of 2000 sheep if only one team were employed in the agricultural work of the said land.' The meaning of the representation as alleged was that the capacity of the land during winter, with such food as could be grown by the proper use in ploughing of one team of horses regularly employed throughout the year, was 2000 sheep. The purchasers asked for rescission of the contract of sale on the grounds of misrepresentation. The trial judge (SIM, J.) decided in favour of the vendor on the claim and counterclaim. This decision was reversed by the Court of Appeal of New Zealand and the vendor appealed.

HELD, by the Judicial Committee of the Privy Council (present: VISCOUNT DUNEDIN, LORD ATKINSON, LORD PHILLIMORE, LORD CARSON and LORD MERRIVALE), that the vendor's statement made prior to the sale was nothing more than an expression of opinion honestly held, and the fact that it was mistaken did not entitle the purchasers to rescission.

LORD MERRIVALE. In the present case, as in those cited, the material facts of the transaction, the knowledge of the parties respectively, and their relative positions, the words of representation used, and the actual condition of the subject-matter spoken of, are relevant to the two enquiries necessary to be made. What was the meaning of the representation? Was it price? In ascertaining what meaning was conveyed to the minds of the purchasers by the vendor's statement as to the 2000 sheep, the most material fact to be remembered is that, as both parties were aware, the vendor had not and, so far as appears, no other person had, at any time carried on sheepfarming upon the unit of land in question. That land as a distinct holding never constituted a sheep-farm.

. . . As was said by SIM, J.: 'In ordinary circumstances, any statement made by an owner who has been occupying his own farm as to its carrying capacity would be regarded as a statement of fact .. This, however, is not such a case. The purchasers knew all about Hogan's block and knew also what sheep the farm was carrying when they inspected it. In these circumstances . . . the purchasers were not justified in regarding anything said by the vendor as to the carrying capacity as being anything more than an expression of his opinion on that subject.'

In this view of the matter their Lordships concur:

NOTE
A statement as to the state of a man's mind may be a statement of fact. Such statement may be made with reference to intention or opinion. If it is proved that the intention was not formed, or the opinion was not held, at the time of the statement, there is misrepresentation. But if the expressed opinion was actually held but was mistaken, there is no misrepresentation.

Routledge v. McKay
[1954] 1 W.L.R. 615; [1954] 1 All E.R. 855
Court of Appeal

The buyer (fourth party) bought a motor cycle combination from the seller (fifth party) by private sale. When the seller himself had previously bought the machine second-hand, the date of the original registration book shown in the registration book was 9th September 1941. Unknown to the seller, the machine had in fact been registered first in 1930. A few days before the sale took place in answer to a question the seller told the buyer that it was a 1941 or 1942 model. At the time of the sale, the parties drew up and signed a memorandum of agreement, but this document made no mention of the date of the model. In this action the buyer (as fourth party) claimed against the seller (as fifth party) for breach of contract.

HELD, by SIR RAYMOND EVERSHED, M.R., and DENNING and ROMER, L.JJ., that the statement as to the year of the model made orally and in the registration book did not constitute a term of the contract of sale, nor was it a term of a collateral contract; that, accordingly, there was no breach of contract.

SIR RAYMOND EVERSHED, M.R. But I will assume that the warranty was given, not when the bargain was struck, but on Oct. 23, 1949, on which date alone, according to the evidence, any representation about the date of the motor cycle combination was made at all.

If that representation is to be a warranty it has to be contractual in form. In other words, so far as I can see, once the existence of a warranty as part of the actual bargain is excluded, it must be a separate contract, and the overwhelming difficulty which faces the fourth party is that when the representation was made there was then no bargain, and it is, therefore, in my view, impossible to say that it could have been collateral to some other contract. Even apart from that, it seems to me that on the evidence there is nothing to support the conclusion, as a matter of law and bearing in mind LORD MOULTON'S observations in *Heilbut, Symons & Co.* v. *Buckleton*, that in answering the question posed about the date of the motor cycle combination there was anything more intended than a mere representation.

Derry v. Peek

[1889] 14 App. Cas. 337; [1886–90] All E.R. Rep. 1
House of Lords
A tramway company was empowered by a special Act of Parliament to operate certain tramways by using animal power. The Act further provided that, with the consent of the Board of Trade, mechanical power might be used. The directors of the company, wishing to raise more capital, included the following statement in a prospectus: '. . . the company has the right to use steam or mechanical motive power instead of horses, and it is fully expected that by means of this a considerable saving will result . . .'. The plaintiff, who was induced by this statement to buy shares in the company, brought this action against the directors for damages for fraudulent misrepresentation. STIRLING, J., dismissed the action on the grounds that the statement was made *bona fide* without any intention to deceive. On appeal to the Court of Appeal it was held that the directors were liable because the statements were untrue and that the directors knew them to be untrue or had no reasonable ground for believing them to be true, it being

immaterial whether there was any intention to deceive. The directors appealed to the House of Lords.

HELD, by LORD HALSBURY, L.C., LORD WATSON, LORD BRAMWELL, LORD FITZGERALD and LORD HERSCHELL that the judgment of the Court of Appeal should be reversed on the ground that to sustain an action for deceit there must be proof of fraud and nothing short of that will suffice.

LORD HERSCHELL. I think the authorities establish the following propositions: First, in order to sustain an action for deceit, there must be proof of fraud, and nothing short of that will suffice. Secondly, fraud is proved when it is shown that a false representation has been made (*i*) knowingly, or (*ii*) without belief in its truth, or (*iii*) recklessly, careless whether it be true or false. Although I have treated the second and third as distinct cases, I think the third is but an instance of the second, for one who makes a statement under such circumstances can have no real belief in the truth of what he states. To prevent a false statement being fraudulent, there must, I think, always be an honest belief in its truth. And this probably covers the whole ground, for one who knowingly alleges that which is false has obviously no such belief. Thirdly, if fraud be proved, the motive of the person guilty of it is immaterial. It matters not that there was no intention to cheat or injure the person to whom the statement was made.

NOTE
In *Akerhielm* v. *de Mare* [1959] a company prospectus contained the following statement: 'About a third of the capital has already been subscribed in Denmark.' This statement was untrue, but the directors of the company believed it to be true at the time of the issue of the prospectus. It was held by the Privy Council that the statement was made in the honest belief in its truth and was, accordingly not fraudulent. Cf. *Edgington* v. *Fitzmaurice* [1885].

Whittington v. Seale-Hayne
[1900] L.T. 49
Chancery Division
The plaintiffs, who were breeders and exhibitors of very valuable

and prize poultry, entered into oral negotiations with the defendant's agent for the lease of certain premises. The plaintiff alleged that the defendant, by his agents, represented that the premises were in a thoroughly sanitary condition, and were also in a good state of repair. The defendant denied that such representations had been made. The plaintiffs, relying on the alleged representations, entered into an agreement for the lease of the premises for a term of 21 years. The lease, which was not read by the plaintiffs, contained a covenant which was not in the agreement, namely, 'to execute all such works as are or may under or in pursuance of any Act or Acts of Parliament already passed or hereafter to be passed be directed or required by any local or public authority to be executed at any time during the said term upon or in respect of the said premises whether by the landlord or tenant thereof.' The plaintiffs engaged a manager who, with his wife and eight children, went to live on the premises. The plaintiff erected outbuildings and stocked the premises with valuable poultry. The insanitary conditions of the premises caused the manager and his family to become very ill and caused the poultry to die or become valueless for breeding. The local authority required the drains to be put in order and the house on the premises to be rendered fit for human habitation. The plaintiffs claimed (*i*) rescission of the lease, and (*ii*) an indemnity against the following costs and charges, incurred by them: Value of stock lost, £750; loss of profit on sales, £100; loss of breeding season, £500; removal of storage and rent, £75; services on behalf of the manager, £100; incidental losses, £100. The defendant contended that an indemnity applied only to whatever was actually required to be done under the contract, such as the payment of rent and taxes and the repairs. There was no obligation on the plaintiffs, he contended, to erect outbuildings or to stock the premises with poultry and, the defendant argued, the plaintiff could not, therefore, recover the expenses thus incurred.

HELD, by FARWELL, J., that the lease should be rescinded for innocent misrepresentation, but that the indemnity was payable only with regard to the amount spent on rates and the cost of repairs ordered by the local authority. The claims for indemnity under the other heads must fail because they did not arise from obligations created by the lease. These claims were really for damages pure and simple and could not be allowed in case of innocent misrepresentation.

FARWELL, J. The question then arises to what extent the doctrine, that a plaintiff who succeeds in an action for rescission on the ground of innocent misrepresentation is entitled to be placed *in statu quo ante*, is to be applied. Counsel for the plaintiffs say that in such a case the successful party is to be placed in exactly the same position as if he had never entered into the contract. The defendant admits liability so far as regards anything which was paid under the contract, but not in respect of any damages incurred by reason of the contract; and I think the defendant's view is the correct one . . . When the plaintiffs say they are entitled to have the misrepresentations made good, it may mean one of two things. It may mean that they are entitled to have the whole of the injury incurred by their entering into the contract made good, or that they are entitled to be repaid what they have paid under their contract – e.g., to make good in the present case would mean to have the drains put right, but to make good by way of compensation for the consequences of the misrepresentations is the same thing as asking for damages . . . I think BOWEN, L.J.'s is the correct view. At p. 592 of 34 Ch. Div., (*Newbigging* v. *Adam*), he says: 'But when you come to consider what is the exact relief to which a person is entitled in a case of misrepresentaion, it seems to me to be this, and nothing more, that he is entitled to have the contract rescinded, and is entitled accordingly to all the incidents and consequences of such rescission. It is said that the injured party is entitled to be placed *in statu quo*. It seems to me that when you are dealing with innocent misrepresentation that you must understand that proposition that he is to be placed *in statu quo* with this limitation – that he is not to be replaced in exactly the same position in all respects, otherwise he would be entitled to recover damages, but is to be replaced in his position so far as regards the rights and obligations which have been created by the contract into which he has been induced to enter.'

Howard Marine & Dredging Co. Ltd. v. Ogden & Sons, Ltd.

[1978] Q.B. 574; [1978] 2 All E.R. 1134
Court of Appeal
The defendants, contractors, were negotiating with the plaintiffs for the hire of two barges which the plaintiffs owned. At a meeting

in the defendants' office, the plaintiffs' marine manager, Mr. O'Loughlin, said in response to questions that the payload was 1,600 tonnes. In fact the payload was only 1,055 tonnes. With regard to another contract, the defendants had calculated on the basis that the barges would carry 1,200 tonnes. At the time of the false statement, the marine manager did not have any papers giving the correct figures. His answer was based on his honest recollection of the 1,800 tonnes given in Lloyd's Register as the deadweight. That figure was, however, incorrect. The marine manager had at some time seen the shipping documents which showed that the deadweight of the barges was 1,195 tonnes. But that figure had not registered in his mind. As a result of the false statement the defendants were unable to carry out certain other contract work of carrying excavated material out to sea for dumping. They then refused to pay the hire charges. The plaintiffs then withdrew the barges and sued for payments due. The defendants counterclaimed for damages under s. 2 (1) of the *Misrepresentation Act*, 1967 and for negligence. Section 2 (1) provides as follows: 'Where a person has entered into a contract after a misrepresentation has been made to him by another party thereto and as a result thereof he has suffered loss, then, if the person making the misrepresentation would be liable to damages in respect thereof had the misrepresentation been made fraudulently, that person shall be so liable notwithstanding that the misrepresentation was not made fraudulently, unless he proves that he had reasonable grounds to believe and did believe up to the time the contract was made that the facts represented were true.' On appeal to the Court of Appeal:

HELD, by BRIDGE and SHAW, L.JJ. (LORD DENNING, M.R., dissenting), that the defendants were entitled to succeed on their counterclaim because (*i*) the plaintiffs' marine manager had not reasonable grounds as required by s. 2 (1) in that he should not have disregarded the deadweight capacity given in the shipping documents and (*ii*) the defendants were in breach of their duty of care in making the statement.

BRIDGE, L.J. [After stating the provisions of s. 2(1) of the 1967 Act.] The first question then is whether Howards would be liable in damages in respect of Mr. O'Loughlin's misrepresentation if it had been made fraudulently, that is to say, if he had known that it was untrue. An affirmative answer to that question is inescapable. The judge found in terms that what Mr. O'Loughlin said about the capacity of the barges was said with the object of getting the hire contract for Howards, in other words with the intention that it should be acted on. This was clearly right. Equally clearly the misrepresentation was in fact acted on by Ogdens. It follows, therefore, on the plain language of the 1967 Act that, although there was no allegation of fraud, Howards must be liable unless they proved that Mr. O'Loughlin had reasonable ground to believe what he said about the barges' capacity. . . .

. . . If the representee proves a misrepresentation which, if fraudulent, would have sounded in damages, the onus passes immediately to the representor to prove that he had reasonable ground to believe the facts represented. In other words the liability of the representor does not depend on his being under a duty of care the extent of which may vary according to the circumstances in which the representation is made. In the course of negotiations leading to a contract the 1967 Act imposes an absolute obligation not to state facts which the representor cannot prove he had reasonable ground to believe.

NOTE

Cf. *Archer* v. *Brown* [1984], in which the defendant had defrauded the plaintiff by selling to him the share capital in a company when he had sold the same shares to other victims. The defendant was imprisoned for these offences. The plaintiff financed the purchase by borrowing some £30,000 from a bank. The plaintiff also entered into an agreement by which he was to be joint managing director at a salary of £16,750 per annum. On discovering the fraud, the plaintiff claimed the return of the £30,000, all damages resulting from the deceit including interest of £13,528 on the bank loan and damages for deceit or breach of contract. The defendant contended that the plaintiff was restricted to the remedy of rescission. It was held that the plaintiff was entitled to damages as well as rescission because the misrepresentation was fraudulent. But even if it had been innocent, the plaintiff would still be entitled to damages under s. 2 of the Misrepresentation Act 1967. A plaintiff may claim under either contract or tort, provided he does not duplicate his claim. Although the measure of damages is different in tort, it makes no difference which measure is applied in this case – the damages are the same. The plaintiff was entitled to recover the bank interest because the defendant knew how the plaintiff proposed to raise the money. The plaintiff was not entitled to damages for loss of prospective earnings with the company, but he was entitled to £2,500 for loss of employment and to £1,000 for the expenses incurred in seeking new employment after discovery of the fraud.

Hedley Byrne & Co. Ltd. v. Heller & Partners Ltd.

[1964] A.C. 465; [1963] 2 All E.R. 575

House of Lords

A bank inquired by telephone of the defendant merchant bankers concerning the financial position of a customer for whom the defendants were bankers. The bank said that they wanted to know in confidence and without responsibility on the part of the defendants the respectability and standing of Easipower, Ltd., and whether this company would be good for an advertising contract for £8,000 to £9,000. Some months later, the bank wrote to the defendants asking in confidence the defendant's opinion of the respectability and standing of Easipower Ltd., by stating whether the defendants considered the company trustworthy, in the way of business, to the extent of £100,000 per annum. The defendant's replies to the effect that the company was respectable and considered good for its normal business engagements, were communicated to the plaintiffs, who were customers of the bank. In reliance on these replies, the plaintiffs, who were advertising agents, placed orders for the company with television and newspaper companies. The plaintiffs assumed responsibility for paying for the advertising time and space, intending to recover under their contract with the company. Easipower Ltd. went into liquidation and the plaintiffs lost over £17,000 on the advertising contracts. The plaintiffs sued the defendants for this amount alleging that the defendants' replies to the bank were given negligently. McNAIR, J., dismissed the claim and the plaintiff's appeal to the Court of Appeal was dismissed. On appeal to the House of Lords:

HELD, by LORD REID, LORD MORRIS, LORD HODSON, LORD DEVLIN and LORD PEARCE, that although in the present case, but for the respondents' disclaimer, the circumstances might have given rise to a duty of care on their part, yet their disclaimer of responsibility for their replies on the occasion of the first inquiry was adequate to exclude the assumption by them of a legal duty of care, with the consequence that they were not liable in negligence.

LORD REID. The appellants founded on a number of cases in contract where very clear words were required to exclude the duty of care which would otherwise have flowed from the contract. To that argument there are, I think, two answers. In the case of a contract it is necessary to exclude liability for negligence, but in this case the question is whether an undertaking to assume a duty to take care can be inferred; and that is a very different matter. Secondly, even in cases of contract general words may be sufficient if there was no other kind of liability to be excluded except liability for negligence: the general rule is that a party is not exempted from liability for negligence 'unless adequate words are used' —*per* SCRUTTON, L.J., in *Rutter* v. *Palmer*. It being admitted that there was a duty to give an honest reply, I do not see what further liability there could be to exclude except liability for negligence: there being no contract, there was no question of warranty.

Esso Petroleum Co. Ltd v. Mardon

[1976] Q.B. 801; [1976] 2 All E.R. 5
Court of Appeal

In 1961 the plaintiffs, Esso, acquired a site for a proposed petrol filling station on a busy main street. Esso had calculated that the estimated annual consumption of petrol would be 200,000 gallons from the third year of operation. The local planning authority then required the forecourt of the station to be sited at the rear of the plot, with the result that it was not visible from the main road and was accessible only from side streets. Subsequently Esso negotiated with the defendant for the grant of a tenancy of the station. An experienced Esso representative told the defendant that the throughput would be 200,000 gallons in the third year of operation. This statement was made in good faith. On the basis of the representation as to throughput, the defendant entered into a tenancy agreement in April 1963 and another, at reduced rent, in September 1964. Because of the planning change, the maximum annual throughput could only be in the region of 70,000 gallons. As a result, the defendant lost all his capital and also incurred a substantial overdraft. He was unable to pay Esso for petrol supplied up to August 1966. Esso brought this action, claiming possession of the station and the money due for the petrol. The defendant counterclaimed for damages in respect of the representation made by the Esso representative that the potential throughput was 200,000 gallons. He alleged (*i*) that it was a warranty, for breach of which he was entitled to damages, and (*ii*) that it amounted to negligent misrepresentation in breach of Esso's duty of care in advising as to potential throughput. The trial judge rejected the claim for breach of warranty, but held that Esso were liable in damages for breach of their duty of care to the defendant. The judge limited damages to the loss suffered between April 1963 and September 1964 on the ground that the misrepresentation made in 1963 had not induced the defendant to enter the agreement of September 1964. The defendant appealed.

HELD, by LORD DENNING, M.R., ORMROD and SHAW, L.JJ., (*i*) where a party with special knowledge and expertise concerning the subject-matter of pre-contract negotiations makes a forecast based on that knowledge and expertise with the intention of inducing the other party to enter into the contract, and in reliance on the forecast the other party did enter into the contract, the forecast could be construed as a warranty that it was reliable, i.e., that it had been made with reasonable skill and care. Since the estimate had been made negligently it was therefore unsound and Esso were liable for breach of warranty. (*ii*) There were no grounds for excluding liability for negligence in relation to statements made in the course of negotiations which culminated in the making of a contract. (*iii*) The measure of damages was the loss suffered by the defendant including that suffered after the agreement of September 1964, since that was also attributable to the original misrepresentation.

ORMROD, L.J. A variety of tests have been suggested to determine the intention of the parties. For example, it is said that to constitute a warranty a representation must be of fact and not of opinion; or a statement about existing facts as opposed to future facts such as a forecast. To quote again, in *De Lassalle* v. *Guildford* A. L. Smith M.R. said: 'In determining whether it was so intended, a decisive test is whether the vendor assumes to assert a fact of which the buyer is ignorant, or merely states an opinion or judgment upon a matter of which the vendor has no special knowledge, and on which the buyer may be expected also to have an opinion and to exercise his judgment.'

But he went too far in speaking of the 'decisive test' which was strongly disapproved of by Lord Moulton in the *Heilbut Symons* case.

In my judgment, these tests are no more than applied common sense. A representation of fact is much more likely to be intended to have contractual effect than a statement of opinion; so it is much easier to infer that in the former case it was so intended, and more difficult in the latter. Similarly, where statements of future fact or forecasts are under consideration, it will require much more cogent evidence to justify the conclusion that such statements were intended to be contractual in character. It is, therefore, with respect to counsel for Esso's argument, not an answer to say, simply, that the statement relied on was an expression of opinion or a forecast and therefore cannot be a warranty. In my view, following Lord Moulton in the *Heilbut Symons* case, the test is whether on the totality of the evidence the parties intended or must be taken to have intended that the representation was to form part of the basis of the contractual relations between them. *Bissett* v. *Wilkinson* fits into this scheme. After a considerable conflict of judicial opinion in Australia, the Privy Council decided finally that the representation that 'the land which was the subject matter of the agreement had a carrying capacity of two thousand sheep if only one team was employed in the agricultural work of the said land' was not to be taken as a warranty. It was a statement about the potential of the land in question based not on experience or special expertise and made in the course of negotiations with a buyer who was not ignorant of such matters. As Cheshire and Fifoot point out, where the party making the representation has a special knowledge or skill, the inference that the parties intended it to have contractual effect will more readily be drawn.

Misrepresentation Act 1967

1. Removal of certain bars to rescission for innocent misrepresentation
Where a person has entered into a contract after a misrepresentation has been made to him, and—

(*a*) the misrepresentation has become a term of the contract; or

(*b*) the contract has been performed;

or both, then, if otherwise he would be entitled to rescind the contract without alleging fraud, he shall be so entitled, subject to the provisions of this Act, notwithstanding the matters mentioned in paragraphs (*a*) and (*b*) of this section.

2. Damages for misrepresentation.

(1) Where a person has entered into a contract after a misrepresentation has been made to him by another party thereto and as a result thereof he has suffered loss, then, if the person making the misrepresentation would be liable to damages in respect thereof had the misrepresentation been made fraudulently, that person shall be so liable notwithstanding that the misrepresentation was not made fraudulently, unless he proves that he had reasonable ground to believe and did believe up to the time the contract was made the facts represented were true.

(2) Where a person has entered into a contract after a misrepresentation has been made to him otherwise than fraudulently, and he would be entitled, by reason of the misrepresentation, to rescind the contract, then, if it is claimed, in any proceedings arising out of the contract, that the contract ought to be or has been rescinded, the court or arbitrator may declare the contract subsisting and award damages in lieu of rescission, if of opinion that it would be equitable to do so, having regard to the nature of the misrepresentation and the loss that would be caused by it if the contract were upheld, as well as to the loss that rescission would cause to the other party.

(3) Damages may be awarded against a person under subsection (2) of this section whether or not he is liable to damages under subsection (1) thereof, but where he is so liable any award under the said subsection (2) shall be taken into account in assessing his liability under the said subsection (1).

3. Avoidance of provision excluding liability for misrepresentation

If a contract contains a term which would exclude or restrict —

(*a*) any liability to which a party to a contract may be subject by reason of any misrepresentation made by him before the contract was made; or

(*b*) any remedy available to another party to the contract by reason of such a misrepresentation,

that term shall be of no effect except in so far as it satisfies the requirement of reasonableness as stated in section 11(1) of the Unfair Contract Terms Act 1977; and it is for those claiming that the term satisfies that requirement to show that it does.

4. . . . .

5. Saving for past transactions
Nothing in this Act shall apply in relation to any misrepresentation or contract of sale which is made before the commencement of this Act.

6. Short title, commencement and extent
(1) This Act may be cited as the Misrepresentation Act 1967.

(2) This Act shall come into operation at the expiration of the period of one month beginning with the date on which it is passed.

(3) This Act, except section 4(2), does not extend to Scotland.

(4) This Act does not extend to Northern Ireland.

9. Mistake at common law

A buys B's horse; he thinks the horse is sound, and he pays the price of a sound horse: he would certainly not have bought the horse if he had known as the fact is that the horse is unsound. If B made no representation as to the soundness and has not contracted that the horse is sound A is bound, and cannot recover back the price: Bell v. Lever Bros., per LORD ATKIN.

Summary

1. Mistake and contractual validity

The general rule is that if the mind of one of the parties, or of both parties, at the time of contracting, is affected by mistake, then, at common law, the contract remains valid and enforceable notwithstanding the mistake: see *Bell* v. *Lever Bros.* [1931]; *Harrison & Jones* v. *Bunton & Lancaster*[1953]; *Crowshaw* v. *Pritchard* [1899]. It is only in the special circumstances referred to below that the common law validity of a contract may be affected.

There are two broad categories of mistake which may affect the validity of a contract in the eyes of the common law, namely, operative mistake and mistake of identity.

2. Operative mistake

There is operative mistake when a mistake of fact prevents the formation of any contract at all. Where it occurs, the courts will declare the agreement void: but where the mistake does not prevent the formation of agreement, the contract is good and valid in the eyes of the common law.

Operative mistake may occur as follows:

(*a*) Common mistake as to the existence of the subject-matter of the contract: *Courturier* v. *Hastie* [1852]; Sale of Goods Act 1979, s.6.

(*b*) Common mistake as to a fact or quality fundamental to the entire agreement: *Bell* v. *Lever Bros.* [1931].

(*c*) Mutual mistake as to the identity of the subject-matter of the contract: *Raffles* v. *Wichelhaus* [1864].

(*d*) Unilateral mistake by the offeror in expressing his intention, the mistake being known to the offeree: *Hartog* v. *Colin & Shields* [1939].

(*e*) Unilateral mistake as to the nature of a document signed or sealed: *Saunders* v. *Anglia Building Society* [1971].

3. Mistaken identity

Where there is unilateral mistake as to the identity of the other contracting party, the mistaken is different in character from the above-mentioned examples of operative mistake. In this connection, we are not concerned with the question whether a contract is void but, rather, whether a voidable title to goods has passed to a fraudulent buyer. Where a fraudulent person conceals his true identity in order to gain possession of goods without payment, he obtains a voidable title to the goods. Any attempt by the rogue to resell the goods will be governed by s.23 of the Sale of Goods Act 1979 which provides that: 'When the seller of goods has a voidable title to them, but his title has not been avoided at the time of the sale, the buyer acquires a good title to the goods, provided he buys them in good faith and without notice of the seller's defect in title'. See *Lewis* v. *Averay* [1972]; *Phillips* v. *Brooks* [1919]; *Ingram* v. *Little* [1960].

Couturier v. Hastie

[1843–60] All E.R. Rep. 280
House of Lords

H sold to A, on *del credere* commission, a cargo of corn. The bought note described it as being of average quality 'when shipped'. The price included freight and insurance to a safe port in the U.K. Before the date of the sale, the corn became over-heated and was sold abroad during the voyage. On hearing of this sale, A repudiated the contract and H's principal sued H for the price. HELD, by LORD CRANWORTH, L.C., and other Lords. At the time they made their contract, the parties contemplated that there was, actually in existence, a cargo to be bought and sold, but in fact, at that time, there was no such cargo. Therefore A was entitled to repudiate the contract and, accordingly, the principal's action against H failed. (This decision affirms that of the Court of Exchequer.)

LORD CRANWORTH, L.C. The contract plainly imports that there was something which was to be sold at the time of the contract, and something to be purchased. No such thing existing, I am of opinion, that the Court of Exchequer Chamber has come to the only reasonable conclusion on it, and consequently that there must be judgment for the respondents.

NOTE

Common mistake as to the existence of the subject-matter is now governed — so far as sale of goods is concerned — by s.6 of the Sale of Goods Act 1979. This section provides that: 'Where there is a contract for the sale of specific goods, and the goods without the knowledge of the seller have perished at the time when the contract was made, the contract is void'.

For the case where the seller is deemed to have warranted that the goods exist, see *McRae* v. *Commonwealth Disposals Commission* [1951].

Bell v. Lever Bros. Ltd.

[1932] A.C. 161; [1931] All E.R. Rep. 1
House of Lords

The appellant was appointed chairman of one of the subsidiaries of the respondent company. He subsequently engaged in certain private business activities in breach of his service contract for which he could have been dismissed without compensation. Neither party realising that this was the appellant's position, they entered another agreement by which the appellant agreed to resign his position prematurely in return for the sum of £30,000 by way of compensation for loss of office. Neither party was aware that it was then open to the company to dismiss the appellant without compensation: both parties believed erroneously that a fresh agreement was necessary to discharge the service contract. On discovering the mistake, the company sought to recover the £30,000 on the grounds that the compensation agreement was void for mistake. The company succeeded at first instance and before the Court of Appeal. The appellants appealed to the House of Lords.

HELD, by LORD HAILSHAM, LORD BLANESBURGH, LORD WARRINGTON, LORD ATKIN and LORD THANKERTON, that the compensation contract was valid and binding, the mistake of the parties not being sufficient to render the contract void. The agreement to terminate a broken contract is not essentially different from an agreement to terminate an unbroken contract, even where the breach gave the innocent party the right to declare the contract at an end.

LORD ATKIN. The agreement which is said to be void is the agreement contained in the letter of March 19, 1929, that Bell would retire from the board of the Niger Co. and its subsidiaries, and that in compensation od his doing so Levers would pay him as compensation for the termination of his agreements and consequent loss of office the sum of £30,000 in full satisfaction and discharge of all claims and demands of any kind against Lever Bros., the Niger Co., or its subsidiaries. The agreement which, as part of the contract, was terminated, had been broken so that it could be repudiated. Is an agreeement to terminate a broken contract different in kind from an agreement to terminate an unbroken contract, assuming that the breach has given the one party the right to declare the contract at an end? I feel the weight of the respondents' contention that a contract immediately determinable is a different thing from a contract for an unexpired term and that the difference in kind can be illustrated by the immense price of release from the longer contract as compared with the shorter. And I agree that an agreement to take an assignment of a lease for five years is not the same thing as to take an assignment of a lease for three years, still less a term for a few months. But on the whole I have come to the conclusion that it would be wrong to decide that an agreement to terminate a definite specified contract is void if it turns out that the contract had already been broken and could have been terminated otherwise. The contract released is the identical contract in both cases; and the party paying for release gets exactly what he bargained for. It seems immaterial that he could have got the same result in another way: or that, if he had known the true facts, he would not have entered into the bargain. A buys B's horse; he thinks the horse is sound and he pays the price of a sound horse: he would certainly not have bought the horse if he had known as the fact is that the horse is unsound. If B has made no representation as to soundness and has not contracted that the horse is sound A is bound, and cannot recover back the price. A buys a picture from B: both A and B believe it to be the work of an old master, and a high price is paid. It turns out to be a modern copy. A has no remedy in the absence of representation or warranty. A agrees to take on lease or to buy from B an unfurnished dwelling-house. The house is in fact uninhabitable. A would never have entered into the bargain if he had known the fact. A has no remedy: and the position is the same whether B knew the fact or not, so long as he made no representation or gave no warranty. A buys a roadside garage business from B abutting on a public thoroughfare: unknown to A, but known to B, it has already been decided to construct a by-pass road which will divert substantially the whole of the traffic from passing A's garage. Again A has no remedy. All these cases involve hardship on A and benefit B, as most people would say, unjustly. They can be supported on the ground that it is of paramount importance that contracts should be observed: and that if parties honestly comply with the essentials of the formation of contracts, i.e., agree in the same terms on the same subject matter they are bound: and must rely on the stipulations of the contract for protection from the effect of facts unknown to them.

NOTE

In *Bell* v. *Lever Bros.* [1931] the mistake was not sufficient to affect the validity of the contract. Similarly, in *Harrison & Jones* v. *Bunton & Lancaster* [1953], the mistake was not operative. In the Harrison case, there was a contract for the sale of a quantity of Calcutta Kapok 'Sree' brand. Both the buyer and the seller thought this to be tree kapok, whereas, in fact, it contained an admixture of bush cotton. The true nature of 'Sree' brand kapok was generally known in the trade.

Cf. *Galloway* v. *Galloway* [1914] in which the parties, believing themselves to be married, entered into a separation agreement under seal by which the man undertook to make money payments to the woman. It was later discovered that the marriage was not valid. The woman claimed the promised payments. She failed because the deed was void for mistake.

Mutual mistake

The above-mentioned cases dealt with the question of common mistake, i.e., where each party is suffering from the same misapprehension. Common mistake must be distinguished from mutual mistake, i.e., where the parties have negotiated completely at cross-purposes, so that there is no consensus.

If the court discovers that the sense of the promise given by one party was quite different from the sense in which it was accepted, there will be operative mutual mistake. For example, in *Raffles* v. *Wichelhaus* [1864], there was a contract for the sale of 125 bales of cotton 'to arrive ex *Peerless* from Bombay'. There were two ships named *Peerless* leaving Bombay at about the same time: the buyer meant one and the seller meant the other. It was held that the contract was void.

Hartog v. Colin & Shields

[1939] 3 All E.R. 566
King's Bench Division
The defendants made an offer in writing to sell to the plaintiff 30,000 Argentinian hare skins, the price being quoted in pence per pound. Immediately before this offer the parties had negotiated in terms of prices per piece, i.e., prices per skin, as was general in the

trade. The offer was accepted before the defendants discovered that they had made a mistake in expressing their offer. The defendants refused to deliver the skins, claiming that there was no binding contract. The plaintiff brought this action for breach of contract to deliver the skins.

HELD, by SINGLETON, J., that there was no contract, the plaintiff having snapped up the defendants' offer knowing that there was a mistake in expressing its terms.

SINGLETON, J. I am satisfied that it was a mistake on the part of the defendants or their servants which caused the offer to go forward in that way, and I am satisfied that anyone with any knowledge of the trade must have realised that there was a mistake. . . . That is the view I formed, having heard the witnesses. I do not form it lightly. I have seen the witnesses and heard them, and in this case can form no other view than that there was an accident. The offer was wrongly expressed, and the defendants by their evidence, and by the correspondence, have satisfied me that the plaintiff could not reasonably have supposed that that offer contained the offerers' real intention. Indeed, I am satisfied to the contrary. That means that there must be judgment for the defendants.

NOTE
In the *Hartog* case, the defendants asked for a declaration that the contract was void for mistake at common law and, in the alternative, for the equitable remedy of rescission. Since the court declared the contract void, there was no need to consider the question of rescission.

Where such a mistake in the offer is not known, nor deemed to be known, by the offeree, the acceptance will conclude a binding contract, the mistake having no effect. For example, in *Crowshaw* v. *Pritchard* [1899] a builder made a mistake in calculating his offer price to do certain building work. The offer was accepted and, later, when the builder discovered his mistake, he wrote to the offeree saying that, in the circumstances, he must withdraw the offer. The offeree then had the work carried out by another builder for a higher price than in the original offer. It was held that the mistake did not affect the contract. In the course of his judgment, Bigham J said, 'They had made a mistake, and they wanted to get out of their bargain because they had made a mistake; "and we fear that we have made an error. Under these circumstances, we must withdraw our estimate." It is too late to withdraw the estimate, which I regard as a complete offer to do the work, after it has been accepted and made the basis of a contract between the parties.' The builder was liable to pay damages amounting to the difference between his offer price and the price actually paid to the subsequent builder who actually did the work.

Saunders v. Anglia Building Society

[1971] A.C. 1004; [1970] 3 All E.R. 961
House of Lords

The plaintiff was an elderly widow who had made a will leaving all her possessions to her nephew, Walter Parkin. Her house was leasehold with more than 900 years to go. She gave the deeds of the house to Parkin because she had left it to him in her will and she knew that he wanted to raise money on it. She was content to allow him to do this provided she was able to remain in the house during her lifetime. When Parkin told his friend the first defendant, that the plaintiff had left the house to him in her will, they came to an arrangement by which the first defendant, who was heavily in debt, could raise some money. According to the arrangement, a document was drawn up by solicitors by which the plaintiff was to sell the house to the first defendant for £3,000. The understanding between Parkin and the first defendant was that after signature by the plaintiff, no purchase price would be paid over, and the first defendant would then mortgage the property to raise money. The first defendant took the document to the plaintiff who, at that time was seventy-eight years old, to get her signature. She did not read the document because she had broken her spectacles. She asked him what it was for, and he replied, 'It is a deed of gift for Wally (Parkin) for the house.' She thought at the time that Parkin was going to borrow money on the deeds and that the first defendant was arranging this for him. After the plaintiff had signed the document no money was paid to her, although the document provided that she acknowledged receipt of £3,000 paid by the first defendant. The first defendant then obtained a loan of £2,000 from the second defendant, a building society, on the security of the deeds. For this purpose, Parkin gave a reference to the building society, falsely stating that he was a reliable person.

Subsequently, the first defendant defaulted in the instalment payments to the building society, which then sought to recover possession of the house. The plaintiff then brought this action, contending that she was not bound by the assignment on the grounds that it was not her deed. STAMP, J., held that the assignment was not her deed and ordered the building society to deliver up the title deeds to the plaintiff. (It is noteworthy that, had matters been allowed to rest at this decision, the only person to benefit would be Parkin, for the building society had given an undertaking to allow the plaintiff to remain in the house for the rest of her life.) The building society appealed to the Court of Appeal. It was held by LORD DENNING, M.R., RUSSELL and SALMON, L.JJ., that the plea of *non est factum* could not be supported and that the appeal must be allowed. The executrix of the plaintiff's estate appealed to the House of Lords.

HELD, by LORD REID, LORD HOBSON, VISCOUNT DILHORNE, LORD WILBERFORCE and LORD PEARSON, that the plaintiff fell very short of making the clear and satisfactory case which is required of those who seek to have a legal act declared void and of establishing a sufficient discrepancy between her intentions and her act.

LORD REID. The plea of *non est factum* obviously applies when the person sought to be held liable did not in fact sign the document. But at least since the sixteenth century it has also been held to apply in certain cases so as to enable a person who in fact signed a document to say that it is not his deed. Obviously any such extension must be kept within narrow limits if it is not to shake the confidence of those who habitually and rightly rely on signatures when there is no obvious reason to doubt their validity. Originally this extension appears to have been made in favour of those who were unable to read owing to blindness or illiteracy and who therefore had to trust someone to tell them what they were signing. I think that it must also apply in favour of those who are permanently or temporarily unable through no fault of their own to have without explanation any real understanding of the purport of a particular document, whether that be from defective education, illness or innate incapacity.

But that does not excuse them from taking such precautions as they reasonably can. The matter generally arises where an innocent third party has relied on a signed document in ignorance of the circumstances in which it was signed, and where he will suffer loss if the maker of the document is allowed to have it declared a nullity. So there must be a heavy burden of proof on the person who seeks to invoke this remedy. He must prove all the circumstances necessary to justify its being granted to him, and that necessarily involves him proving that he took all reasonable precautions in the circumstances. I do not say that the remedy can never be available to a man of full capacity. But that could only be in very exceptional circumstances; certainly not where his reason for not scrutinising the document before signing it was that he was too busy or too lazy. In general I do not think that he can be heard to say that he signed in reliance on someone he trusted. But particularly when he was led to believe that the document which he signed was not one which affected his legal rights, there may be cases where this plea can properly be applied in favour of a man of full capacity.

The plea cannot be available to anyone who was content to sign without taking the trouble to try to find out at least the general effect of the document. Many people do frequently sign documents put before them for signature by their solicitor or other trusted advisers without making any enquiry as to their purpose or effect. But the essence of the plea *non est factum* is that the person signing believed that the document he signed had one character or one effect whereas in fact its character or effect was quite different. He could not have such a belief unless he had taken steps or been given information which gave him some grounds for his belief. The amount of information he must have and the sufficiency of the particularity of his belief must depend on the circumstances of each case. Further the plea cannot be available to a person whose mistake was really a mistake as to the legal effect of the document, whether that was his own mistake or that of his adviser. That has always been the law and in this branch of the law at least I see no reason for any change.

NOTE
The general rule is that a person is bound by the terms of any instrument which he has signed or sealed even though he did not read it, or did not understand its contents. An exception arises where a person signs or seals a document under a mistaken belief as to the nature of the document and the mistake was due to either (*1*) the blindness, illiteracy, or senility of the person signing, or (*2*)

a trick or fraudulent misrepresentation as to the nature of the document, provided that person took all reasonable precautions before signing.

Lewis v. Averay

[1972] 1 Q.B. 198; [1971] 3 All E.R. 907
Court of Appeal, Civil Division

The plaintiff put an advertisement in a newspaper, offering to sell his car for £450. In reply to the advertisement, a man (who turned out to be a rogue) telephoned and asked if he could see the car. That evening, he came to see the car, tested it and said that he liked it. The rogue and the plaintiff then went to the flat of the plaintiff's fiancée, where the rogue introduced himself as Richard Greene, making the plaintiff and his fiancée believe that he was the well-known film actor of that name. The rogue wrote a cheque for the agreed sum of £450, but the plaintiff was, at first, not prepared to let him take the car until the cheque was cleared. When the rogue pressed to be allowed to take the car with him, the plaintiff asked: "Have you anything to prove that you are Mr. Richard Greene?" Whereupon, the rogue produced a special pass of admission to Pinewood Studios, bearing the name of Richard A. Greene and a photograph, which was clearly of the man claiming to be Richard Greene. The plaintiff was satisfied that the man was really Mr. Richard Greene, the film actor. He let the rogue take the car in return for the cheque. A few days later, the plaintiff discovered that the cheque was from a stolen book and that it was worthless. In the meantime, the rogue sold the car to the defendant who paid £200 for it in entire good faith. The rogue then disappeared. The plaintiff brought this action against the defendant, claiming damages for conversion. The county court judge found in favour of the plaintiff. The defendant appealed. On the essential question whether there was a contract of sale by which property in the car passed from the plaintiff to the rogue:
HELD, by LORD DENNING, M.R., PHILLIMORE and MEGAW, L.JJ., that the fraud rendered the contract between the plaintiff and the rogue voidable (and not void) and that, accordingly, the defendant obtained good title since he bought in good faith and without notice of the fraud, the plaintiff having failed to avoid the contract in time.

LORD DENNING, M.R.: I think the true principle is that which underlies the decision of this court in *King's Norton Metal Co. Ltd.* v. *Eldridge, Merrett & Co. Ltd.* and of HORRIDGE, J. in *Phillips* v. *Brooks Ltd.*, which has stood for these last 50 years. It is this: when two parties have come to a contract — or rather what appears, on the face of it, to be a contract — the fact that one party is mistaken as to the identity of the other does not mean that there is no contract, or that the contract is a nullity and void from the beginning. It only means that the contract is voidable, that is, liable to be set aside at the instance of the mistaken person, so long as he does so before third parties have in good faith acquired rights under it.

Applied to the cases such as the present, this principle is in full accord with the presumption stated by PEARCE, L.J. and also by DEVLIN, L.J. in *Ingram* v. *Little*. When a dealing is had between a seller like Mr. Lewis and a person who is actually there present before him, then the presumption in law is that there is a contract, even though there is a fraudulent impersonation by the buyer representing himself as a different man than he is. There is a contract made with the very person there, who is present in person. It is liable no doubt to be avoided for fraud but it is still a good contract under which title will pass unless and until it is avoided. In support of that presumption, DEVLIN, L.J., quoted, not only the English case of *Phillips* v. *Brooks*, but other cases in the United States where: 'The Courts hold that if A appeared in person before B, impersonating C, an innocent purchaser from A gets the property in the goods against B.' That seems to me to be right in principle in this country also.

In this case Mr. Lewis made a contract of sale with the very man, the rogue, who came to the flat. I say that he 'made a contract' because in this regard we do not look into his intentions, or into his mind to know what he was thinking or into the mind of the rogue. We look to the outward appearances. On the face of the dealing, Mr Lewis made a contract under which he sold the car to the rogue, delivering the car and the log book to him, and took a cheque in return. The contract is evidenced by the receipts which were signed. It was, of course, induced by fraud. The rogue made false representations as to his identity. But it was still a contract, though voidable for fraud. It was a contract under which this property passed to the rogue, and in due course passed from the rogue to Mr. Averay, before the contract was avoided.

Although I very much regret that either of these good and reliable gentlemen should suffer, in my judgment it is Mr. Lewis who should do so. I think the appeal should be allowed and judgment entered for the defendant.

NOTE

Where a fraudulent person conceals his true identity in order to get possession of goods from a seller and having got possession of the goods, resells them, the question of title to the goods arises. Do the goods belong to the original seller who was defrauded and never received the price? Or do the goods belong to the subsequent buyer, who may have paid for the goods in all good faith?

The rogue who concealed his identity obtains a voidable title to the goods and the resale is governed by s.23 of the Sale of Goods Act 1979 and previously governed by a similar provision in s.23 of the 1893 Act. Section 23 provides that: 'When the seller of goods has a voidable title to them, but his title has not been avoided at the time of the sale, the buyer acquires a good title to the goods, provided he buys them in good faith and without notice of the seller's defect in title'.

Lord Denning's judgment contains an analysis and comparison of two conflicting cases, namely, *Ingram* v. *Little* [1960] and *Phillips* v. *Brooks* [1919], by which he explained his preference for the latter. *Ingram* v. *Little* must now be regarded as being of doubtful authority.

Phillips v. Brooks, Ltd.

[1919] 2 K.B. 243; [1918–19] All E.R. Rep 246
King's Bench Division

One North went into the plaintiff's shop and asked to see some pearls and rings. He selected pearls at £2,550 and a ring at £450 and then produced a cheque book and wrote a cheque for £3,000. As he signed he said 'You see who I am; I am Sir George Bullough.' This was the name of a man well-known in London at the time. The plaintiff used a directory to check the address given by North. The plaintiff then asked North whether he would like to take the jewellery with him and he replied, 'You had better have the cheque cleared first; but I should like to take the ring as it is my wife's birthday tomorrow.' North took the ring with him. When the plaintiff presented the cheque it was returned marked "No account." In the meantime, North pawned the ring with the defendants who took it in good faith and advanced £350 on it. The plaintiff brought this action to recover the ring or its value.

HELD, by HORRIDGE, J., that the plaintiff intended to contract with the person present in front of him, i.e. North. Consequently, the property in the ring passed to North, who gave good title to the defendants.

HORRIDGE, J. I have carefully considered the evidence of the plaintiff, and have come to the conclusion that, although he believed the person to whom he was handing the ring was Sir George Bullough, he in fact contracted to sell and deliver it to the person who came into his shop, and who was not Sir George Bullough but a man of the name of North, who obtained the sale and delivery by means of false pretence that he was Sir George Bullough. It is quite true the plaintiff in re-examination said he had no intention of making any contract with any other person than Sir George Bullough; but I think that I have myself to decide what is the proper inference to draw where a verbal contract is made and an article delivered to an individual describing himself as somebody else. After obtaining the ring the man North pledged it in the name of Firth with the defendants, who *bona fide* and without notice advanced £350 upon it. The question, therefore, in this case is whether or not the property had so passed to the swindler as to entitle him to give a good title to any person who gave value and acted *bona fide* without notice.

NOTE
In *Lewis* v. *Averay* [1972] the Court of Appeal preferred the principle applied in *Phillips* v. *Brooks* [1919] to that which was applied by the Court of Appeal in *Ingram* v. *Little* [1960].

Ingram v. Little
[1961] 1 Q.B. 31; [1960] 3 All E.R. 332
Court of Appeal
A swindler called on the plaintiffs in answer to their advertisement for the sale of a car. At first refusing to part with the car in return

for a cheque, the plaintiffs changed their minds, taking the cheque, after the swindler had convinced them that he was a certain Mr. P.G.M. Hutchinson of Stanstead House, Stanstead Road, Caterham, Surrey. The plaintiffs had checked the name and address in a telephone directory, and it was with the person of that name and address that they intended to deal. The cheque was dishonoured and the car was traced to the defendants, who had taken it in good faith and had paid for it. The plaintiffs brought this action to recover the car or its value.

HELD, by SELLERS and PEARCE, L.JJ. (DEVLIN, L.J., dissenting), that the plaintiffs' offer was made to the person whom the swindler pretended to be, namely, Mr P.G.M. Hutchinson, and the swindler knew this. Consequently, the offer was not capable of being accepted by the swindler; therefore, there was no contract for the sale of the car. The plaintiffs were entitled to recover the car or its value from the defendants.

PEARCE, L.J. The question in such cases is this. Has it been sufficiently shown in the particular circumstances that, contrary to the prima facie presumption, a party was not contracting with the physical person to whom he uttered the offer, but with another individual whom (to the other party's knowledge) he believed to be the physical person present? The answer to that question is a finding of fact.

DEVLIN, L.J., dissenting. Why should the question whether the defendant should or should not pay the plaintiff damages for conversion depend on voidness or voidability and on inferences to be drawn from a conversation in which the defendant took no part? The true spirit of the common law is to override theoretical distinctions when they stand in the way of doing practical justice. For the doing of justice the relevant question in this sort of case is not whether the contract was void or voidable, but which of two innocent parties shall suffer for the fraud of a third. The plain answer is that the loss should be divided between them in such proportion as is just in all the circumstances. If it be pure misfortune, the loss should be borne equally; if the fault or imprudence of either party has caused or contributed to the loss, it should be borne by that party in the whole or in the greater part.

NOTE

Ingram v. *Little* is of doubtful authority since the decision in *Lewis* v. *Averay* [1972].

Consider the passage in the judgment of Devlin L.J. in which he says, 'for the doing of justice the relevant question in this sort of case is not whether the contract was void or voidable, but which of two innocent parties shall suffer for the fraud of a third'.

10. Mistake in equity

In order to see whether the lease can be avoided for this mistake it is necessary to remember that mistake is of two kinds: first, mistake which renders the contract void, that is, a nullity from the beginning, which is the kind of mistake which was dealt with by the courts of common law, and, secondly, mistake which renders the contract not void, but voidable, that is, liable to be set aside on such terms as the court thinks fit, which is the kind of mistake which was dealt with by the courts of equity: Solle v. Butcher, per DENNING, L.J.

Summary

In appropriate circumstances, equity may afford relief to a party who has incurred contractual obligations by mistake. Equitable relief, according to the circumstances, may be rescission on terms, rectification or refusal to award specific performance.

1. Rescission on terms

Where there is common mistake, but the contract remains valid at common law, mistake notwithstanding, rescission may be available to a party who has been adversely affected. In such cases, rescission will be ordered subject to the claimant entering into a new contract with the defendant containing fair and just terms as ordered by the court: *Solle* v. *Butcher* [1950]; *Grist* v. *Bailey* [1966].

2. Rectification

Where a written contract does not express the actual agreement between the parties, the court may order the rectification of the written document so as to bring it into conformity with the actual agreement. A claimant must prove (*a*) the agreement and (*b*) that there was a mistake in expressing the terms of that agreement in a subsequent written document: *Craddock* v. *Hunt* [1923]; *Joscelyne* v. *Nissen* [1970].

3. Refusal of specific performance

A court will not usually award specific performance against a defendant who was under some material misapprehension at the time of contracting and (*a*) it would, therefore, be unduly harsh to compel the defendant to comply specifically with the contract, or (*b*) the mistake was caused by a misrepresentation by the plaintiff, or (*c*) the plaintiff knew of the defendant's mistake: *Tamplin* v. *James* [1880]; *Webster* v. *Cecil* [1861]; *Grist* v. *Bailey* [1966].

Solle v. Butcher

[1950] 1 K.B. 671; [1949] 2 All E.R. 1107
Court of Appeal

The landlord held a long lease of a house which he repaired and restored after war-damage. He then entered into an agreement to let a flat in the house for £250 a year. Both landlord and tenant knew that the controlled rent had been £140 before the restoration work had been done. But they both erroneously believed that the flat had undergone a change of identity due to the substantial nature of the repairs and restoration, and that the Rent Restriction Acts no longer applied to it. (Had he not been mistaken in this way, the landlord could have taken the necessary steps to have the controlled rent raised to £250 immediately after the repairs had been completed and before letting it to the tenant.) On discovering the mistake, the tenant brought this action to obtain a declaration that the controlled rent was £140 a year. The landlord contended that the lease should be rescinded on the grounds that both parties entered it under mistake. HELD, by BUCKNILL and DENNING, L.JJ. (JENKINS, L.J., dissenting), that the structural alterations were not such as to change the identity of the flat and that the misapprehension of the parties in this connexion was a mistake of fact. The landlord was, therefore, entitled to have the lease set aside in equity on terms that the tenant should be granted a new lease at the full permitted rent (but not exceeding £250 a year) if he so wished.

DENNING, L.J. The Landlord says with truth that it is unfair that the tenant should have the benefit of the lease for the outstanding five years of the term at £140 a year when the proper rent is £250 a year. If he cannot give notice of increase now, can he not avoid the lease? The only ground on which he can avoid it is on the ground of mistake. It is quite plain that the parties were under a mistake. They thought that the flat was not tied down to a controlled rent, whereas in fact it was. In order to see whether the lease can be avoided for this mistake it is necessary to remember that mistake is of two kinds: first, mistake which renders the contract void, that is, a nullity from the beginning, which is the kind of mistake which was dealt with by the courts of common law, and, secondly, mistake which renders the contract not void, but voidable, that is, liable to be set aside on such terms as the court thinks fit, which is the kind of mistake which was dealt with by the courts of equity.... . While presupposing that a contract was good at law, or at any rate not void, the court of equity would often relieve a party from the consequences of his own mistake, so long as it could do so without injustice to third parties. The court had power to set aside the contract whenever it was of the opinion that it was unconscientious for the other party to avail himself of the legal advantage which he had obtained.

NOTE

In *Solle* v. *Butcher*, the Court of Appeal applied *Cooper* v. *Phibbs* (1867), an appeal from the Chancery Court to the House of Lords. In *Cooper* v. *Phibbs*, the appellant had taken a three-year lease of a salmon fishery from the respondent. At the time both parties believed that the fishery belonged to the respondent, indeed, he had spent a considerable sum on improvements. It was subsequently discovered that the fishery was the property of the appellant, who now sought to have the lease set aside for mistake. It was held by the House of Lords that the appellant was entitled to have the lease rescinded on terms that the respondent would have a lien on the property to the extent of the money spent on improvements. Lord Westbury said, 'If parties contract under a mutual mistake and misapprehension as to their relative and respective rights, the result is that that agreement is liable to be set aside as having proceeded upon a common mistake.'

Grist v. Bailey

[1967] Ch. 532; [1966] 2 All E.R. 875
Chancery Division

The defendant entered into a written agreement to sell a house to the plaintiff 'subject to the existing tenancy' for £850. At the time of this agreement, the parties were under a common mistake as to the existence of the tenancy. They both believed the house to be in the occupation of the statutory tenant. But, unknown to them, the tenant had died and the house was occupied by his son who did not wish to claim the statutory tenancy for himself. When the defendant discovered this, he refused to complete, because without a statutory tenant, the house was worth about £2,250. The plaintiff brought this action for specific performance of the agreement to sell for £850, and the defendant counterclaimed for rescission on the grounds of the common mistake of the parties.

HELD, by GOFF, J., that the counterclaim for rescission must succeed. The common mistake was fundamental and there was no fault on the part of the defendant.

GOFF, J. The result, in my judgment, is that the defendant is entitled to relief in equity, and I do not feel that this is a case for simply refusing specific performance. Accordingly, the action fails, and on the counterclaim I order rescission. It is clear that this being equitable relief may be granted unconditionally or on terms, and counsel on behalf of the defendant has offered to submit to a condition that the relief I have ordered should be on condition that the defendant is to enter into a fresh contract at a proper vacant possesssion price, and if required by the plaintiff, I will impose that term.

Craddock Brothers v. Hunt

[1923]2 Ch. 136; [1923] All E.R. Rep. 394
Court of Appeal
A piece of land was knocked down to the plaintiff at an auction sale, the piece being accurately described in the particulars of sale. The defendant's agent was present at the sale. By error, a certain plot included in the particulars of sale was omitted from the subsequent written contract and the conveyance. By a further error on the part of the vendor, this same plot was included in the conveyance of an adjoining piece of land to the defendant. The conveyance to the plaintiff was made the day before the conveyance to the defendant. The defendants made no claim to the plot now in dispute until about seven months after the conveyance, during which period the plaintiffs had treated it as being in their ownership. On becoming aware of the mistake, the plaintiffs claimed a declaration that they were entitled to have the plot in dispute conveyed to them and, if necessary, rectification of the conveyance to them.
HELD, by LORD STERNDALE, M.R., and WARRINGTON, L.J., (YOUNGER, L.J., dissenting), that, (*i*) the defendant was a trustee of the plot in dispute for the plaintiff, (*ii*) the conveyance to the plaintiff should be rectified and (*iii*) the defendant must execute a conveyance to the plot in dispute to the plaintiff.

LORD STERNDALE, M.R. I can see no conscience or honesty in the defendant's claim, and I think he should be declared a trustee for the plaintiffs of land to which he has by mistake got a title which he knew had been knocked down to them and which he never thought was intended to be sold to him or had been bought by him.

WARRINGTON, L.J. The jurisdiction of courts of equity in this aspect is to bring the written document executed in pursuance of an antecedent agreement into conformity with that agreement. The conditions to its exercise are that there must be an antecedent contract and the common intention of embodying or giving effect to the whole of that contract by the writings and there must be clear evidence that the document by common mistake failed to embody such contract and either contained provisions not agreed upon, or omitted something that was agreed upon or other wise departed from its terms. If these conditions are fulfilled, then it seems to me, on principle that the instrument so rectified should have the same force as if the mistake had not been made.

NOTE

Rectification will not be granted unless it can be shown (*a*) that a complete and certain agreement was reached between the parties, and (*b*) that the agreement was unchanged at the time it was put into writing, and the writing did not correspond with the agreement previously reached. In other words, rectification may be available where parties make a mistake when they reduce an oral agreement into writing.

The equitable remedy of rectification is not available to a party who carelessly fails to read the terms of the contract and is consequently mistaken as to those terms: *Agip* v. *Navigazione Alta Italia* [1984]. Cf. *Saunders* v. *Anglia Building Soc.* [1971].

Rectification is not available to a party who made a mistake in expressing the terms of his offer. In *Higgins* v. *Northampton Corporation* [1927] a builder submitted a tender to the corporation for the building of certain houses. After the acceptance of the tender, the builder discovered that he had stated the wrong price for the work owing to faulty calculations. The tender had been accepted without knowledge of the mistake. The builder failed in his claim for rectification. Cf. *Hartog* v. *Colin & Shields* [1939].

Joscelyne v. Nissen

[1970] 2 Q.B. 86; [1970] 1 All E.R. 1213
Court of Appeal, Civil Division
This case concerns a dispute between a father and his daughter. The
father lived in a house from which he carried on a car hire business.
In 1960 he received notice to quit. The daughter, in order to help her
father, bought the house and let her husband's house furnished to pay
the mortgage. She, together with her husband, moved into the house
to live with her parents. The car hire business deteriorated owing to
the amount of time the father had to devote to his sick wife. In order
to improve things, the father and the daughter agreed in writing that
the business should be transferred to the daughter on condition that
the daughter would permit the father during his life to have the right
to reside in the ground floor of the house 'free of all rent and
outgoings of every kind in any event.' In pursuance of this agreement,
the daughter for a time paid the gas, electricity and coal bills and the
cost of home help for the father. Trouble occurred between the
daughter and her parents and she stopped the above-mentioned
payment, being advised that they were not covered by the written
agreement. The father obtained an order for rectification of the
written agreement in the county court. The daughter appealed.
HELD, by RUSSELL, SACHS and PHILLIMORE, L.JJ., that this
was a proper case for rectification based on antecedent expressed
accord on a point adhered to in intention by the daughter and father
as parties to the subsequent written contract and since both parties
were in agreement up to the moment when they executed the written
agreement that the daughter should pay all outgoings on the house,
and the written agreement did not conform with that agreement, the
court had jurisdiction to rectify the written contract, although there
may have been no concluded and binding contract between the
parties until the written contract was executed.

RUSSELL, L.J. [who read the judgment of the Court]. In our
judgment the law is as expounded by SIMONDS, J. in *Crane's* case,
with the qualification that some outward expression of accord is
required. We do not wish to attempt to state in any different phrases
that with which we entirely agree, except to say that it is in our view
better to use only the phrase 'convincing proof' without echoing an
old fashioned word such as 'irrefragable' and without importing from

the criminal law the phrase 'beyond all reasonable doubt.' Remembering always the strong burden of proof that lies on the shoulders of those seeking rectification, and that the requisite accord and continuance of accord of intention may be the more difficult to establish if a complete antecedent concluded contract be not shown, it would be a sorry state of affairs if when that burden is discharged a party to a written contract could, on discovery that the written language chosen for the document did not on its true construction reflect the accord of the parties on a particular point, take advantage of the fact.

NOTE

In *Crane* v. *Hegeman-Harris Co.* [1939] 1 All E.R. 662, SIMONDS, J., said: 'Before I consider the facts and come to a conclusion whether the defendants are right in their contention, it is necessary to say a few words upon the principles which must guide me in this matter. I am clear that I must follow the decision of CLAUSON, J., as he then was, in *Shipley Urban District Council* v. *Bradford Corpn.*, the point of which is that, in order that this court may exercise its jurisdiction to rectify a written instrument, it is not necessary to find a concluded and binding contract between the parties antecedent to the agreement which it is sought to rectify. The judge held, and I respectfully concur with his reasoning and his conclusion, that it is sufficient to find a common continuing intention in regard to a particular provision or aspect of the agreement. If one finds that, in regard to a particular point, the parties were in agreement up to the moment when they executed their formal instrument, and the formal instrument does not conform with that common agreement, then this court has jurisdiction to rectify, although it may be that there was, until the formal instrument was executed, no concluded and binding contract between the parties. That is what the judge decided, and, as I say, with his reasoning I wholly concur, and I can add nothing to his authority in the matter, except that I would say that, if it were not so, it would be a strange thing, for the result would be that two parties binding themselves by a mistake to which each had equally contributed, by an instrument which did not express their real intention, would yet be bound by it. That is a state of affairs which I hold is not the law, and, until a higher court tells me it is the law, I shall continue to exercise the jurisdiction which CLAUSON, J., as I think rightly, held might be entertained by this court. Secondly, I want to say this upon the principle of the jurisdiction. It is a jurisdiction which is to be exercised only upon convincing proof that the

concluded instrument does not represent the common intention of
the parties. That is particularly the case where one finds prolonged
negotiations between the parties eventually assuming the shape of a
formal instrument in which they have been advised by their respective
skilled legal advisers. The assumption is very strong in such a case
that the instrument does represent their real intention, and it must
be only upon proof which LORD ELDON, I think, in a somewhat
picturesque phrase described as 'irrefragable' that the court can act.
I would rather, I think, say that the court can only act if it is satisfied
beyond all reasonable doubt that the instrument does not represent
their common intention, and is further satisfied as to what their
common intention was. For let it be clear that it is not sufficient to
show that the written instrument does not represent their common
intention unless positively also one can show what their common
intention was.'

Tamplin v. James

[1880], 15 Ch.D. 215; [1874–80] All E.R. Rep. 560
Court of Appeal
The plaintiffs put up for auction certain property consisting of an inn
and an adjoining shop. Accurate plans and particulars of the property
were displayed in the auction room, but the property was not sold at
the auction. The defendant, who was present at the auction,
afterwards offered £750 for it and the offer was accepted. The
defendant signed a contract for purchase and paid a deposit, but he
then refused to complete on the grounds that he mistakenly believed
that certain gardens formed part of the property he had agreed to
buy. The defendant knew the property well and knew that, previously,
the gardens in question had been held and occupied with the inn and
the shop respectively. The defendant had not seen the plans displayed
in the auction room which showed quite clearly that the gardens were
not part of the lot sold to the defendant. The plaintiff obtained a
decree of specific performance and the defendant appealed.
HELD, by JAMES, BRETT and COTTON L.JJ., the description of
the property was accurate and the defendant's mistake was caused
only by his failure to take reasonable care to ascertain what he was
buying: accordingly, the defendant must be held to his bargain.

JAMES, L.J. The vendors did nothing to mislead. In the particulars of sale they described the property as consisting of nos. 454 and 455 on the tithe map, and this was quite correct. The purchaser says that the tithe map is on so small a scale as not to give sufficient information, but he never looked at it. He must be presumed to have looked at it, and at the particulars of sale. He says he knew the property, and was aware that the gardens were held with the other property in the occupation of the tenants, and he asked no questions about it. If a man will not take reasonable care to ascertain what he is buying, he must take the consequences. The defence on the ground of mistake cannot be sustained.

NOTE

He who comes to equity must come with clean hands. Therefore, in *Tamplin* v. *James*, where the mistake was caused by the defendant's own carelessness, specific performance was awarded notwithstanding the mistake. Similarly, where a party accepted an offer, knowing that it was mistakenly expressed, he will not succeed if he claims specific performance. In *Webster* v. *Cecil* [1861] the purchaser offered to buy certain land for £2,000 but the owner rejected the offer. The owner then wrote to the purchaser offering to sell the land for £1,250 and the purchaser accepted by return of post. The owner immediately gave notice to the purchaser that he had written £1,250 in error for £2,250. The purchaser claimed specific performance but it was refused because he must have known of the mistake in the expression of the owner's offer.

11. Inequality of bargaining power

> *As no court has ever attempted to define fraud, so no court has ever attempted to define influence, which includes one of the many varieties:* Allcard v. Skinner, per LINDLEY, L.J.

Summary

1. Undue influence

A contract or gift may be set aside where it was made under undue influence.

2. Where undue influence must be proved

The general rule is that the party alleging undue influence must prove it: see, e.g., *Williams* v. *Bayley* (1866). This class of case depends on the principle that no one should be allowed to retain any benefit arising from his own fraud or wrongful act: *Allcard* v. *Skinner* [1887] per Cotton, L.J.

3. Where undue influence is presumed (abuse of influence)

If a meticulous examination of the facts pertaining to the relations between the parties is such as to raise a presumption of undue influence the court will set aside the transaction if it was to the manifest disadvantage to the person influenced: *National Westminster Bank* v. *Morgan* [1985]. The court will set aside the transaction unless there is sufficient evidence to rebut the transaction, e.g., to the effect that the party influenced had competent independent advice.

In this kind of case the court interferes, not on the ground that any wrongful act has been committed by the influencer, but on the ground of public policy, and to prevent the relations which existed between the parties and the influence arising therefrom being abused: *Allcard* v. *Skinner* [1887]; *Lloyds Bank* v. *Bundy* [1974]; *National Westminster Bank* v. *Morgan* [1985]. It is not necessary to show that the influencer was in a relationship of domination over the other party to the transaction in question: *Goldsworthy* v. *Brickell* [1987].

4. Economic duress

The court will recognise economic duress as a factor which may render a contract voidable, provided that the duress amounts to a coercion of will which vitiates consent: *Pao On* v. *Lau Yiu Long* [1980]; *North Ocean Shipping Co.,* v. *Hyundai Construction Co. The Atlantic Baron* [1979]. The party claiming to have been coerced must show that he repudiated the transaction as soon as the pressure on him was relaxed.

Allcard v. Skinner

[1887] 36 Ch.D 145; [1886–90] All E.R.Rep.90
Court of Appeal

In 1868 the plaintiff, an unmarried woman, was introduced to a Church of England sisterhood. In 1870 she became a novice and in 1871 she was admitted a full member of the sisterhood, embracing the vows of poverty, obedience and chastity. The plaintiff, without independent advice, made gifts of money and stock to the defendant, who was the lady superior of the sisterhood. In 1879 the plaintiff left the sisterhood and became a member of the Church of Rome. Soon afterwards, she spoke to her brother about getting back her money and he told her that it would be better to leave it alone. She was similarly advised by a Roman Catholic priest. Then, in 1880, her solicitor advised her that the sum was too large to leave with the sisterhood without asking for its return, but she replied that she preferred not to bother about it. In 1884 the plaintiff heard that one of the sisters had left the sisterhood and that her money had been returned to her at her request. As a result of this news, the plaintiff decided to make an attempt to get her money back from the sisterhood. In the same year, 1884, the plaintiff asked for her money. The lady superior refused to return it and the plaintiff brought this action against her for its recovery in 1885. The plaintiff claimed to recover the entire capital sum which she had given to the lady superior, but the trial judge gave judgment for the defendant. The plaintiff appealed, limiting her appeal to certain railway stock which was transferred to the lady superior and was still standing in the lady superior's name.

HELD, by COTTON, LINDLEY and BOWEN, L.JJ., (*i*) that the lady superior's equitable title was imperfect because, at the time of the gift, the plaintiff was bound by her vows, and the rules of the sisterhood, to make absolute submission to the defendant as lady superior; but (*ii*) (COTTON, L.J., dissenting) the plaintiff was not entitled to recover the funds because of the delay in making her claim.

COTTON, L.J. The question is: Does the case fall within the principles laid down by the decisions of the Court of Chancery in setting aside voluntary gifts executed by parties who at the time were under such influence as, in the opinion of the court, enable the donor afterwards to set the gift aside? These decisions may be divided into two classes – (*i*) Where the court has been satisfied that the gift was the result of influence expressly used by the donee for the purpose; (*ii*) Where the relations between the donor and donee have at or shortly before the execution of the gift been such as to raise a presumption that the donee had influence over the donor. In such a case the court sets aside the voluntary gift, unless it is proved that in fact the gift was the spontaneous act of the donor acting under circumstances which enabled him to exercise an independent will, and justifies the court in holding that the gift was the result of a free exercise of the donor's will. The first class of cases may be considered as depending on the principle that no one shall be allowed to retain any benefit arising from his own fraud or wrongful act. In the second class of cases the court interferes, not on the ground that any wrongful act has in fact been committed by the donee, but on the ground of public policy, and to prevent the relations which existed between the parties and the influence arising therefrom being abused.

LINDLEY, L.J. It would obviously be to encourage folly, recklessness, extravagance, and vice if persons could get back property made away with, whether by giving it to charitable institutions, or by bestowing it on less worthy objects. On the other hand, to protect people from being forced, tricked, or misled, in any way, by others into parting with their property, is one of the most legitimate objects of all laws; and the equitable doctrine of undue influence has grown out of and been developed by the necessity of grappling with insidious forms of spiritual tyranny and with the infinite varieties of fraud. As no court has ever attempted to define fraud, so no court has ever attempted to define undue influence, which includes one of the many varieties. The undue influence which courts of equity endeavour to defeat is the undue influence of one person over another; not the influence of enthusiasm on the enthusiast who is carried away by it, unless indeed such enthusiasm is itself the result of external undue influence. But the influence of one mind over another is very subtle, and of all influences religious influence is the most dangerous and the most powerful. To counteract it courts of equity have gone very far. They have not shrunk from setting aside gifts made to persons in a position to exercise undue influence over the donors, although there has been no proof of the actual exercise of such influence; and the courts have done this on the avowed ground of the necessity of going this length in order to protect persons from the exercise of such influence under circumstances which render proof of it impossible. The courts have required proof of its non-exercise, and, failing that proof, have set aside gifts otherwise unimpeachable.

Lloyds Bank Ltd. v. Bundy

[1975] Q.B. 326; [1974] 3 All E.R. 757
Court of Appeal, Civil Division
The defendant was an elderly farmer. His home was his farmhouse which had belonged to his family for several generations. It was his only asset. The defendant, his son and a company formed by the son were all customers of the same branch of the plaintiff's bank. The company ran into difficulties and the defendant guaranteed the company's overdraft for £1,500 and charged his farmhouse to the bank to secure that sum. The company ran into further difficulties and the defendant executed a further guarantee for £5,000 and a further charge for £6,000. The defendant's solicitor had advised that this was the most that he should commit to the son's business, since the house was worth only £10,000. The company's business went from bad to worse and the son went to the bank for further money. Accordingly, the bank's new assistant manager and the son went to visit the defendant. The assistant manager took with him a form of guarantee and a form of charge for up to £11,000 already prepared for the defendant's signature. The assistant manager realised that the defendant relied on him to advise on the transaction 'as bank manager.' He knew that the defendant's farmhouse was his only asset. The defendant, to help his son's business, executed the forms of guarantee and charge which the assistant manager had produced. About five months later, a receiving order was made against the son. The bank then attempted to enforce the guarantee and charge against the defendant. They brought this action for possession of the defendant's farmhouse. The trial judge gave judgment for the bank and the defendant appealed.
HELD, by LORD DENNING, M.R., CAIRNS, L.J. and SIR ERIC SACHS, that there was a confidential relationship between the defendant and the bank which imposed on the bank a duty of fiduciary care, *i.e.* to ensure that the defendant formed an independent and informed judgment on the proposed transaction before committing himself. The bank should have advised the

defendant to obtain independent advice whether the company's affairs had any prospect of becoming viable. The bank was in breach of its fiduciary duty and, accordingly, the guarantee and charge would be set aside and the action for possession dismissed.

SIR ERIC SACHS. It was inevitably conceded on behalf of the bank that the relevant relationship can arise as between banker and customer. Equally, it was conceded on behalf of the defendant that in the normal course of transactions by which a customer guarantees a third part's obligations, the relationship does not arise. The onus of proof lies on the customer who alleges that in any individual the line has been crossed and the relationship has arisen. . . . Undue influence is a phrase which is commonly regarded – even in the eyes of a number of lawyers – as relating solely to occasions when the will of one person has become so dominated by that of another that, to use the learned county court judge's words, 'the person acts as the mere puppet of the dominator'. Such occasions, of course, fall within what Cotton, L.J., in *Alcard* v. *Skinner* described as the first class of cases to which the doctrine on undue influence applies. There is, however, a second class of such cases. This is referred to by Cotton, L.J., as follows:

> 'In the second class of cases the Court interferes, not on the ground that any wrongful act has been committed by the donee, but on the ground of public policy, and to prevent the relations which existed between the parties and the influence arising therefrom being abused'

It is thus to be emphasised that as regards the second class the exercise of the court's jurisdiction to set aside the relevant transaction does *not* depend on proof of one party being 'able to dominate the other as though a puppet'.

There remains to mention that counsel for the bank, whilst conceding that the relevant special relationship could arise between banker and customer, urged in somewhat doom-laden terms that a decision taken against the bank on the facts of this particular case would seriously affect banking practice. With all respect to that submission, it seems necessary to point out that nothing in this judgment affects the duties of a bank in the normal case where it obtains a guarantee, and in accordance with standard practice explains to the person about to sign, its legal effect and the sums involved. When, however, a bank, as in the present case, goes further and advises on more general matters germane to the wisdom of the transaction, that indicates that it may — not necessarily must — be crossing the line into the area of confidentiality so that the court may then have to examine all the facts including, of course, the history leading up to the transaction, to ascertain whether or not that line has, as here, been crossed. It would indeed be rather odd if a bank which *vis-à-vis* a customer attained a special relationship in some ways akin to that of a 'man of affairs' — something which can be a matter of pride and enhance its local reputation — should not, where a conflict of interest has arisen as between itself and the person advised, be under the resulting duty now under discussion. Once, as was inevitably conceded, it is possible for a bank to be under that duty, it is, as in the present case, simply a case for 'meticulous examination' of the particular facts to see whether that duty has arisen. On the special facts here it did arise and it has been broken.

NOTE

In his judgment, Sir Eric Sachs explained that the conclusion that the defendant established that, as between himself and the bank, the relevant transaction fell within the second category of undue influence, is one reached on the single issue pursued on behalf of the defendant. Sir Eric Sachs did not express an opinion as regards the wider areas covered by Lord Denning. Cairns, L.J., agreed with Sir Eric Sachs, whose judgment must be regarded as the leading judgment. For an examination of Lord Denning's general principle of 'inequality of bargaining power', see *National Westminster Bank* v. *Morgan* [1985] in the House of Lords.

In *Williams* v. *Bayley* [1866] a son forged his father's name to a promissory note, and, by means of it, raised money from the bank of which they were both customers. On discovering the forgery, the bank put pressure on the father to charge his property to the bank with payment of the note. In effect, the bank said to the father, 'Take your choice — give us security for your son's debt. If you do take that on yourself it will all go smoothly; if you do not, we shall be bound to exercise pressure'. It was held by the House of Lords that the charge was invalid because of the undue pressure exerted by the bank.

National Westminster Bank v. Morgan

[1985] A.C. 686 [1985] 1 All E.R. 821
House of Lords

A husband and wife were joint owner of their home. The husband was unsuccessful in a business venture and was unable to meet the repayments due under a mortgage secured over the home. The then mortgagee commenced proceedings to take possession. The husband tried to save the situation by entering a refinancing arrangement with a bank. The refinancing was secured by a legal charge in favour of the bank. The bank manager made a brief visit to the home so that the wife could execute the charge. The wife made it clear to the bank manager that she had little faith in her husband's business ability and that she did not want the charge to cover his business liabilities. The bank manager assured her that the charge secured only the amount advanced to refinance the mortgage. Nevertheless, it was the bank's intention to treat it as limited to the amount required to refinance the mortgage. This assurance was given in good faith but was incorrect. The terms of the charge were unlimited in extent and extended to all of the husband's liabilities to the bank.

The wife did not receive independent legal advice before signing the charge. The husband fell into arrears with payments and the bank obtained an order for possession of the home. The husband then died without owing the bank on any business advances. The wife appealed against the order for possession contending that the charge should be set aside as it had been signed as a result of undue influence from the bank. The bank argued that undue influence could be raised only when the transaction was manifestly disadvantageous to the defendant. The bank contended that the refinancing arrangement had averted the earlier possession by the previous mortgagee and that this was manifestly advantageous to the wife. The Court of Appeal found in favour of the wife on the grounds that a special relationship had been created which the bank was unable to rebut because of the failure to advise the wife to seek independent legal advice. The bank appealed to the House of Lords.

HELD, by LORD SCARMAN, LORD KEITH, LORD ROSKILL, LORD BRIDGE and LORD BRANDON, that the appeal should be allowed and possession of the house be given to the bank. A transaction could not be set aside on the grounds of undue influence unless it is shown that the transaction was to the manifest disadvantage of the person subjected to the dominating influence.

The Court of Appeal erred in law in holding that the presumption of undue influence can arise from the evidence of the relationship of the parties without also evidence that the transaction itself was wrongful in that it constituted an advantage taken of the person subjected to the influence which, failing proof to the contrary, was explicable only on the basis that undue influence had been exercised to procure it. The bank manager never crossed the line. The transaction was not unfair to the wife. The bank was, therefore, under no duty to ensure that she had independent advice. It was an ordinary banking transaction whereby the wife sought to save her home; and she obtained an honest and truthful explanation of the bank's intention which, notwithstanding the terms of the mortgage deed, was correct; for the bank had not sought to make the wife liable, nor to make the home a security, for any business debt of the husband.

LORD SCARMAN. The wrongfulness of the transaction must, therefore, be shown: it must be one in which an unfair advantage has been taken of another. The doctrine is not limited to transactions of gift. A commercial relationship can become a relationship in which one party assumes a role of dominating influence over the other. In *Poosathurai*'s case the Board recognised that a sale at an undervalue could be a transaction which a court could set aside as unconscionable if it was shown or could be presumed to have been procured by the exercise of undue influence. Similarly, a relationship of banker and customer may become one in which the banker acquires a dominating influence. If he does and a manifestly disadvantageous transaction is proved, there would then be room for the court to presume that it resulted from the exercise of undue influence.

This brings me to *Lloyds Bank Ltd v. Bundy*. It was, as one would expect, conceded by counsel for the wife that the relationship between banker and customer is not one which ordinarily gives rise to a presumption of undue influence; and that in the ordinary course of banking business a banker can explain the nature of the proposed transaction without laying himself open to a charge of undue influence. This proposition has never been in doubt, though some, it would appear, have thought that the Court of Appeal held otherwise in *Lloyds Bank Ltd v. Bundy*. If any such view has gained currency, let it be destroyed now once and for all time. . . .

A meticulous examination of the facts of the present case reveals that Mr Barrow never 'crossed the line'. Nor was the transaction unfair to the wife. The bank was, therefore, under no duty to ensure that she had independent advice. It was an ordinary banking transaction whereby the wife sought to save her home; and she obtained an honest and truthful explanation of the bank's intention which, notwithstanding the terms of the mortgage deed which in the circumstances the trial judge was right to dismiss as 'essentially theoretical', was correct; for no one has suggested that Mr Barrow or the bank sought to make the wife liable, or to make her home the security, for any debt of her husband other than the loan and interest necessary to save the house from being taken away from them in discharge of their indebtedness to the building society.

For these reasons, I would allow the appeal. In doing so, I would wish to give a warning. There is no precisely defined law setting limits to the equitable jurisdiction of a court to relieve against undue influence. This is the world of doctrine, not of neat and tidy rules. The courts of equity have developed a body of learning enabling relief to be granted where the law has to treat the transaction as unimpeachable unless it can be held to have been procured by undue influence. It is the unimpeachability at law of a disadvantageous transaction which is the starting point from which the court advances to consider whether the transaction is the product merely of one's own folly or of the undue influence exercised by another. A court in the exercise of this equitable jurisdiction is a court of conscience. Definition is a poor instrument when used to determine whether a transaction is or is not unconscionable: this is a question which depends on the particular facts of the case.

NOTE

In *Goldsworthy* v. *Brickell* [1987] the Court of Appeal took the view that it is not necessary for the party in whom the trust is reposed to actually dominate the other party. The test applied by the trial judge was approved. He said that the influence acquired (by the defendant in that case) was based on and arising out of a particular association and an advisory capacity well short of domination which, nevertheless, made it his duty to take care of the plaintiff in any transaction between them.

North Ocean Shipping Co. v. Hyundai Construction Co. The Atlantic Baron

[1979] Q.B. 705; [1978] 3 All E.R. 1170
Queen's Bench Division
Hyundai shipbuilders agreed to build a tanker for the shipping company for $US30,950,000 payable in five instalments. The contract required the builder to open a letter of credit for the repayment of instalments in the event of their default in performance. After the payment of the first instalment, the builders claimed an increase of 10 per cent on the remaining instalments. There was no legal basis for this claim and the shipping company rejected it, but later agreed to pay the extra 10 per cent in return for which the builders agreed to increase their letter of credit correspondingly. All further instalments were paid as agreed. There was no protest over the additional 10 per cent until six months after delivery of the ship was accepted. The shipping company brought this action to recover the additional 10 per cent. They argued that the agreement to pay the additional money was void for lack of consideration and that the 10 per cent was recoverable as money had been received or, alternatively, that the agreement to pay it was made under economic duress and, accordingly, voidable.
HELD, by MOCATTA, J., that the agreement to pay the additional 10 per cent was binding since it was supported by the builder's promise to increase the letter of credit. Further, although the agreement to pay the additional money might have been voidable for economic duress, the failure on the part of the shipping company to protest until more than six months after delivery amounted to an affirmation of the agreement. The shipping company was not, therefore, entitled to the return of the money representing the additional 10 per cent.

MOCATTA, J. First, I do not take the view that the recovery of money paid under duress other than to the person is necessarily limited to duress to goods falling within one of the categories hitherto established by the English cases. I would respectfully follow and adopt the broad statement of principle laid down by Isaacs, J. cited earlier and frequently quoted and applied in the Australian cases. Secondly, from this it follows that the compulsion may take the form of 'economic duress' if the necessary facts are proved. A threat to break a contract may amount to such 'economic duress'. Thirdly, if there has been such a form of duress leading to a contract for consideration, I think the contract is a voidable one which can be avoided and the excess money paid under it recovered.

NOTE

Mocatta, J. referred to the principle laid down by Isaacs, J. in *Smith* v. *William Charlick* [1924]: 'It is conceded that the only ground on which the promise to repay could be implied is "compulsion". The payment is said by the respondent not to have "voluntary" but "forced" from it within the contemplation of the law. . . "Compulsion" in relation to a payment of which refund is sought, and whether it is also variously called "coercion", "extortion", "exaction" or "force", includes every species of duress or conduct analogous to duress, actual or threatened, exacted by or on behalf of the payee and applied to the person or property or any right of the person who pays . . . Such compulsion is a legal wrong, and the law provides a remedy by raising a fictional promise to repay.'

In the Privy Council case *Pao On* v. *Lau Yiu Long* [1980] Lord Scarman said: 'There is nothing contrary to principle in recognising economic duress as a factor which may render a contract voidable, provided always that the basis of such recognition is that it must always amount to a coercion of will which vitiates consent.'

A party seeking to have a contract set aside for economic duress must be able to show that he repudiated the transaction as soon as the pressure on him was relaxed: see *Alec Lobb Garages* v. *Total Oil G.B.* (1983). Failure to do so will amount to an affirmation of the contract: *North Ocean Shipping Co.* v. *Hyundai Construction Co. The Atlantic Baron* [1978].

12. Restraint of trade

Restraints of trade and interference with individual liberty of action, may be justified by the special circumstances of a particular case. It is sufficient justification, and indeed, it is the only justification, if the restriction is reasonable reasonable, that is, in reference to the interests of the parties concerned and reasonable in reference to the interests of the public, so framed and so guarded as to afford adequate protection to the party in whose favour it is imposed, while at the same time it is in no way injurious to the public; the Nordenfelt case, per LORD MACNAGHTEN.

Summary

1. Restraint of trade

A contract in restraint of trade is one which contains a provision by which one of the parties agrees to suffer a restriction with regard to the carrying on of his trade or profession. Or it may be a contract by which both parties agree to suffer restriction in the way they carry on business.

Contracts in restraint of trade may be classified as follows:

(*a*) Where an employee agrees that he will not compete with his employer's business.

(*b*) Where the vendor of a business undertakes that he will not compete with the purchaser after the sale.

(*c*) Where business firms or trade associations give mutual undertakings for the regulation of their business relations, e.g., for the control of output, prices or the business use of a piece of land.

Contracts in restraint of trade are *prima facie* void but will be upheld if it can be shown that the restraint is reasonable. The question of reasonableness is tested at two levels, first, as between the parties and, second, as regards the interests of the public: *Nordenfelt* v. *Maxim Nordenfelt Co.* [1894]. Where a restraint provision cannot be shown to be reasonable, the court will declare it to be void. The rest of the contract remains valid and binding.

2. Contracts of employment

An employer is entitled to the benefit of a restraint clause which prevents the use of confidential information or trade secrets by an employee, apprentice or articled clerk. The employer must be able to show that the restraint is no wider than is necessary for the protection of both parties, taking into account the public interest: *Morris* v. *Saxelby* [1916], *Fitch* v. *Dewes* [1921], *Home Counties Dairies* v. *Skilton* [1970].

3. Sale of the goodwill of a business

Where a business is sold, the trade connections will always be an important item. The buyer is entitled to the protection of a restraint clause by which the vendor agrees that he will not set up in competition with the business he has sold to the purchaser. Restraints of this class are valid only so far as they protect a definite proprietary interest: *Nordenfelt* v. *Maxim Nordenfelt Co.* [1894].

4. Contracts regulating trade

Agreements between business organisations or trade associations governing the regulation of trade will not be regarded as reasonable unless each party derives some advantage from the restraint provision: *English Hop Growers* v. *Dering* [1928], *Esso Petroleum Co.* v. *Harper's Garage* [1968].

5. Severance

Where part of a contract is declared void as being in restraint of trade, the rest of the contract remains valid and will be upheld. In other words, the void clause will be severed from the rest of the contract: *Attwood* v. *Lamont* [1920]. Where a restraint provision contains several distinct restraints, some of which are reasonable and some of which are not, the unreasonable elements will be severed and the rest of the provision upheld: *Goldsoll* v. *Goldman* [1915].

Nordenfelt v. Maxim Nordenfelt Guns and Ammunition Co. Ltd.

[1894] A.C. 535; [1891–4] All E.R. Rep. 1
House of Lords.
The defendant, Thorsten Nordenfelt, had established a business for the manufacture and sale of guns and ammunition. His dealings were world-wide. He sold the business to a company which was formed for the specific purpose of buying it. The contract of sale contained a restraint clause intended to protect the business in the hands of the company. Two years later, the company transferred the business to the Maxim Nordenfelt Company with the concurrence of the defendant. On the occasion of the transfer, the defendant entered another restraint agreement in substitution for that which was entered into with the original purchasers. The restraint was that the defendant should not, during the term of 25 years from the formation of the company, engage in the trade or business of a manufacturer of guns, explosives or ammunition. Subsequently, the defendant engaged in business which was contrary to the restraint agreement. The company brought this action claiming an injunction restraining him from further breach. The defendant contended that the restraint agreement was void as being in restraint of trade and going beyond what was reasonably necessary for the protection of the company's interests. The plaintiff company succeeded before the Court of Appeal and the defendant appealed to the House of Lords.
HELD, by LORD HERSCHELL, L.C., LORD WATSON, LORD ASHBOURNE, LORD MACNAGHTEN and LORD MORRIS, that the restraint agreement, unlimited in space, not to carry on for the space of twenty five years 'the trade or business of a manufacturer of guns, gun-mountings or carriages, gunpowder, explosives or ammunition,' in a contract by which the defendant assigned his interest in the business to the plaintiff company was valid on the ground that the area supplied by the company was practically unlimited, since the customers would be governments of countries all over the world, and so the restraint was reasonable and not wider than the protection of the company required. The company succeeded in its claim for an injunction.

LORD HERSCHELL, L.C. When the nature of the business and the limited number of customers is considered, I do not think the covenant can be held to exceed what is necessary for the protection of the covenantees.

LORD MACNAGHTEN. The public have an interest in every person's carrying on his trade freely; so has the individual. All interference with individual liberty of action in trading, and all restraints of trade of themselves, if there is nothing more, are contrary to public policy, and, therefore, void. That is the general rule. But there are exceptions. Restraints of trade and interference with individual liberty of action, may be justified by the special circumstances of a particular case. It is a sufficient justification, and indeed, it is the only justification, if the restriction is reasonable — reasonable, that is, in reference to the parties concerned and reasonable in reference to the interests of the public, so framed and so guarded as to afford adequate protection to the party in whose favour it is imposed, while at the same time it is in no way injurious to the public.

Herbert Morris Ltd. v. Saxelby

[1916] 1 A.C. 688; [1916–17] All E.R. Rep. 305
House of Lords
The defendant covenanted in a contract of service with the plaintiffs, his former employers, that he would not at any time during a period of seven years from the date of his ceasing to be employed carry on or be concerned, directly or indirectly, in the United Kingdom, with the sale or manufacture of pulley blocks, overhead runways or overhead travelling cranes. In this action, the plaintiffs sought to restrain the defendant from breach of covenant. The action was dismissed by SARGENT, J., whose decision was affirmed by the Court of Appeal. The plaintiffs appealed to the House of Lords.
HELD, by LORD ATKINSON, LORD SHAW, LORD PARKER OF WADDINGTON and LORD SUMNER, that, having regard to all the circumstances, the convenant was not reasonable in reference to the interests of the parties and was prejudicial to the interests of the public, and, therefore, it was void and unenforceable.

LORD ATKINSON. I think it has been generally assumed that the law upon this subject of the validity or invalidity of contracts in restraint of trade has been authoritatively determined by the decision of the House in *Nordenfelt* v. *Maxim Nordenfelt Guns and Ammunition Co.,* and that it is laid down in the clearest and most happily selected language in the oft-quoted passage of the judgment of LORD MACNAGHTEN, so that it is, I think, no longer necessary to refer to the earlier authorities. The passage runs thus ([1894] A.C. at p. 565):

'The true view at the present time is, I think, this: The public have an interest in every person's carrying on his trade freely; so has the individual. All interference with individual liberty of action in trading and all restraint of trade themselves, if there is nothing more, are contrary to public policy, and therefore void. That is the general rule. But there are exceptions; restraints of trade and interference with individual liberty of action may be justified by the special circumstances of a particular case. It is sufficient justification, and, indeed, it is the only justification if the restriction is reasonable – reasonable that is in reference to the interests of the parties concerned, and reasonable in reference to the interests of the public, so framed and so guarded as to afford adequate protection to the party in whose favour it is imposed, while at the same time it is in no way injurious to the public. That, I think, is the fair result of all the authorities.'

It will be observed that LORD MACNAGHTEN uses the plural, 'parties concerned,' in the earlier portion of this passage, meaning, apparently, to include both the covenantor and covenantee, while in the latter portion of the passage he merely speaks of 'protection' being given to the covenantee, which does not injure the public. But in the opening lines of the passage he had already said that the individual (here the covenantor), as well as the public, have an interest in freedom of trading.

If it be assumed, as I think it must be, that no person has an abstract right to be protected against competition per se in his trade or business, then the meaning of the entire passage would appear to me to be this: If the restraint affords to the person in whose favour it is imposed nothing more than reasonable protection against something which he is entitled to be protected against, then as between the parties concerned the restraint is to be held to be reasonable in reference to their respective interests, but, notwithstanding this, the restraint may still be held to be injurious to the public and therefore void, the onus of establishing to the satisfaction of the judge who tries the case facts and circumstances which show that the restraint is of the reasonable character mentioned resting upon the person alleging that it is of that character, and the onus of showing that, notwithstanding that it is of that character, it is nevertheless injurious to the public, and, therefore, void resting in the like manner on the party alleging the latter...

In all cases such as the present one has to ask oneself what are the interests of the employer that are to be protected, and against what is he entitled to have them protected? He is undoubtedly entitled to have his interest in his trade secrets protected, such as secret processes of manufacture which may be of vast value. And that protection may be secured by restraining the employee from divulging these secrets or putting them to his own use. He is also entitled not to have his old customers by solicitation or such other means enticed away from him. But freedom from all competition per se apart from both these things, however lucrative it might be to him, he is not entitled to be protected against. He must be prepared to encounter that even at the hands of a former employee.

NOTE

A restraint clause which purports to prevent an employee using his skill in competition with his employer after leaving the employment is void, even where the skill was acquired in that employer's service.

In deciding what is reasonable, the court will consider the relevant circumstances, particularly, the nature of the employer's business, the status of the employee, the area covered by the restraint and the duration of the restraint.

Fitch v. Dewes

[1921] 2 A.C. 158; [1921] All E.R. Rep 13
House of Lords

The respondent was a solicitor practising in Tamworth in Warwickshire. In 1899 the appellant entered the employment of the respondent as a junior clerk and continued in that employment until 1914. In 1903 the appellant was articled to the respondent. In 1908 there was an agreement between the respondent and the appellant which provided that if the appellant was successful in his final law examination he should serve the respondent as managing clerk.

There was a further agreement made in 1912 by which the appellant agreed to serve the respondent as managing clerk for a period of three years from 31st December 1911. This agreement contained the following restraint clause: 'The said Thomas Birch Fitch hereby expressly agrees with the said John Hunt Dewes that he will not on the expiration or sooner determination of the said term of three years or any extended term as herein provided either alone or jointly with any other person or persons directly or indirectly be engaged or manage or concerned in the office, profession or business of a solicitor within a radius of seven miles of the town hall of Tamworth, but nothing herein contained shall at any time prevent the said Thomas Birch Fitch from carrying on the legal business of the North Warwickshire Miners' Association at Tamworth or within the aforesaid radius thereof.' When the respondent sought to enforce the restraint clause the appellant contended that it was against public policy and void.

HELD, by LORD BIRKENHEAD, L.C., VISCOUNT CAVE, LORD SUMNER, LORD PARMOOR and LORD CARSON, the question whether or not the unlimited restriction as to time was void as being in restraint of trade and so against public policy, depended on (*i*) whether it was against the public interest and (*ii*) whether it exceeded what was required for the respondent's protection. And that, on the facts of this case, the unlimited restriction as to time was not against the public interest and that it was reasonable to give to the respondent the specified protection.

LORD BIRKENHEAD, L.C. It has for long now been accepted that such an agreement as this, if it is impeached, is to be measured by reference to two considerations. First: Is it against the public interest? And, second: Does that which has been stipulated for exceed what is required for the protection of the covenantee? It might perhaps be more properly stated, as it has sometimes been with the highest authority stated, does it exceed what is necessary for the protection of both the parties? But the impeachment which is in fact made in this case demands the consideration of this question only: Does the restriction which is attacked exceed that which was reasonably necessary for the protection of the covenantee? The answer to these questions is to be found in an examination of the circumstances, and counsel for the appellant was undoubtedly right when he said towards the close of his argument that in order to determine whether or not in a particular case such a restriction did exceed that which was so reasonable it became necessary to understand the facts of the particular case.

NOTE
An employee can be restrained from using a list of customers of his former employer: *Robb* v. *Green* (1895).

Home Counties Dairies Ltd. v. Skilton

[1970] 1 W.L.R. 526; [1970] 1 All E.R. 1227
Court of Appeal, Civil Division
In June 1963 the respondent became employed as a roundsman in a dairyman's business. The agreement made between employer and employee in July 1964, when the employee had already been employed for one year, contained the following two clauses among others. Clause 12 provided that: 'During his employment hereunder the Employee shall not, without the previous consent of the Employer, enter the service of or be employed in any capacity or for any purpose whatsoever by any person, firm or company carrying on any dairy business.' Clause 15 provided that: 'The Employee expressly agrees not at any time during the period of one year after the determination of his employment under this agreement (whether the same shall have been determined by notice or otherwise) either on his own account or representative or agent of any person or company, to serve or sell milk or dairy produce to, or solicit orders for milk or dairy produce from any person or company who at any time during the last six months of his employment shall have been a customer of the Employer and served by the Employee in the course of his employment.' In March 1969, the employer sold the goodwill of his business to the appellant company which agreed to take over all employees. At the end of March the employee gave a week's notice to end his employment with the employer. In April, he entered the employment of another dairyman whose business was in the same area and immediately began to serve the same milk round that he had worked during the course of his previous employment. The respondent company then brought this action to enforce clause 15 of the agreement.
HELD, by HARMAN, SALMON and CROSS, L.JJ., that the agreement, on its true construction, was an agreement not to serve another employer as a milk roundsman calling on the customers of

the old milk round whom he had served in the previous six months. And that, the restraint contained in clause 15 was not unreasonable and was binding on the respondent.

HARMAN, L.J. When a man sells the goodwill of his business, one of the principal items will be his trade connections, and the buyer is entitled to protect that by restraining the vendor from setting up in competition with the very thing which he has agreed to buy. In the case of a master and servant, aside from confidential information, the servant is entitled to make use of the skill and knowledge he has acquired in the master's service and may not be prevented from competing with it. There has certainly been in the course of time a swing in the view taken by the court in these matters, and many cases in which an injunction was granted in the last century would not succeed now. Nevertheless, if the object be merely to protect the master's legitimate interest in his goodwill and the restraint does not have as its paramount object to restrain competition, nor have the effect of hindering the employee in activities outside the area of the master's trade, a restraint can still be imposed.

Esso Petroleum Co., Ltd. v. Harper's Garage (Stourport), Ltd.
[1968] A.C. 269; [1967] 1 All E.R. 699
House of Lords

The respondent garage company had entered into what is known as a solus agreement with the appellants in respect of each of the respondents' two garages. By these agreements, the respondents undertook, *inter alia*, to sell Esso petrol and no other in each of their garages. The first agreement (the Corner Garage agreement) was expressed to remain in force for a period of twenty-one years from 1st July 1962. In October 1962 the respondents charged the Corner Garage by way of legal mortgage, covenanting to repay the appellants £7,000 with interest by quarterly instalments over a period of twenty-one years, and undertaking that they would not be entitled to redeem the mortgage otherwise than by payments over the full period of twenty years. The respondents covenanted by the same deed to sell Esso petrol and no other during the continuance of the mortgage. The second agreement (the Mustow Green agreement) was expressed to remain in force for a period of four years and five months from 1st July 1963. By this agreement, the respondents undertook, *inter alia*, to keep open at all reasonable hours to sell Esso petrol and not to dispose of the garage except to a person willing to enter into a similar solus agreement with the appellant. The appellants appealed to the House of Lords against the Court of Appeal decision that the doctrine of restraint of trade could apply to covenants in mortgage deeds and that the restrictions in the solus agreements and the mortgage deed were unreasonable and, consequently, void. (At the time of the action, the respondents had tendered repayment of the mortgage.)

HELD, by LORD REID, LORD MORRIS OF BORTH-Y-GEST, LORD HODSON, LORD PEARCE and LORD WILBERFORCE, that contracts or covenants regulating the trading use made of a particular piece of land are not necessarily outside the doctrine of restraint of trade and that the doctrine may apply to mortgages; that the solus agreements and the provisions in the mortgage deed relating to trading were within the scope of the doctrine of restraint of trade and must therefore be justified if they are to be enforceable: that a restriction is justified only if it is reasonable; that the Mustow Green restrictions were reasonable because the period of four years and five months was reasonable, taking into account the advantages derived by the respondents; that the Corner Garage agreement and the restrictive provisions in the mortgage deed were unreasonable because the period of duration, twenty-one years, was unreasonable, and these provisions were, accordingly, unenforceable.

LORD REID. It is now generally accepted that a provision in a contract which is to be regarded as in restraint of trade must be justified if it is to be enforceable, and that the law on this matter was correctly stated by LORD MACNAGHTEN in the *Nordenfelt* case. He said: 'Restraints of trade and interference with individual liberty of action, may be justified by the special circumstances of a particular case. It is a sufficient justification, and indeed, it is the only justification, if the restriction is reasonable — reasonable, that is, in reference to the interests of the parties concerned and reasonable in reference to the interests of the public, so framed and so guarded as to afford adequate protection to the party in whose favour it is imposed, while at the same time it is in no way injurious to the public.' So in every case it is necessary to consider, first whether the restraint went farther than to afford adequate protection to the party in whose favour it was granted, secondly whether it can be justified as being in the interests of the party restrained, and thirdly whether it must be held contrary to the public interest. I find it difficult to agree with the way in which the court has in some cases treated the interests of the party restrained. Surely it can never be in the interest of a person to agree to suffer a restraint unless he gets some compensating advantage, direct or indirect; and LORD MACNAGHTEN said 'of course the quantum of consideration may enter into the question of the reasonableness of the contract'.

Where two experienced traders are bargaining on equal terms and one has agreed to a restraint for reasons which seem good to him, the court is in grave danger of stultifying itself if it says that it knows that trader's interest better than he does himself. There may well be cases, however, where, although the party to be restrained has deliberately accepted the main terms of the contract, he has been at a disadvantage as regards other terms: for example, where a set of conditions has been incorporated which has not been the subject of negotiation – there the court may have greater freedom to hold them unreasonable.

The Court of Appeal held that these ties were for unreasonably long periods. They thought that, if for any reason the respondents ceased to sell the appellants' petrol, the appellants could have found other suitable outlets in the neighbourhood within two or three years. I do not think that that is the right test. In the first place there was no evidence about this, and I do not think that it would be practicable to apply this test in practice. It might happen that, when the respondents ceased to sell their petrol, the appellants would find such an alternative outlet in a very short time; but looking to the fact that well over ninety per cent. of existing filling stations are tied and that there may be great difficulty in opening a new filling station, it might take a very long time to find an alternative. Any estimate of how long it might take to find suitable alternatives for the respondents' filling stations could be little better than guesswork.

I do not think that the appellants' interest can be regarded so narrowly. They are not so much concerned with any particular outlet as with maintaining a stable system of distribution throughout the country, so as to enable their business to be run efficiently and economically. In my view there is sufficient material to justify a decision that ties of less than five years were insufficient, in the circumstances of the trade when these agreements were made, to afford adequate protection to the appellants' legitimate interests. If that is so, I cannot find anything in the details of the Mustow Green agreement which would indicate that it is unreasonable. It is true that, if some of the provisions were operated by the appellants in a manner which would be commercially unreasonable, they might put the respondents in difficulties. I think, however, that a court must have regard to the fact that the appellants must act in such a way that they will be able to obtain renewals of the great majority of their very numerous ties, some of which will come to an end almost every week. If in such circumstances a garage owner chooses to rely on the commercial probity and good sense of the producer, I do not think that a court should hold his agreement unreasonable because it is legally capable of some misuse. I would therefore allow the appeal as regards the Mustow Green agreement.

The Corner Garage agreement, however, involves much more difficulty. Taking first the legitimate interests of the appellants, a new argument was submitted to your lordships that, apart from any question of security for their loan, it would be unfair to the appellants if the respondents, having used the appellants' money to build up their business, were entitled after a comparatively short time to be free to seek better terms from a competing producer. There is no material, however, on which I can assess the strength of this argument, and I do not find myself in a position to determine whether it has any validity. A tie for twenty-one years stretches far beyond any period for which developments are reasonably foreseeable. Restrictions on the garage owner which might seem tolerable and reasonable in reasonably foreseeable conditions might come to have a very different effect in quite different conditions: the public interest comes in here more strongly. Moreover, apart from a case where he gets a loan, a garage owner appears to get no greater advantage from a twenty year tie than he gets from a five year tie. So I would think that there must at least be some clearly established advantage to the producing company— something to show that a shorter period would not be adequate—before so long a period could be justified; but in this case there is no evidence to prove anything of the kind. Moreover, the other material which I have thought it right to consider does not appear to me to assist the appellant here. I would therefore dismiss the appeal as regards the Corner Garage agreement.

NOTE
The requirement that, in contracts regulating trade, there must be mutual advantage is illustrated clearly by *English Hop Growers* v.

Dering (1928). In this case, a member of a growers' association was held bound by his agreement to deliver his entire crop of hops to the association for onward sale. The arrangement by which the growers eliminated competition between themselves by putting the marketing and price-fixing into the hands of the Association divided the overall benefit or loss in any one year fairly amongst the members.

In all of the cases mentioned in this chapter, any void restraint covenant was severed from the contract: the remaining provisions being valid and enforceable. Sometimes the question will arise as to whether any distinct element within a restraint clause can be severed from that clause. For example, in *Goldsoll* v. *Goldman* [1915] there was a restrictive agreement by which two jewellery dealers attempted to end competition between each other. The plaintiffs were dealers in jewellery (substantially imitation jewellery) and the defendant undertook that he would not for a period of two years be concerned directly or indirectly in the business of real or imitation jewellery, 'in the County of London, England, Scotland, Ireland, Wales, or any part of the United Kingdom of Great Britain and Ireland and the Isle of Man or in France, the United States of America, Russia or Spain, or within 25 miles of the Potsdamer Strasse, Berlin or St Stefan's Kirche, Vienna'. It was decided by the Court of Appeal that (*a*) the area of restraint was unreasonable and should be severed so that it is limited to the United Kingdom and the Isle of Man; (*b*) the restraint with regard to real jewellery was unreasonable and should be severed from the restraint with regard to imitation jewellery, which was reasonable; and (*c*) after severance in these two respects, the restraint covenant, as so limited, was enforceable against the defendant.

The *Goldsoll* case should be compared with *Attwood* v. *Lamont* [1920] in which the separate elements of an employee's covenant could not be severed because the totality of these elements constituted a single covenant for the protection of the employer's department-store business. The Court of Appeal held that the clause must stand or fall in its unaltered form and that it was unreasonably wide for the protection of the employer's business from the activities of the employee, who was a tailor's cutter.

13. Illegality and public policy

The principle of public policy is this; ex dolo malo non oritur actio. *No court will lend its aid to a man who founds his cause of action upon an immoral or illegal act:* Holman v. Johnson per LORD MANSFIELD, C.J.

Summary

1. Public policy

It is a principle of public policy that no court will lend its aid to a man who founds his cause of action upon an immoral or illegal act: *Holman* v. *Johnson* [1775]. This principle may be stated in the form of the maxim *ex turpi causa non oritur actio.*

2. Effect of illegality

If a contract is expressly or by necessary implication forbidden by statute, or if it is *ex facie* illegal, or if both parties know that though *ex facie* legal it can only be performed by illegality or is intended to be performed illegally, the law will not help the plaintiffs in any way that is a direct or indirect enforcement of rights under the contract; and for this purpose both parties are presumed to know the law: per PEARCE, L.J. in *Archbolds* v. *Spanglett* [1961]. If a contract is *ex facie* legal and is performed in an illegal manner, e.g., contrary to statute, the contract may be enforced by a party who had no knowledge of the other's intention to perform illegally: *Archbolds* v. *Spanglett* [1961]. But, in the case of an *ex facie* legal contract which is performed in an illegal manner with both parties participating in the illegal performance, neither party can enforce the contract: *Ashmore* v. *Dawson* [1973].

3. Examples of illegal contracts

The following kinds of contract may be rendered unenforceable by considerations of public policy:

(*a*) Contracts expressly or impliedly prohibited by statute: *Phoenix Insurance* v. *Adas* [1987]; see also *Archbolds* v. *Spanglett* [1961].

(*b*) Contracts performed in a manner prohibited by statute: *Archbolds* v. *Spanglett* [1961]; *Ashmore* v. *Dawson* [1973]; *St John Shipping Corporation* v. *Joseph Rank:* [1957].

(*c*) Contracts containing an immoral element: *Pearce* v. *Brooks* [1866].

(*d*) Contracts to defraud the Revenue or a rating authority: *Alexander* v. *Rayson* [1936]; *Napier* v. *National Business Agency* [1951]. See also *Saunders* v. *Edwards* [1987].

(*e*) Contracts involving corruption in public life: *Parkinson* v. *College of Ambulance* [1925].

4. Actions in tort

Where an action in tort arises out of a contract between the same parties and which contains an illegal element, the conduct of the parties and their relative moral culpability may be relevant in determining whether, as a matter of public policy, the court will take notice of the illegality so as to allow an *ex turpi causa* defence: *Saunders* v. *Edwards* [1987].

Archbolds (Freightage) Ltd. v. S. Spanglett, Ltd.

[1961] 1 Q.B. 374; [1961] All E.R. 417
Court of Appeal
There was a contract between the plaintiffs and the defendants by
which the defendants agreed to carry by road certain goods which
were owned by a third party. The vehicle in which the goods were
carried had a 'C' licence. The Road and Rail Traffic Act 1933
prohibits the use of goods vehicles on a road except with an 'A'
licence. The defendants knew at the time of the contract that a
vehicle with a 'C' licence was to be used: but the plaintiffs did not
know this. As a result of negligence on the part of the defendants,
the goods were stolen in transit. The plaintiff claimed damages for
breach of contract and negligence.
HELD, by SELLERS, PEARCE and DEVLIN, L.JJ. that the
plaintiffs were not debarred by the illegality of the defendants'
performance of the contract of carriage from recovering damages
for breach because (*i*) the contract of carriage was not forbidden by
statute nor was it impliedly prohibited by the statute and (*ii*) the
defendants, not knowing that there was only a 'C' licence for the
vehicle, were innocent parties to the contract of carriage which was
not *ex facie* illegal.

PEARCE, L.J. The object of the Rail and Road Traffic Act, 1933,
was not, in this connexion, to interfere with the owner of goods or
his facilities for transport, but to control those who provide the
transport with a view to promoting its efficiency. Transport of goods
was not made illegal but the various licence-holders were prohibited
from encroaching on one another's territory, the intention of the act
being to provide an orderly and comprehensive service. Penalties
were provided for those licence-holders who went outside the
bounds of their allotted sphere. These penalties apply to those using
the vehicle but not to the goods owner. Though the latter could be
convicted of aiding and abetting any breach, the restrictions were not
aimed at him. Thus a contract of carriage was, in the sense used by
DEVLIN, J., in the *St. John Shipping* case 'collateral' and it was not
impliedly forbidden by the statute.
  This view is supported by common sense and convenience. If the
other view were held it would have far-reaching effects. For instance,
if a carrier induces me (who am in fact ignorant of any illegality) to

entrust goods to him and negligently destroys them, he would only have to show that (though unknown to me) his licence had expired or did not properly cover the transportation or that he was uninsured and I should then be without a remedy against him. Or again, if I ride in a taxicab and the driver leaves me stranded in some deserted spot, he would only have to show that he was (though unknown to me) unlicensed or uninsured, and I should be without remedy. This appears to me an undesirable extension of the implications of a statute.

In *Vita Food Products* v. *Unus Shipping Co.* [1956] LORD WRIGHT said: 'Each case has to be considered on its merits. Nor must it be forgotten that the rule by which contracts not expressly forbidden by statute or declared to be void are in proper cases nullified for disobedience to a statute is a rule of public policy only, and public policy understood in a wider sense may at times be better served by refusing to nullify a bargain save on serious and sufficient grounds.' If the court too readily implies that a contract is forbidden by statute, it takes it out of its own power (so far as the contract is concerned) to discriminate between guilt and innocence. If, however, the court makes no such implication, it still leaves itself with a general power, based on public policy, to hold those contracts unenforceable which are *ex facie* unlawful, and also to refuse its aid to guilty parties in respect of contracts which to the knowledge of both can only be performed by a contravention of the statute or which though apparently lawful are intended to be performed illegally or for an illegal purpose (for example, *Pearce* v. *Brooks* [1866]).

NOTE
In *Pearce* v. *Brooks* [1866] there was a contract by which a firm of coachbuilders hired out a carriage to a prostitute. They knew that she intended to use the vehicle as part of her display to attract men. She feel into arrears with the hire payments. The coachbuilders claimed the sum due. It was held that the contract was unenforceable for illegality.

In *St. John Shipping Corporation* v. *Joseph Rank* [1957] it was held that a contract for the carriage of goods by sea was not made illegal when the ship's master allowed lading beyond the deadline, which is an offence. DEVLIN J. said that a contract will be declared illegal only if the prohibited act is at the centre of it.

Archbolds v. *Spanglett* should be compared with *Ashmore* v. *Dawson* [1973] in which the plaintiffs had manufactured a large piece of engineering equipment weighing 25 tons, which the defendants agreed to carry to a certain point of shipment. The plaintiffs transport manager was present when the equipment was loaded. He knew that the vehicle provided by the defendants was overloaded contrary to the statutory regulations. He made no objection, nor did he explain (what he well knew) that the appropriate vehicle would have been a 'low loader'. On its way to the port the vehicle toppled over and the equipment was damaged. The plaintiffs brought this action for damages for negligence and/or breach of contract. It was held by the Court of Appeal that even if the contract was lawful in its inception, it was performed in an unlawful manner and the plaintiffs, through their transport manager had participated in the illegality. Accordingly, the plaintiffs could not succeed in their claim for damages.

In *Phoenix Insurance* v. *Adas* [1987] the Court of Appeal had to decide whether the Insurance Companies Act, 1974, prohibited certain contracts of insurance. KERR, L.J., approached the problem as follows. (*i*) Where a statute prohibits both parties from concluding or performing a contract when both or either of them have no authority to do so, the contract is impliedly prohibited. (*ii*) But where a statute merely prohibits one party from entering into a contract without authority and/or imposes a penalty on him if he does so (i.e., a unilateral prohibition) it does not follow that the contract itself is impliedly prohibited so as to render it illegal and void. Whether or not the statute has this effect depends on considerations of public policy in the light of the mischief which the statute is designed to prevent, its language, scope and purpose, the consequences for the innocent party, and any other relevant considerations . . . . (*iii*) The Insurance Companies Act 1974 only imposes a unilateral prohibition on unauthorised insurers. If this were merely to prohibit them from carrying on 'the business of effecting contracts of insurance' of a class for which they have no authority, then it would be clearly open to the court to hold that considerations of public policy preclude the implication that such contracts are prohibited and void. But unfortunately the unilateral prohibition is not limited to the business of 'effecting contracts of insurance' but extends to the business of 'carrying out contracts of insurance'. This is a form of statutory prohibition, albeit only unilateral, which is not covered by any authority.

The court cannot enforce a contract against an unauthorised insurer when he is expressly forbidden by statute from carrying it out. In this situation there is no room for the introduction of considerations of public policy. Where a statute prohibits both contract and performance, that is the public policy.

Alexander v. Rayson

[1936] 1 K.B. 169; [1935] All E.R. Rep 185
Court of Appeal
In July 1929 the defendant, Mrs. Rayson approached the plaintiff with a view to taking an under lease of a flat at a rent of £1,200 a year, the rent to cover the provision of services. The plaintiff, accordingly, sent to the defendant two documents: the first being a draft sub-lease of the flat at a rent of £450 a year and the second being a draft agreement for various services in connection with the flat for the payment of an additional sum of £750 a year. The sub-lease itself provided for services which were substantially the same as those in the service agreement with the exception of the provision and maintenance of a frigidaire. (The plaintiff had stated to the rating assessment committee that £450 was the only amount he received for rent, services and rates. His assessment was then reduced from £720 to £270. But the committee subsequently discovered the existence of the agreement and the assessment of £720 was restored.) The annual sum of £1,200 was paid by the defendant quarterly up to and including the instalment due at Midsummer 1934. But the defendant refused to pay the quarterly instalment of the £750 which fell due in September 1934, contending that the plaintiff had failed to comply with his obligations in respect of the services to be rendered under the sub-lease and under the agreement. The defendant tendered the sum of £112 10s. as the quarterly rent due under the sub-lease. The plaintiff refused this tender and brought this action claiming the sum of £300, being the quarterly instalment payable under the two documents. The defendant contended, *inter alia*, that the agreement was void for illegality and that its enforcement would be contrary to public policy in that its execution was obtained by the plaintiff for the purposes of defrauding the Westminster City Council by deceiving them as to the true rateable value of the premises and by inducing them to believe that the true rent received by the plaintiff was £450 and by concealing from them the terms of the agreement. The trial judge held that the agreement was not unenforceable for illegality. The defendant appealed.
HELD, by GREER, ROMER and SCOTT, L.JJ., that the landlord

had intended to use the sub-lease and the agreement for an illegal purpose and had, accordingly, put himself in the same position in law as though he had intended that the flat, when let, should be used for an illegal purpose. He was, therefore, not entitled to enforce the sub-lease or the agreement. It made no difference that he had failed to defraud the rating authority and could no longer use the documents for an illegal purpose.

ROMER, L.J., [who read the judgment of the court]. It is settled law that an agreement to do an act that is illegal or immoral or contrary to public policy, or to do any act for a consideration that is illegal, immoral, or contrary to public policy, is unlawful and therefore void. But it often happens that an agreement which, in itself, is not unlawful, is made with the intention of one or both parties to make use of the subject-matter for an unlawful purpose, that is to say, a purpose that is illegal, immoral, or contrary to public policy. The most common instance of this is an agreement for the sale or letting of an object, where the agreement is unobjectionable on the face of it, but where the intention of one or both of the parties is that the object shall be used by the purchaser or hirer for an unlawful purpose. In such a case any party to the agreement who had the unlawful intention is precluded from suing upon it *ex turpi causa non oritur actio*. The action does not lie because the court will not lend its help to such a plaintiff.

Napier v. National Business Agency, Ltd.

[1951] 2 All E.R. 264
Court of Appeal
The plaintiff was employed by the defendant company as secretary and accountant. The plaintiff was remunerated by means of a salary of £13 a week together with £6 a week for expenses. It was known to both parties that the plaintiff's expenses could never be as much as £6 a week. In fact, not more than £1 a week could be treated as fairly representing his expenses. The plaintiff was paid his salary subject to income tax deduction by means of the P.A.Y.E. system and the defendant company made the appropriate deductions before paying him. The defendant company showed in its returns to the Inland

Revenue Commissioners the payment of £6 a week as being a reimbursement of expenses to the plaintiff. After being summarily dismissed by the defendant company, the plaintiff claimed repayment, in lieu of notice, of £13 a week for the notice period. At first instance it was held that the contract was against public policy as being intended to defraud the revenue and that, therefore, the plaintiff was unable to enforce any part of it. The plaintiff appealed. HELD, by SIR RAYMOND EVERSHED, M.R., DENNING and HODSON, L.JJ., that the agreement to pay £6 a week as expenses was intended to evade tax and that the agreement was therefore against public policy and, further, that the agreement relating to the salary of £13 a week was not severable from the expenses agreement, and was similarly unenforceable.

SIR RAYMOND EVERSHED, M.R. If those were the facts, what is the inference? It must surely be that, by making an agreement in that form the parties to it were doing that which they must be taken to know would be liable to defeat the proper claims of the Inland Revenue and to avoid altogether, or at least to postpone, the proper payment of income tax. If that is the right conclusion, it seems to me equally clear (subject to one point which I will mention in a moment) that the agreement must be regarded as contrary to public policy. There is a strong legal obligation based on all citizens to make true and faithful returns for tax purposes, and, if parties make an agreement which is designed to do the contrary, *i.e.* to mislead and to delay, it seems to me impossible for this court to enforce that contract at the suit of one party to it.

That being so, the further point arises whether the terms of the agreement relating to the two branches of the plaintiff's reward can be severed, *i.e.*, whether the plaintiff can reject the tainted part of the contract relating to the £6 a week for expenses, and sue only, as he has done, in respect of the £13 a week for remuneration simply so called. I think the answer to that point is in the negative. The contract is, to my mind, not severable. It cannot properly be treated as consisting of two separate and distinct bargains, and, therefore, although it is true that the plaintiff sues only in respect of £13 a week, he is really seeking to enforce a contract which is tainted to the extent I have mentioned. It being so tainted I think that the court will not enforce it at his suit. I think that this appeal fails and should be dismissed.

Parkinson v. College of Ambulance, Ltd.

[1925] 2 K.B. 1; [1924] All E.R. Rep 325
King's Bench Division

One Harrison, the second defendant in this case, was the secretary of the defendant company. He fraudulently represented to the plaintiff that he had power to nominate persons to receive titles of honour and that he or the company could arrange for the grant to the plaintiff of a knighthood if the plaintiff would make a donation to the company funds. In response to this false and fraudulent representation, the plaintiff made a donation of £3,000 to the company. The plaintiff brought this action to recover £3,000 as damages for deceit, or, in the alternative, as money had and received by the defendants to the use of the plaintiff, or, in the further alternative, as damages for breach of warranty of authority.

HELD, by LUSH, J., that the contract between the plaintiff and the defendants by which the plaintiff gave the money on the strength of the representations that he would receive a knighthood, was against public policy and, therefore, illegal; as the parties were *in pari delicto* an action for damages could not be maintained by the plaintiff, nor could he recover the money on the ground that it was had and received by the defendants to his use.

LUSH, J. The first question to consider is this. The contract being against public policy, and being of the character that I have described, can the plaintiff still rely on the fraud of Harrison and recover damages against him; and can he, as against the college, recover the £3,000 which the college had received through that fraud, as money had and received to his use? I am not prepared to hold – it is not necessary that I should decide the question – that in every case where a contract is against public policy, where one of the parties to it is defrauded by the other, he is prevented from recovering. It may be that whenever one party to a contract which is not improper in itself is unaware that it is illegal and is defrauded, the parties may not be *in pari delicto*. However that may be, I am of opinion that if the contract has any element of turpitude in it the parties are *in pari delicto* and no action for damages can be maintained by the party defrauded. It is not correct to say, as was contended before me, that it is only if the contract is of a criminal nature that the plaintiff is precluded from recovering.

Saunders v. Edwards

[1987] 2 All E.R. 651
Court of Appeal, Civil Division

The defendant sold the lease of a flat to the plaintiffs. During negotiations the defendant fraudulently misrepresented that the flat included a roof terrace. The defendant had created access from the flat to the flat roof over which he had no rights. The plaintiffs paid £45,000 for the flat together with certain chattels. The plaintiffs suggested and the defendant agreed that, in order to reduce stamp duty, the purchase price should be apportioned as £40,000 for the flat and £5,000 for the chattels, – both parties knew that the chattels were worth much less. On discovering that the flat did not include a roof terrace, the plaintiffs brought an action for damages for fraudulent misrepresentation and damages for the disappointment and inconvenience suffered in not having the roof terrace. At first instance, the plaintiffs were awarded damages for fraudulent misrepresentation and a further sum of £500 for inconvenience and disappointment. In each case, the damages was to carry interest from the date of the writ. The defendant appealed, claiming that the plaintiffs' claim required them to rely on their own illegal conduct in regard to the false apportionment of the purchase price in order to reduce stamp duty.

HELD, by KERR, NICHOLLS and BINGHAM, L.JJ., where a claim in tort arose out of a fraudulent contract between the parties, their conduct and relative moral culpability could be relevant in determining whether, as a matter of public policy, the court would take notice of the illegality. On the present facts, the *ex turpi causa* defence must fail and the plaintiffs are entitled to damages.

KERR, L.J. The plaintiffs have an unanswerable claim for damages for fraudulent misrepresentation. The possible illegality involved in the apportionment of the price in the contract is wholly unconnected with their cause of action. The plaintiffs' loss caused by the defendant's fraudulent misrepresentation would have been the same even if the contract had not contained this illegal element. Their claim for damages is in no way seeking to enforce the contract or any relief in connection with it. The moral culpability of the defendant greatly outweighs any on the part of the plaintiffs. He cannot be allowed to keep the fruits of his fraud.

14. Minors' contracts

It is not sufficient for the plaintiff to say, 'I have discharged the onus which rests upon me if I simply show that the goods supplied were suitable to the condition in life of the infant at the time.' There is another branch of the definition which cannot be disregarded. Having shown that the goods were suitable in the life of the infant he must then go on to show that they were suitable to his actual requirements at the time of sale and delivery. Unless he establishes that fact either by evidence adduced by himself or by cross-examination of the defendant's witnesses, as the case may be, in my opinion he has not discharged the burden which the law imposes upon him: Nash *v.* Inman, per SIR HERBERT COZENS-HARDY, M.R.

Summary

1. Definition

The age of majority at common law is 21 years. But, by s. 1 of the Family Law Reform Act, 1969, the age of capacity for the purpose of any rule of law is 18 years. A person will be deemed to attain the age of 18 at the commencement of the eighteenth anniversary of his birth: Family Law Reform Act, 1969, s. 9.

2. Minors' contracts — the general rule

The general rule at common law is that a contract between a minor and a person of full age is enforceable by the minor but not against him. Such a contract could become binding on the minor only if he ratified it on or after reaching full age.

This rule applies to all contracts entered into by a minor except contracts of continuing obligation, contracts for necessaries and contracts for training or beneficial service. These are exceptional cases for which there are special rules as set out below.

3. Contracts of continuing obligation

This category includes marriage settlements, tenancy agreements, partnership agreements and agreements to take shares in company which are not fully paid up. Any such contract is binding on a minor unless he repudiates it before reaching majority or within a reasonable time thereafter: *Edwards* v. *Carter* [1893]. After repudiation, the minor can recover money paid or property transferred only where there has been total failure of consideration: *Steinberg* v. *Scala* [1923].

4. Contracts for necessaries

Where necessaries are sold and delivered to a minor he must pay a reasonable price for them: Sale of Goods Act, 1979, s. 3(2): 'necessaries' means goods suitable to the condition in life of the minor and to his actual requirements at the time of the sale and delivery: Sale of Goods Act 1979, s. 3(3). See *Nash* v. *Inman* (1908). At common law, 'necessaries' includes goods and services for the minor and his dependants according to his condition in life. Contracts for necessaries are, thus binding on a minor to the extent that he must pay a reasonable price.

5. Beneficial contracts of service

A minor is bound by a contract of employment which, on the whole, is to his advantage: *Doyle* v. *White City Stadium* [1935]. He is not bound by a contract whose terms are onerous or unreasonable.

6. Restitution

Section 3 of the Minors' Contracts Act, 1987, confers on the court a new power to order restitution against minors who unjustly or unfairly acquire property under an unenforceable or void contract.

This section provides that where 'a person (the plaintiff) has . . . entered into a contract with another (the defendant), and that the contract is unenforceable against the defendant (or he repudiates it) because he was a minor when the contract was made, the court may, if it is just and equitable to do so, require the defendant to transfer to the plaintiff any property acquired by the defendant under the contract, or any property representing it'.

7. Guarantees

Where a guarantee is given in respect of an obligation of a party to a contract, and the obligation is unenforceable against him (or he repudiates the contract) because he was a minor when the contract was made, the guarantee will not for that reason alone be unenforceable against the guarantor: Minors' Contracts Act 1987, s. 2.

Edwards v. Carter

[1893] A.C. 360; [1891–4] All E.R. Rep. 1259
House of Lords
An infant covenanted by a marriage settlement, dated 16th October
1883, to settle after-acquired property. The infant came of age on
19th November 1883. In 1887 the infant became entitled under his
father's will to a large sum of money to which the covenant in the
marriage settlement should have applied. But in July 1888 the infant
repudiated the settlement. The trustees of the settlement brought
this action to enforce the covenant to settle after-acquired property.
It was held by the Court of Appeal (reversing a decision of ROMER,
J.) that an infant must repudiate, if at all, within a reasonable time
after he attains his majority, and what is a reasonable time is a
question of fact to be determined in the light of all the circumstances,
and in the circumstances of the present case, four and a half years
was not a reasonable time. The respondent then appealed to the
House of Lords.
HELD, by LORD HERSCHELL, L.C., LORD WATSON, LORD
HALSBURY, LORD MACNAGHTEN, LORD MORRIS and
LORD SHAND, that the law gives an infant the privilege of
repudiating obligations undertaken during minority within a
reasonable time after coming of age. The law lays no obligation upon
the infant, it merely confers upon him a privilege which he might or
might not avail himself of as he chooses. If he chooses to be inactive
his opportunity is lost, if he chooses to be active the law comes to his
assistance. In the present case the period of four years and eight
months which the infant permitted to elapse before he took any steps
in the matter could not possibly be regarded as a reasonable time
and, therefore, the covenant was binding.

LORD HERSCHELL, L.C. The first question is whether the infant
was entitled to wait until an actual sum of money came to him to
which this covenant could apply before he made the repudiation. I
think that is a proposition which it is absolutely impossible to regard
seriously—that this covenant being binding unless he repudiates it
within a reasonable time he is entitled to wait and see how in respect
of any particular sum of money the covenant will operate, and when
he has made up his mind whether with regard to that sum of money

it will be beneficial to him or not, he can then, and not till then, be said to have his proper opportunity of making the determination.

Then it is said that in considering whether a reasonable time has elapsed you must take into account the fact that he did not know what were the terms of the settlement and that it contained this particular covenant. He knew that he had executed a deed – he must be taken to have known that the deed though binding upon him could be repudiated when he came of age, and it seems to me that in measuring a reasonable time whether in point of fact he had or had not acquainted himself with the nature of the obligations which he had undertaken is wholly immaterial – the time must be measured in precisely the same way whether he had so made himself acquainted or not. I do not say that he was under any obligation to make himself acquainted with the nature of the deed, which, having executed it as an infant, he might or might not at his pleasure repudiate when he came of age – all I say is this, that he cannot maintain that the reasonable time when measured must be a longer time because he has chosen not to make himself acquainted with the nature of the deed which he has executed.

Having put aside these two contentions the only question comes to be, has a reasonable time been exceeded? The learned judges in the court below expressed their opinion that the period which elapsed, a period between four and five years, was more than a reasonable time. It is not at all necessary for your Lordships to lay down what would have been a reasonable time in this case – it is enough to say that, in my opinion, it is impossible to hold that the learned judges in the court below in saying that more than a reasonable time had elapsed have in any way erred.

Steinberg v. Scala (Leeds), Ltd.

[1923] 2 Ch. 452; [1923] All E.R. Rep. 239
Court of Appeal

The plaintiff, an infant, applied for shares in the defendant company. She paid the amounts due on application and on allotment. She also paid on two calls. The plaintiff attended no company meetings and she received no dividend. The plaintiff later repudiated the contract to take the shares and brought this action to recover the moneys paid to the defendant company. It was held by ROCHE, J., that the plaintiff was entitled to the relief she claimed. The defendant company appealed.

HELD, that the plaintiff, being an infant, was entitled to repudiate the contract, but that she could not recover the sums paid to the defendant company because there had not been a total failure of consideration.

LORD STERNDALE, M.R. She [the plaintiff] became aware of the fact that as she was an infant she could rescind the contract and she did so. There is no doubt that she was entitled to do so, and entitled to have the register rectified by taking her name off it. But then there came another question. She wanted the £250 back, and, to a certain extent, I think the argument for the plaintiff has rather proceeded on the assumption that the question whether she can rescind and the question whether she can recover her money are the same questions. They are two quite different questions, as is stated by TURNER, L.J., in his judgment in *Ex parte Taylor*. He says (8 De G.M. & G. at p. 257): 'It is clear that an infant cannot be absolutely bound by a contract entered into during his minority. He must have a right upon his attaining his majority to elect whether he will adopt the contract or not.' Then he goes on: 'It is, however, a different question, whether, if an infant pays money on the footing of a contract, he can afterwards recover it back. If an infant buys an article which is not a necessary, he cannot be compelled to pay for it, but if he does pay for it during his minority he cannot on attaining his majority recover the money back.' That seems to me to be only stating in other words the principle which is laid down in a number of other cases that, although the contract may be rescinded the money paid cannot be recovered unless there has been an entire failure of the consideration for which the money has been paid. Therefore, it seems to me, that is the question to which we have to address ourselves: Has there been here a total failure of the consideration for which the money was paid?

The plaintiff has the shares; I do not mean to say she has the certificates; she could have had them at any time if she had applied for them; she has had the shares allotted to her, and there is evidence that the shares were of some value, that they had been dealt in at from 9s. to 10s. a share. Her shares were only half-paid up and, therefore, if she had attempted to sell them she would only have got half of that money, but that is quite a tangible and substantial sum.

In those circumstances is it possible to say that there is a total

failure of consideration? If the plaintiff were a person of full age
suing to recover the money back on the ground, and the sole ground,
that there had been failure of consideration, it seems to me it would
have been impossible for the plaintiff to succeed because he or she
would have got the very thing for which the money was paid and
would have got a thing of tangible value.

Nash v. Inman

[1908] 2 K.B. 1; [1908–10] All E.R. Rep. 317
Court of Appeal
The plaintiff had supplied to the defendant clothing to the value of
£145 10*s.* 3*d.* at a time when the defendant was a Cambridge
undergraduate. The clothes supplied by the plaintiff included eleven
fancy waistcoats. The defendant raised the defence of infancy at the
time the goods were supplied and that the goods were not
'necessaries'. The defendant's father had amply supplied the
defendant with proper clothes according to his condition in life. It
was held by RIDLEY, J. that there was no evidence that the goods
were 'necessaries' and judgment was entered for the defendant. The
plaintiff appealed.
HELD, by SIR HERBERT COZENS-HARDY, M.R.,
FLETCHER MOULTON and BUCKLEY, L.JJ., that there was no
evidence that the goods supplied were necessary to the defendant's
requirements; that, on the contrary, the defendant was amply
supplied with suitable and necessary clothes. The trial judge was
correct in the view that he took.

SIR HERBERT COZENS-HARDY, M.R. In substance the
position is this. The plaintiff sues the defendant for goods sold and
delivered. The defendant pleads infancy at the date of the sale, and
his plea is proved. What is the consequence of that? The
consequence of that is that the contract may turn out to be void, for
since the Infants' Relief Act, 1874, all contracts for goods supplied
to infants are absolutely void, subject, inter alia, to these provisions
of s. 2 of the Sale of Goods Act, 1893: 'Capacity to buy and sell is
regulated by the general law concerning capacity to contract, and to
transfer and acquire property: Provided that where necessaries are
sold and delivered to an infant, or minor, or to a person who by

reason of mental incapacity or drunkenness is incompetent to contract, he must pay a reasonable price therefor.' The section then defines 'necessaries' as follows: 'Necessaries in this section means goods suitable to the condition in life of such infant, or minor, or other person, and to his actual requirements at the time of the sale and delivery.' What is the effect of that? The plaintiff, as I have already stated, sues for goods sold and delivered and the defendant pleads infancy. The plaintiff must then reply, 'the goods sold were "necessaries" within the meaning of the definition in s. 2 of the Sale of Goods Act, 1893.' It is not sufficient, in my view, for him to say, 'I have discharged the onus which rests upon me if I simply show that the goods supplied were suitable to the condition in life of the infant at the time.' There is another branch of the definition which cannot be disregarded. Having shown that the goods were suitable to the condition in life of the infant he must then go on to show that they were suitable to his actual requirements at the time of the sale and delivery. Unless he establishes that fact either by evidence adduced by himself or by cross-examination of the defendant's witnesses, as the case may be, in my opinion he has not discharged the burden which the law imposes upon him.

NOTE
The provisions of section 2 of the Sale of Goods Act 1893 were re-enacted in section 3 of the Sale of Goods Act 1979.

Doyle v. White City Stadium , Ltd.
[1935] 1 K.B. 110; [1934] All E.R. Rep. 252
Court of Appeal
In March 1932 the plaintiff, an infant, applied to the British Boxing Board of Control for a licence as a boxer. The material part of his application is as follows: 'I hereby apply for a licence as a boxer, and if this licence is granted me I declare to adhere strictly to the rules of the British Boxing Board of Control (1929) as printed, and abide by any further rules or alterations to existing rules as may be passed.' As a result of his application, the Board issued to him a boxer's licence. Shortly afterwards, the original rule that a boxer's money was to be stopped only when he was disqualified for committing a

deliberate foul was replaced by a new rule which provided that in any case of disqualification, boxers were to receive only certain specified expenses. On 12th July 1933 the plaintiff fought Jack Petersen for the heavyweight championship of Great Britain at White City. It was part of the plaintiff's contract that he would receive £3,000 win, lose or draw. In the second round of this fight, the plaintiff was disqualified for fouling. The stewards of the British Boxing Board of Control decided to withhold all of the £3,000 with the exception of £5 a week to be paid to the plaintiff and £5 a week to be paid to the plaintiff's mother for a period of six months. The plaintiff brought this action against White City Stadium, Ltd., and the British Boxing Board of Control to recover the £3,000. MACKINNON, J., held that the contract between the plaintiff and the Board by which the licence was granted to the plaintiff, and by which he became liable to observe the rules of the Board, was for the benefit of the plaintiff and was not, therefore, voidable by him, but that the amended rule of the Board by which the £3,000 had been forfeited had not been brought to the plaintiff's notice, and judgment was given against the Board for £3,000. The Board appealed.

HELD, by LORD HANWORTH, M.R., SLESSER and ROMER, L.JJ., (*i*) that the contract between the plaintiff and the Board, regarded as a whole, was beneficial to the plaintiff and was, therefore, a contract which would be binding on an infant; (*ii*) that the amendment of the Board's rule did not fundamentally alter the purpose of the original rule; the rules did not provide that an amendment would be binding only where it was brought to the notice of the plaintiff; the plaintiff was, therefore, bound by the rule as amended.

LORD HANWORTH, M.R. I turn now to three cases which to my mind are binding upon this court. The first is *De Francesco* v. *Barnum*. In that case FRY, L.J., says this: 'I approach this subject with the observation that it appears to me that the question is this, Is the contract for the benefit of the infant? Not, Is any one particular stipulation for the benefit of the infant? Because it is obvious that the contract of apprenticeship or the contract of labour must, like any other contract, contain some stipulations for the benefit of the one contracting party, and some for the benefit of the other. It is not because you can lay your hand on a particular stipulation which you may say is against the infant's benefit, that therefore the whole contract is not for the benefit of the infant. The court must look at the whole contract, having regard to the circumstances of the case, and determine, subject to any principles of law which may be ascertained by the cases, whether the contract is or is not beneficial. That appears to me to be in substance a question of fact.' In *Corn* v. *Matthews* the matter came again before the Court of Appeal and LORD ESHER definitely said: 'It seems to me that the judgment of FRY, L.J., is one with which one would agree, and, although it makes the major premise larger than it had been previously enunciated in such cases, it does not alter the law applicable to them.' He repeats what FRY, L.J., had said, and particularly that the mere fact that some of the conditions in the deed are against an apprentice does not enable the court on that ground to say that the agreement is void. He says this, that the question is whether or not the terms are such as would on the whole be beneficial to the infant, and it seemed to him in the particular case that there was a term which was unfair to the infant and solely in favour of the master. The term was one that if there was either a strike, or what we call a lock-out now, the master could cease to pay the apprentice's wages though the master himself had caused the lock-out, and it was on that ground, and that ground only, that they held the term to be unreasonable and against the interest of the infant; but *Corn* v. *Matthews* is one which definitely confirms the principles laid down by FRY, L.J.

Then in *Clements* v. *London and North-Western Rail Co.*, we have once more the statement made that the whole contract is to be looked at. That was a case in which the infant, when being employed by the railway company, joined an insurance society formed among the employees of the railway company towards the funds of which the railway company contributed, and in return for being a member and getting that contribution, and so on, the infant agreed not to bring any proceedings under the Employers' Liability Act. He set aside, in other words, a very considerable advantage given to him by statute, but it was held by LORD ESHER that the contract was one which was for the benefit of the infant, and he says: 'I am of opinion, without going again through the cases that have been cited, that the answer to this proposition depends on whether, on the true construction of the contract as a whole, it was for his advantage. If it was not so, he can repudiate it; but if it was for his advantage, it was not a voidable contract, but one binding on him, which he had no right to repudiate.' A. L. SMITH, L.J., in his judgment in that case quotes the passage from *Corn* v. *Matthews* and says: 'In my judgment, the agreement, instead of being detrimental to the infant is, on the whole, manifestly to his advantage.' It was, therefore, held effective and binding. Those case are binding upon us. The learned judge on the question of fact has held that these terms are favourable and to the advantage of the infant, and it seems, therefore, that the rules cannot be held to be defeated by reason of the plea of infancy.

Minors' Contracts Act 1987

1987 Chapter 13
An Act to amend the law relating to minors' contracts. [9th April 1987]

Be it enacted by the Queen's most Excellent Majesty, by and with the advice and consent of the Lords Spiritual and Temporal, and Commons, in this present Parliament assembled, and by the authority of the same, as follows:

1. Disapplication of Infants Relief Act 1874 etc.
The following enactments shall not apply to any contract made by a minor after the commencement of this Act —

(*a*) the Infants Relief Act 1874 (which invalidates certain contracts made by minors and prohibits actions to enforce contracts ratified after majority); and
(*b*) section 5 of the Betting and Loans (Infants) Act 1892 (which invalidates contracts to repay loans advanced during minority).

2. Guarantees
Where —

(*a*) a guarantee is given in respect of an obligation of a party to a contract made after the commencement of this Act, and
(*b*) the obligation is unenforceable against him (or he repudiates the contract) because he was a minor when the contract was made,

the guarantee shall not for that reason alone be unenforceable against the guarantor.

3. Restitution
(1) Where —

(*a*) a person ('the plaintiff') has after the commencement of this Act entered into a contract with another ("the defendant"), and

(*b*) the contract is unenforceable against the defendant (or he repudiates it) because he was a minor when the contract was made,

the court may, if it is just and equitable to do so, require the defendant to transfer to the plaintiff any property acquired by the defendant under the contract, or any property representing it.

(2) Nothing in this section shall be taken to prejudice any other remedy available to the plaintiff.

4. Consequential amendment and repeals

(1) In section 113 of the Consumer Credit Act 1974 (that Act not to be evaded by use of security) in subsection (7) —

(*a*) after the word 'indemnity', in both places where it occurs, there shall be inserted 'or guarantee',

(*b*) after the words 'minor, or' there shall be inserted 'an indemnity is given in a case where he'; and

(*c*) for the word 'they' there shall be substituted 'those obligations'.

(2) The Infants Relief Act 1874 and the Betting and Loans (Infants) Act 1892 are hereby repealed (in accordance with section 1 of this Act).

5. Short title, commencement and extent

(1) This Act may be cited as the Minors' Contracts Act 1987.

(2) This Act shall come into force at the end of the period of two months beginning with the date on which it is passed.

(3) This Act extends to England and Wales only.

15. Discharge by performance

> *The law is that, where there is a contract to do work for a lump sum, until the work is completed the price of it cannot be recovered*: Sumpter *v.* Hedges, per A. L. SMITH, L.J.

Summary

1. Discharge of contract

When the obligations of both parties are at an end, the contract is said to be discharged. Discharge of contract may occur in any of the following ways namely, by performance, by agreement, by frustration or by acceptance of breach. Each of these will be dealt with in the following chapters.

2. Discharge by performance

The general rule is that a contractual obligation is discharged by complete performance of the undertaking. Where performance falls short of the completed undertaking, there is no discharge of the obligation or of the contract. The practical effect of this rule is that, where a contract provides for payment by one party after performance by the other, no action for payment may be maintained until performance is complete: *Cutter* v. *Powell* [1795]. Nor will an action for proportional payment be available on a *quantum meruit* basis: *Sumpter* v. *Hedges* [1898]. However, provided that entire completion is not a condition precedent to payment, a party who has performed his side of the bargain substantially but not completely, may sue on the contract: *Hoenig* v. *Isaacs* [1952].

Cutter v. Powell

[1795] 6 T.R. 320

King's Bench

The plaintiff sued as administratrix of her deceased husband's estate. The defendant had, in Jamaica, subscribed and delivered to T Cutter, the intestate, a note as follows: 'Ten days after the ship Governor Parry, myself master, arrives at Liverpool, I promise to pay to Mr. T. Cutter the sum of thirty guineas, provided he proceeds, continues and does his duty as second mate in the said ship from hence to the port of Liverpool. Kingston, July 31, 1793.' The *Governor Parry* sailed from Kingston on 2nd August 1793 and arrived in Liverpool on 9th October. But T. Cutter died on 20th September, until which date he did his duty as second mate. The plaintiff claimed payment on a *quantum meruit*.

HELD, by LORD KENYON, C.J., ASHURST, GROSE and LAWRENCE, JJ., that, according to the express terms of the contract, the sum of thirty guineas was payable only on completion of the whole voyage. A term to the effect that proportional payment should be made in case of partial performance could not be implied. The plaintiff could not, therefore, succeed in her claim on a *quantum meruit*.

LORD KENYON, C.J. But it seems to me at present that the decision of this case may proceed on the particular words of this contract and the precise facts here stated, without including marine contracts in general. That where the parties have come to an express contract none can be implied has prevailed so long as to be reduced to an axiom in the law. Here the defendant expressly promised to pay the intestate thirty guineas, provided he proceeded, continued and did his duty as second mate in the ship from Jamaica to Liverpool; and the accompanying circumstances disclosed in the case are that the common rate of wages is four pounds per month, when the party is paid in proportion to the time he serves: and that this voyage is generally performed in two months. Therefore if there had been no contract between these parties, all that the intestate could have recovered on a *quantum meruit* for the voyage would have been eight pounds; whereas here the defendant contracted to pay thirty guineas provided the mate continued to do his duty as mate during the whole voyage, in which case the latter would have received nearly four times as much as if he were paid for the number of months he served. He stipulated to receive the larger sum if the whole duty were performed, and nothing unless the whole of that duty were performed: it was a kind of insurance. On this particular contract my opinion is formed at present; at the same time I must say that if we were assured that these notes are in universal use, and that the commercial world have received and acted upon them in a different sense, I should give up my own opinion.

Sumpter v. Hedges
[1898] 1 Q.B. 673
Court of Appeal
The plaintiff, a builder, entered into a contract to build two houses and stables on the defendant's land for a lump sum. The plaintiff did about three fifths of the work and then informed the defendant that he had no money and could not go on with the work. (The trial judge found that he had abandoned the contract.) The defendant then completed the buildings himself using certain materials left on site by the plaintiff. The plaintiff was awarded the value of the materials used by the defendant but he failed to recover on a *quantum meruit* for the building work done before the contract was abandoned. The plaintiff appealed.
HELD, by A.L. SMITH, CHITTY and COLLINS, L.JJ., that the plaintiff could not recover on the contract to do work for a lump sum unless and until the work was completed. The plaintiff was not entitled to recover on a *quantum meruit* in the absence of a fresh agreement to pay for the work already done.

A.L. SMITH, L.J. The law is that, where there is a contract to do work for a lump sum, until the work is completed the price of it cannot be recovered. Therefore the plaintiff could not recover on the original contract. It is suggested however that the plaintiff was entitled to recover for the work he did on a *quantum meruit*. But, in order that that may be so, there must be evidence of a fresh contract to pay for the work already done.

COLLINS, L.J. I think the case is really concluded by the finding of the learned judge to the effect that the plaintiff had abandoned the contract. If the plaintiff had merely broken his contract in some way so as not to give the defendant the right to treat him as having abandoned the contract, and the defendant had then proceeded to finish the work himself, the plaintiff might perhaps have been entitled to sue on a *quantum meruit* on the ground that the defendant had taken the benefit of the work done. But that is not the present case. There are cases in which, though the plaintiff has abandoned the performance of a contract, it is possible for him to raise the inference of a new contract to pay for the work done on a *quantum meruit* from the defendant's having taken the benefit of that work, but, in order that that may be done, the circumstances must be such as to give an option to the defendant to take or not to take the benefit of the work done. It is only where the circumstances are such as to give that option that there is any evidence on which to ground the inference of a new contract. Where, as in the case of work done on land, the circumstances are such as to give the defendant no option whether he will take the benefit of the work or not, then one must look to other facts than the mere taking the benefit of the work in order to ground the inference of a new contract. In this case I see no other facts on which such an inference can be founded. The mere fact that a defendant is in possession of what he cannot help keeping, or even has done work upon it, affords no ground for such an inference.

Hoenig v. Isaacs

[1952] 2 All E.R. 176
Court of Appeal

The plaintiff, an interior decorator and designer of furniture, entered into a contract to decorate and furnish a one-roomed flat belonging to the defendant. The agreed price was the sum of £750 to be paid 'net cash, as the work proceeds, and balance on completion.' While the work was in progress, the defendant paid two instalments of £150, and when the plaintiff claimed to have finished he asked for the balance of £450. At this point the defendant complained of faulty design and bad workmanship, paid a further instalment of £100 to the plaintiff and entered into occupation of the flat, using the furniture provided under the contract. The plaintiff sued for the balance of £350, and the Official Referee held that there was substantial compliance with the contract and that the defendant was liable to pay the sum due under the contract less the cost of remedying the defects. The defendant appealed from this decision. HELD, by SOMERVELL, DENNING and ROMER, L.JJ., that, in a contract for work and labour for a lump sum payable on completion, the employer cannot repudiate liability on the ground that the work, when substantially performed, is in some respects not in accordance with the contract. In these circumstances, the employer is liable for the balance due under the contract less the cost of making good defects or omissions. And where the employer takes the benefit of the work by using chattels made under the contract, he cannot treat entire performance as a condition precedent to payment, for the condition is waived by his taking the benefit of the work.

DENNING, L.J. The question of law is whether the plaintiff was entitled in this action to sue for the £350 balance of the contract price. The defendant said that he was only entitled to sue on a *quantum meruit*, and he was anxious to insist on that because he said that the contract price was unreasonably high. He wished, therefore, to reject that price altogether and to pay simply a reasonable price for all the work that was done. That would obviously mean an inquiry into the value of every item, including all the many items which had been done in compliance with the contract as well as the three which fell short of it. The plaintiff resisted that course and refused to claim on a *quantum meruit*. He said that he was entitled to the balance of £350 less a deduction for the defects.

In determining this issue the first question is whether, on the true construction of the contract, entire performance was a condition precedent to payment. It was a lump sum contract, but that does not mean that entire performance was a condition precedent to payment. When a contract provides for a specific sum to be paid on completion of specified work, the Courts lean against a construction of the contract which would deprive the contractor of any payment at all simply because there are some defects or omissions. The promise to complete the work is therefore construed as a term of the contract, but not as a condition. It is not every breach of that term which absolves the employer from his promise to pay the price, but only a breach which goes to the root of the contract, such as an abandonment of the work when it is only half done. Unless the breach does go to the root of the matter, the employer cannot resist payment of the price. He must pay it and bring a cross-claim for the defects and omissions, or, alternatively, set them up in diminution of the price. The measure is the amount by which the work is worth less by reason of the defects and omissions and is usually calculated by the cost of making them good.

16. Discharge by agreement

> *The giving of a cheque of the debtor for a smaller amount than the sum due is very different from 'the gift of a horse, hawk, or robe etc.' mentioned in Pinnel's case*: D. & C. Builders *v.* Rees, per DANCKWERTS, L.J.

Summary

A contract may be discharged by a subsequent binding agreement to that effect. This occurs where there is a mutual waiver or accord and satisfaction. Also, contractual obligations may be discharged by release under seal.

1. Waiver

Where neither party has completely performed his obligations under a contract, that contract may be discharged by a mutual waiver of outstanding obligations. The waiver is binding because each party gives (by his waiver) consideration to the other party. The mutual waiver may be express or implied, see, e.g., *The Hannah Blumenthal* [1983].

2. Accord and satisfaction

Where one party, but not the other, has completed his undertaking, the party to whom the obligation is owed may subsequently agree with the other party to accept something different in place of the original obligation. The subsequent agreement is binding and is known as accord and atisfaction. The new agreement is the accord and the agreed substituted consideration is the satisfaction: *Pinnel's* case [1602]; *D & C Builders* v. *Rees* [1965]. Where a creditor has agreed to release his debtor from liability and the debtor gives no consideration to support the creditor's promise, there is no satisfaction and, consequently, the debtor remains liable for the debt: *Foakes* v. *Beer* [1884].

Pinnel's Case

[1602] 5 Co. Rep. 117a
Court of Common Pleas
Pinnel brought an action of debt on a bond of £16 against Cole for payment of £8 10s. due on 11th November 1600. The defendant pleaded that, at the instance of the plaintiff, he had paid him £5 2s. 2d. on 1st October, and that the plaintiff accepted this sum in full satisfaction of the £8 10s. 'It was resolved by the whole Court, that payment of a lesser sum on the day in satisfaction of a greater, cannot be any satisfaction for the whole, because it appears to the Judges that by no possibility, a lesser sum can be a satisfaction to the plaintiff for a greater sum: but the gift of a horse, hawk or robe, &c. in satisfaction is good. For it shall be intended that a horse, hawk or robe, &c. might be more beneficial to the plaintiff than the money, in respect of some circumstances, or otherwise the plaintiff would not have accepted of it in satisfaction, But when the whole sum is due, by no intendment the acceptance of parcel can be satisfaction to the plaintiff: but in the case at Bar it was resolved, that the payment and acceptance of parcel before the day in satisfaction of the whole, would be a good satisfaction in regard of circumstances of time; for peradventure parcel of it before the day would be more beneficial to him than the whole at the day, and the value of the satisfaction is not material: so if I am bound in £20 to pay you £10 at Westminster and you request me to pay you £5 at the day at York, and you will accept it in full satisfaction of the whole £10 it is a good satisfaction for the whole: for the expenses to pay it at York, is sufficient satisfaction: but in this case the plaintiff had judgment for the insufficient pleading; for he did not plead that he had paid the £5 2s. 2d. in full satisfaction (as by law he ought) but pleaded the payment of part generally; and that the plaintiff accepted it in full satisfaction. And always the manner of the tender and of the payment shall be directed by him who made the tender or payment, and not by him who accepts it. And for this cause judgment was given for the plaintiff.'

NOTE
In *The Hannah Blumenthal* [1983] the question arose as to whether an arbitration agreement could be abandoned by implied mutual waiver. The House of Lords made it clear that abandonment of arbitration by mutual waiver, express or implied, was governed by the normal rules of contract. Thus, in a case where the parties have

allowed their arbitration process to become moribund by neglect, the party claiming waiver must be able to show that the other party so conducted himself as to entitle him to assume and that he did assume, that the arbitration agreement was agreed to be abandoned by mutual waiver.

D. & C. Builders Ltd. v. Rees

[1966] 2 QB. 617; [1965] 3 All E.R. 837
Court of Appeal
In July 1964 the defendant owed £482 13s. 1d. to the plaintiffs for work done by them as jobbing builders. In August and again in October the plaintiffs wrote to the defendant asking for payment. In November 1964 the defendant's wife telephoned the plaintiffs and said, 'My husband will offer £300 in settlement. That is all you'll get. It is to be in satisfaction.' The plaintiffs then discussed the problem between themselves. The company was a small one and it was in desperate financial straits: for this reason the plaintiffs decided to accept the £300. The plaintiffs then telephoned the defendant's wife, telling her that '£300 will not even clear our commitments on the job. We will accept £300 and give you a year to find the balance.' She replied, 'No, we will never have enough money to pay the balance. £300 is better than nothing.' When she was told by the plaintiffs that they had no choice but to accept, she said, 'Would you like the money by cash or by cheque. If it is cash, you can have it on Monday. If by cheque; you can have it tomorrow (Saturday).' The next day, the defendant's wife gave the plaintiffs a cheque for £300, asking for a receipt, and insisting on the words 'in completion of account'. So that the wording of the receipt was as follows: 'Received the sum of £300 from Mr. Rees in completion of the account. Paid, M. Casey.' In evidence, Mr. Casey explained why he gave a receipt in those terms: 'If I did not have the £300 the company would have gone bankrupt. The only reason we took it was to save the company. She knew the position we were in.' The plaintiffs brought this action to recover the balance of £182 13s. 1d. On a preliminary point whether there was accord and satisfaction, it was held by the county court judge that the taking of the cheque for £300 did not discharge the debt of £482 13s. 1d. The defendant appealed.
HELD, by LORD DENNING, M.R., DANCKWERTS and WINN,

L.JJ., that there was no accord and satisfaction and that the plaintiff was entitled to recover the balance.

LORD DENNING, M.R. In the present case, on the facts as found by the judge, it seems to me that there was no true accord. The debtor's wife held the creditor to ransom. The creditor was in need of money to meet his own commitments, and she knew it. When the creditor asked for payment of £480 due to him, she said to him in effect: 'We cannot pay you the £480. But we will pay you £300 if you will accept it in settlement. If you do not accept it on those terms, you will get nothing. £300 is better than nothing.' She had no right to say any such thing. She could properly have said: 'We cannot pay you more than £300. Please accept it on account.' But she had no right to insist on his taking it in settlement. When she said: 'We will pay you nothing unless you accept £300 in settlement,' she was putting undue pressure on the creditor. She was making a threat to break the contract (by paying nothing) and she was doing it so as to compel the creditor to do what he was unwilling to do (to accept £300 in settlement): and she succeeded. He complied with her demand. . . . In these circumstances there was no true accord so as to found a defence of accord and satisfaction. There is also no equity in the defendant to warrant any departure from the due course of law. No person can insist on a settlement procured by intimidation.

DANCKWERTS, L.J. The giving of a cheque of the debtor for a smaller amount than the sum due is very different from 'the gift of a horse, hawk, or robe etc.' mentioned in Pinnel's case. I accept that the cheque of some other person than the debtor, in appropriate circumstances, may be the basis of an accord and satisfaction, but I cannot see how in the year 1965 the debtor's own cheque for a smaller sum can be better than payment of the whole amount of the debt in cash. The cheque is only conditional payment, it may be difficult to cash, or it may be returned by the bank with the letters 'R.D.' on it. . .

I agree also that, in the circumstances of the present case, there was no true accord. Mr. and Mrs. Rees really behaved very badly. They knew of the plaintiff's financial difficulties and used their awkward situation to intimidate them. The plaintiffs did not wish to accept the sum of £300 in discharge of the debt of £482, but were desperate to get some money. It would appear also that the defendant and his wife misled the plaintiff. Mr Rees, in his evidence, said: 'In June (1964) I could have paid £700 odd. I could have settled the whole bill.' There is no evidence that by August, or even by November, their financial situation had deteriorated so that they could not pay the £482. Nor does it appear that their position was altered to their detriment by reason of the receipt given by the plaintiffs. The receipt was given on Nov. 14, 1964. On Nov. 23, 1964 the plaintiffs' solicitors wrote a letter making it clear that the payment of £300 was being treated as a payment on account. I cannot see any ground in this case for treating the payment as a satisfaction on equitable principles.

Foakes v. Beer

[1884] 9 App. Cas. 605; [1881–5] All E.R. Rep. 106
House of Lords
On 11th August 1875 judgment was entered against the defendant and in favour of the plaintiff, for £2,077 17s. 2d. for debt and £13 1s. 10d. for costs. By the *Judgments Act*, 1838, s. 17, 'Every judgment debt shall carry interest at the rate of four pounds per centum per annum from the time of entering the judgment . . . until the same shall be satisfied.' On 21st December 1876 the parties made and signed a memorandum of agreement in the following terms:

'Whereas the said John Weston Foakes is indebted to the said Julia Beer, and she has obtained a judgment in Her Majesty's High Court of Justice, Exchequer Division, for the sum of £2090 19s. And whereas the said John Weston Foakes has requested the said Julia Beer to give him time in which to pay such judgment, which she has agreed to do on the following conditions. Now this agreement witnesseth that in consideration of the said John Weston Foakes paying to the said Julia Beer on the signing of this agreement the sum of £500, the receipt whereof she doth hereby acknowledge in part satisfaction of the said judgment debt of £2090 19s., and on condition of his paying to her or her executors, administrators, assigns or nominee the sum of £150 on the 1st day of July and the 1st day of January or within one calendar month after each of the said days respectively in every year until the whole of the said sum of £2090 19s. shall have been fully paid and satisfied, the first of such payments to be made on the 1st day of

July next. then she the said Julia Beer hereby undertakes and agrees that she, her executors, administrators or assigns, will not take any proceedings whatever on the said judgment.'

The defendant paid all sums as they fell due under this agreement, but the plaintiff claimed interest. CAVE. J., held that, whether the judgment was satisfied or not, the plaintiff was not entitled to issue execution for any sum on the judgment by reason of her agreement that she 'will not take any proceedings whatever on the said judgment.' This decision was upheld by the Queen's Bench Division. But this decision was reversed by the Court of Appeal and the defendant appealed to the House of Lords.

HELD, by the EARL OF SELBOURNE, L.C., LORD BLACKBURN, LORD WATSON and LORD FITZGERALD, that the creditors agreement not to take any proceedings on the judgment is *nudum pactum*, being without consideration, and does not prevent the creditor from taking proceedings to recover the interest payable on the judgment by virtue of s.17 of the *Judgments Act*, 1838.

EARL OF SELBOURNE. Not being under seal, the agreement cannot be legally enforced against the respondent, unless she received consideration for it from the appellant, or unless, though without consideration, it operates by way of accord and satisfaction, so as to extinguish the claim for interest. What is consideration? On the face of the agreement none is expressed, except a present payment of £500, on account and in part of the larger debt then due and payable by law under the judgment. The appellant did not contract to pay the future instalments of £150 each, at the times therein mentioned; much less did he give any new security, in the shape of negotiable paper, or in any other form. The promise *de futuro* was only that of the respondent, that if the half-yearly payments of £150 each were regularly paid, she would 'take no proceedings whatever on the judgment'. No doubt if the appellant had been under no antecedent obligation to pay the whole debt, his fulfilment of the condition might have imported some consideration on his part for that promise. But he was under that antecedent obligation; and payment at those deferred dates, by the forbearance and indulgence of the creditor, of the residue of the principal debt and costs, could not (in my opinion) be a consideration for the relinquishment of interest and discharge of the judgment, unless the payment of the £500, at the time of signing the agreement, was such a consideration. As to accord and satisfaction, in point of fact there could be no complete satisfaction, so long as any future instalment remained payable; and I do not see how any mere payments on account could operate in law as a satisfaction *ad interim*, conditionally upon other payments being afterwards duly made, unless there was a consideration sufficient to support the agreement while still unexecuted. Nor was anything, in fact, done by the respondent in this case, on the receipt of the last payment, which could be tantamount to an acquittance, if the agreement did not previously bind her.

LORD FITZGERALD. The short question then is, in relation to a judgment debt payable immediately, and on which the creditor is entitled to have execution, is the payment by the debtor of a part a sufficient consideration to support a parol agreement by the judgment creditor not to take any proceedings whatever on the judgment for the residue? In my opinion it is not; and I think, therefore, that the judgment of the Court of Appeal should be affirmed.

17. Discharge by frustration

The doctrine of discharge from liability by frustration has been explained in various ways, sometimes by speaking of the disappearance of a foundation which the parties assumed to be at the basis of their contract, sometimes as flowing from the inference of an implied term. Which-ever way it is put, the legal consequence is the same: Joseph Constantine Steamship Line *v.* Imperial Smelting Corporation, per VISCOUNT SIMON, L.C.

Summary

1. Subsequent impossibility

Where performance has become unexpectedly onerous or even impossible, owing to the occurrence of some subsequent event, there is no excuse and no discharge for the party whose performance is affected. If a party wishes to protect himself from the effect of subsequent difficulties or impossibility he should stipulate accordingly when making the bargain: *Paradine* v. *Jane* [1648]. Since the decision in *Taylor* v. *Caldwell* [1863] the strict rule in *Paradine* v. *Jane* has been relaxed by the courts where the doctrine of frustration is applicable.

2. The doctrine of frustration of contract

The doctrine of frustration will apply where, due to some event, the fundamental purpose of the contract is rendered impossible of performance, so that any attempted performance would amount to something quite different from what must have been contemplated by the parties when they made their contract. On the occurrence of such an event, both parties are discharged from any obligations of further performance.

The doctrine may apply where there is destruction of an object necessary to the performance of the contract: *Taylor* v. *Caldwell* [1863]. Or where death or injury prevents performance: *Robinson* v. *Davison* [1871]. Or on the non-occurrence of an event fundamental to the contract: *Krell* v. *Henry* [1903], *Herne Bay Steamboat Co.* v. *Hutton* [1903]. The event must not have been induced by one of the parties: *Joseph Constantine Steamship Line* v. *Imperial Smelting Corporation* [1942]. There will be no frustration where the event, though onerous, is not sufficiently grave: *National Carriers* v. *Panalpina (Northern)* (1981).

3. Effect of frustration

At common law, a contract is terminated at the time of the frustrating event. The parties are excused performance of obligations falling due after the event. Obligations which accrue before the event are not discharged by frustration and must be honoured. Money paid before the event can be recovered in quasi contract where there has been a complete failure of consideration: *Fibrosa Spolka Akcyjina* v. *Fairbairn Lawson Combe Barbour* [1943]. The unfairness inherent in the common law position was cured by the Law Reform (Frustrated Contracts) Act [1943], which gives to the court a power to order the payment, retention or recovery of money as it thinks just, having regard to the circumstances of each case.

Paradine v. Jane

[1648] Aleyn 26
Court of King's Bench

Debt. The plaintiff brought this action to recover rent due under a lease and was met with the defence 'that a certain German prince, by name Prince Rupert, an alien born, enemy to the King and kingdom, had invaded the realm with an hostile army of men; and with the same force did enter upon the defendant's possession, and him expel- led, and held out of possession from the 19 of July 18 Car. till the Feast of the Annunciation, 21 Car. whereby he could not take the profits; . . .'

The Court held that 'when the party by his own contract creates a duty or charge upon himself, he is bound to make it good, if he may, notwithstanding any accident by inevitable necessity, because he might have provided against it by his contract. . . . Now the rent is a duty created by the parties upon the reservation, and had there been a covenant to pay it, there had been no question but the lessee must have made it good, notwithstanding the interruption by enemies, for the law would not protect him beyond his own agreement, no more than in the case of reparations; this reservation then being a covenant in law, and whereupon an action of covenant hath been maintained (as Roll said) it is all one as if there had been an actual covenant. Another reason was added, that as the lessee is to have the advantage of casual profits, so he must run the hazard of casual losses, and not lay the whole burthen of them upon his lessor; and . . . that though the land be surrounded, or gained by the sea, or made barren by wildfire, yet the lessor shall have his whole rent: and judgment was given for the plaintiff.'

Taylor v. Caldwell

[1863] 3 B. & S. 826; [1861–73] All E.R. Rep. 24
Court of Queen's Bench

The defendants agreed to let the plaintiffs have the use of the Surrey Gardens and Music Hall on four specified days for the purpose of giving a series of four concerts and day and night fêtes. After the making of this agreement and before the date fixed for the first concert, the Hall was destroyed by fire. The contract contained no express stipulation with reference to fire. The plaintiffs, who had spent money on advertisements and otherwise in preparing for the concerts, brought this action to recover damages. It was contended that, according to the rule in *Paradine* v. *Jane*, the destruction of the premises by fire did not exonerate the defendants from performing their part of the agreement.

HELD, by BLACKBURN, J., that both parties were excused from performance of the contract.

BLACKBURN, J. There seems no doubt that, where there is a positive contract to do a thing not in itself unlawful, the contractor must perform it or pay damages for not doing it, although in consequence of unforeseen accident, the performance of his contract has become unexpectedly burdensome, or even impossible. But this rule is only applicable when the contract is positive and absolute and not subject to any condition either expressed or implied; and there are authorities which, as we think, establish the principle that where, from the nature of the contract, it appears that the parties must from the beginning have known that it could not be fulfilled unless, when the time for the fulfilment of the contract arrived, some particular specified thing continued to exist, so that when entering into the contract they must have contemplated such continued existence as the foundation of what was to be done, there, in the absence of any expressed or implied warranty that the thing shall exist, the contract is not to be construed as a positive contract, but as subject to an implied condition that the parties shall be excused in case, before breach, performance becomes impossible from the perishing of the thing without default of the contractor.

There seems little doubt that this implication tends to further the great object of making the legal construction such as to fulfil the intention of those who enter into the contract, for, in the course of affairs, men, in making such contracts, in general, would, if it were brought to their minds, say that there should be such a condition ...

In the present case, looking at the whole contract, we find that the parties contracted on the basis of the continued existence of the music hall at the time when the concerts were to be given, that being essential to their performance. We think, therefore, that, the music hall having ceased to exist without fault of either party, both parties are excused, the plaintiffs from taking the gardens and paying the money, the defendants from performing their promise to give the use of the hall and gardens and other things.

Robinson v. Davison

[1871] L.R. 6 Exch. 269; [1861–73] All E.R. Rep. 699
Court of Exchequer
The plaintiff was a professor of music and a giver of musical entertainments, and the defendant was the husband of a celebrated pianist. The plaintiff entered into a contract with the defendant's wife (as her husband's agent) to perform at a concert he had arranged for a specified evening. A few hours before the concert was due to begin the plaintiff received a letter from the defendant's wife informing him that on account of her illness she could not perform at the concert. The plaintiff brought this action for breach of contract.
HELD, by KELLY, C.B., and CHANNEL, BRAMWELL and CLEASBY, BB., that the contract was conditional upon the defendant's wife being well enough to perform and that, consequently, the defendant was excused.

BRAMWELL, B. This is a contract to perform a service which no deputy could perform, and which, in case of death, could not be performed by the executors of the deceased; and I am of the opinion that by virtue of the terms of the original bargain incapacity either of body or mind in the performer, without default on his or her part, is an excuse for non-performance. Of course the parties might expressly contract that incapacity should not excuse, and thus preclude the condition of health from being annexed to their agreement. Here they have not done so; and as they have been silent on that point, the contract must in my judgment be taken to have been conditional, and not absolute. This is the conclusion I come to upon principle, and the cases cited seem to me in accordance with it.

Krell v. Henry

[1903] 2 K.B. 740; [1900–3] All E.R. Rep. 20
Court of Appeal
By a written contract, the defendant agreed to hire from the plaintiff a third-floor flat in Pall Mall for 26th and 27th June 1902. The defendant's purpose was to view the coronation processions which had been proclaimed to pass along the street below on those dates,

but there was no express mention of this in the contract. The agreed price was £75, of which £25 was advanced to the plaintiff at the time the contract was made. The King fell ill and processions did not take place on the days appointed, and the defendant refused to pay the balance of £50 according to the agreement. The plaintiff brought this action to recover it. The defendant denied liability and counter-claimed for the recovery of £25, the amount paid by way of deposit. DARLING, J., following *Taylor* v. *Caldwell*, gave judgment for the defendant on the claim and on the counter-claim. The plaintiff appealed and the defendant abandoned his counter-claim.

HELD, by VAUGHAN WILLIAMS, ROMER and STIRLING, L.JJ., that there was a necessary inference from the circumstances, recognised by both parties, that the coronation procession and the relative position of the rooms was the foundation of the contract; that the express terms of the contract to pay for the use of the flat on the days named, though unconditional, were not used with reference to the possibility of the cancellation of the procession, and consequently, the plaintiff was not entitled to recover the balance of £50.

VAUGHAN WILLIAMS, L.J. Each case must be judged by its own circumstances. In each case one must ask oneself, first, what, having regard to all the circumstances, was the foundation of the contract? Secondly, was the performance of the contract prevented? Thirdly, was the event which prevented the performance of the contract of such a character that it cannot reasonably be said to have been in the contemplation of the parties at the date of the contract? If all these questions are answered in the affirmative (as I think they should be in this case), I think both parties are discharged from further performance of the contract. I think that the coronation procession was the foundation of this contract, and that the non-happening of it prevented the performance of the contract; and, secondly, I think that the non-happening of the procession, to use the words of Sir James Hannen in *Baily* v. *De Crespigny*, was an event 'of such a character that it cannot reasonably be supposed to have been in the contemplation of the contracting parties when the contract was made, and that they are not to be held bound by general words which, though large enough to include, were not used with reference to the possibility of the particular contingency which afterwards happened.' I myself am clearly of opinion that in this case, where we have to ask ourselves whether the object of the contract was frustrated by the non-happening of the coronation and its procession on the days proclaimed, parol evidence is admissible to shew that the subject of the contract was rooms to view the coronation procession, and was so to the knowledge of both parties. When once this is established, I see no difficulty whatever in the case. It is not essential to the application of the principle of *Taylor* v. *Caldwell* that the direct subject of the contract should perish or fail to be in existence at that time. In the present case the condition which fails and prevents the achievement of that which was, in the contemplation of both parties, the foundation of the contract, is not expressly mentioned either as a condition of the contract or the purpose of it; but I think for the reasons which I have given that the principle of *Taylor* v. *Caldwell* ought to be applied. This disposes of the plaintiff's claim for £50 unpaid balance of the price agreed to be paid for the use of the rooms. The defendant at one time set up a cross-claim for the return of the £25 he paid at the date of the contract. As that claim is now withdrawn it is unnecessary to say anything about it.

Herne Bay Steamboat Co. v. Hutton

[1903] 2 K.B. 683; [1900–3] All E.R. Rep. 627
Court of Appeal

The plaintiff steamship company contracted to place their steamboat *Cynthia* at the disposal of the defendant on 28th June 1902, 'for the purpose of viewing the Naval Review and for a day's cruise round the fleet; also on Sunday June 29th 1902, for a similar purpose'. The *Cynthia* was fitted out for this trip but on 25th June the postponement of the review was announced. On 26th June the plaintiffs, telegraphed the defendant: 'What about Cynthia? She is ready to start at six tomorrow. Waiting cash.' There was no reply from the defendant. The plaintiff brought this action for damages for breach of contract. GRANTHAM, J., gave judgment for the defendant on the claim and on the counter-claim. The plaintiff appealed.

HELD, by VAUGHAN WILLIAMS, ROMER and STIRLING, L.JJ., that the defendant was not discharged from his obligations under the contract by the postponement of the Naval Review because (*i*) the object in hiring the vessel was the defendant's alone and of no concern to the plaintiff and (*ii*) the holding of the Naval Review was not the foundation of the contract.

ROMER, L.J. This is not a case where the subject-matter of the contract is a mere licence to the defendant to use the ship for the purpose of seeing the Naval Review and going round the fleet. It is really a contract for hiring the ship by the defendant for a certain voyage, though the object of the hirer is stated — *viz.*, to see the Naval Review and the fleet. But that object was one with which the defendant as hirer of the ship was alone concerned, and not the plaintiffs, the owners.... . The ship had nothing to do with the review or the fleet. It was only a carrier of passengers to see it, and many other ships would have done just as well. It is similar to the hiring of a cab or other vehicle, on which, though the object of the hirer was stated, that statement would not make the object any less a matter for the hirer alone, and would not affect the person who was letting the vehicle for hire. There was not here, by reason of the review not taking place, a total failure of the consideration, nor anything like a total destruction of the subject-matter of the contract.

STIRLING, L.J. It seems to me that the reference in the contract to the review is explained by the object of the voyage, and I am quite unable to treat the reference to the voyage as the foundation of the contract so as to entitle either party to the benefit of the doctrine in *Taylor* v. *Caldwell*. I come to that conclusion more readily as the object of the voyage was not to see the review only, but included a cruise round the fleet. The fleet was there, and the passengers might have been willing to go round it. It seems to me that that was the business of the defendant, whose venture it was. I am therefore unable to agree with the decision of GRANTHAM, J., and I think the defendant was not discharged from the performance of the contract.

Joseph Constantine Steamship Line Ltd. v. Imperial Smelting Corporation Ltd.

[1942] A.C. 154; [1941] 2 All E.R. 165
House of Lords
A ship was chartered to load a cargo at Port Pirie in South Australia and to carry it to Europe. While the vessel was anchored in the roads

246 Casebook on contract law

off Pirie and before she became an 'arrived ship' there was a violent explosion near her auxiliary boiler, causing damage and making it impossible to perform the charterparty. The charterers claimed damages, alleging that the owners had broken the charterparty by their failure to load the cargo. The owners contended that the contract was frustrated by the destructive consequences of the explosion. There was no evidence that the explosion was due to the fault of the owners. It was held by the Court of Appeal that the defence raised by the owners, that the charter was frustrated, must fail unless the owners could prove affirmatively that the frustration occurred without their default. The owners appealed.

HELD, by VISCOUNT SIMON, L.C., VISCOUNT MAUGHAN, LORD RUSSELL OF KILLOWEN, LORD WRIGHT and LORD PORTER, that the onus of proving default lies upon the party denying the frustration. Since there was no evidence that the explosion was attributable to the fault of the owners, the contract was frustrated.

VISCOUNT SIMON. In this connection, it is well to emphasise that, when 'frustration' in the legal sense occurs, it does not merely provide one party with a defence in an action brought by the other. It kills the contract itself and discharges both parties automatically. The plaintiff sues for breach at a past date and the defendant pleads that at that date no contract existed. In this situation, the plaintiff could only succeed if it were shown that the determination of the contract were due to the defendant's 'default', and it would be a strange result if the party alleging this were not the party required to prove it.

The doctrine of discharge from liability by frustration has been explained in various ways, sometimes by speaking of the disappearance of a foundation which the parties assumed to be at the basis of their contract, sometimes as deduced from a rule arising from impossibility of performance, and sometimes as flowing from the inference of an implied term. Whichever way it is put, the legal consequence is the same. The most satisfactory basis, I think, upon which the doctrine can be put is that it depends on an implied term in the contract of the parties. It has the advantage of bringing out the distinction that there can be no discharge by supervening impossibility if the express terms of the contract bind the parties to performance notwithstanding that the supervening event may occur. Every case in this branch of the law can be stated as turning on the question of whether, from the express terms of the particular contract, a further term should be implied which, when its conditions are fulfilled, puts an end to the contract.

If the matter is to be regarded in this way, the question, therefore, is as to the construction of a contract, taking into consideration its express and implied terms. The implied terms in the present case may well be: 'This contract is to cease to be binding if the vessel is disabled by an over-powering disaster, provided that disaster is not brought about by the default of either party.'

LORD WRIGHT. The explanation which has been generally accepted in English law is that impossibility or frustration depends on the court implying a term or exception and treating that as part of the contract. Whatever explanation is adopted cannot affect the decision of this, or, so far as I can see, of any, case. If the question is still open in English law, I should prefer to rest the principle simply on the true meaning of the contract, as it appears to the court. The essential feature of the role is that the court construes the contract, having regard to its language, its nature and the circumstances, as meaning that it depended for its operation on the existence or occurrence of a particular object or state of things as its basis or foundation. If that is gone, the life of the contract in law goes with it, at least as regards future performance. The contract remains only to enforce accrued rights.

NOTE

The basis of the doctrine of frustration should be considered. In *Taylor* v. *Caldwell* [1863] Blackburn, J., said that the contract was 'subject to an implied condition that the party shall be excused in case, before breach, performance becomes impossible from the perishing of the thing without default of the contractor'. In the *Joseph Constantine* case [1942] Viscount Simon, L.C., said: 'The doctrine of discharge from liability by frustration has been explained in various ways, sometimes by speaking of the disappearance of a foundation which the parties assumed to be at the basis of their contract, sometimes as flowing from the inference of an implied term. Which-ever way it is put, the legal consequence is the same.' A helpful statement was made by Lord Wright in *Denny, Mott & Dickson* v. *James Fraser & Co.* [1944]. He said, 'The data for decision are on the one hand the terms and construction of the contract, read in the light of the then existing circumstances, and on the other hand the events which have occurred. It is the court which has to decide what is the true position between the parties.' *See* also Lord Wright's speech in *Joseph Constantine*.

National Carriers, Ltd. v. Panalpina (Northern) Ltd.

[1981] A.C. 675; [1981] 1 All E.R. 161
House of Lords

The plaintiffs, National Carriers, leased a warehouse to the defendants, Panalpina, for a term of ten years. The rent for the first five years was agreed at £6,500 and for the second five years, £13,300. The ten-year term commenced on 1st January 1974. In May 1979 the local authority closed the street giving the only access to the warehouse because there was a dangerous building opposite. The building could not be immediately demolished because it was listed as being of special architectural or historical interest. The street was reopened in January 1981. The closure of the street prevented the defendants from using the warehouse for the only purpose contemplated by the lease, namely, as a warehouse. In May 1979 they stopped paying rent. In July 1979 the plaintiffs brought an action claiming payment of two quarterly instalments due under the lease. The defendants contended that they were not liable to pay the rent because the lease was frustrated by the closure of the street. Judgment was given for the plaintiffs on the ground that the judge was bound by authority to hold that the doctrine of frustration could not apply to a lease. The defendants appealed directly to the House of Lords.

HELD, (1) by LORDS HAILSHAM, WILBERFORCE, SIMON and ROSKILL (LORD RUSSELL *dubitante*), that the doctrine of frustration was capable of applying to an executed lease of land.

HELD, (2) unanimously that, although by the time access was restored, the defendants would have lost two out of ten years' use of the warehouse and their business would have been severely disrupted, it was not sufficiently grave to amount to a frustrating event.

LORD SIMON. The matter must be considered as it appeared at the time when the frustrating event is alleged to have happened.

Commercial men must be entitled to act on reasonable commercial probabilities at the time they are called on to make up their minds. What we know has in fact happened is, however, available as an aid to determine the reasonable probabilities at the time when decision was called for.

Favourably to the appellants' case, the road would remain closed for 'well over a year' from application for listed-building consent to demolition. Still more favourable is that it will in fact remain closed for some twenty months.

The appellants were undoubtedly put to considerable expense and inconvenience. But that is not enough. Whenever the performance of a contract is interrupted by a supervening event, the initial judgment is quantitative: what relation does the likely period of interruption bear to the outstanding period for performance? But this must ultimately be translated into qualitative terms: in the light of the quantitative computation and of all other relevant factors (from which I would not entirely exclude executed performance) would outstanding performance in accordance with the literal terms of the contract differ so significantly from what the parties reasonably contemplated at the time of execution that it would be unjust to insist on compliance with those literal terms? In the instant case, at the most favourable to the appellants' contention, they could, at the time the road was closed, look forward to pristine enjoyment of the warehouse for about two-thirds of the remaining currency of the lease. The interruption would be only one-sixth of the total term. Judging by the drastic increase in rent under the rent review clause (more than doubled), it seems likely that the appellants' occupation towards the end of the first quinquennium must have been on terms very favourable to them. The parties can hardly have contemplated that the fire risk expressly provided for was the only possible source of interruption of the business of the warehouse: some possible interruption from some cause or other cannot have been beyond the reasonable contemplation of the parties. Weighing all the relevant factors, I do not think that the appellants have demonstrated a triable issue that the closure of the road so significantly changed the nature of the outstanding rights and obligations under the lease from what the parties could reasonably have contemplated at the time of its execution that it would be unjust to hold them to the literal sense of its stipulations.

Fibrosa Spolka Akcyjna v. Fairbairn Lawson Combe Barbour, Ltd.

[1943] A.C. 32; [1942] 2 All E.R. 122

House of Lords

The parties entered a contract in July 1939 by which the vendors undertook to manufacture and deliver certain machinery c.i.f. Gdynia. By the terms of the contract (*i*) if dispatch was hindered by any cause beyond the vendor's reasonable control, a reasonable extension of time should be granted, and (*ii*) one third of the purchase price was payable at the time of the order being given. One third of the purchase price was £1,600, and, of this £1,000 only was paid in July 1939. In September 1939 Gdynia was occupied by the enemy, rendering impossible the lawful delivery of the machinery there. The London agents of the purchasers brought this action to recover the £1,000 paid in advance, contending that the contract was frustrated notwithstanding the provision for reasonable extension.

HELD, by VISCOUNT SIMON, L.C., LORD ATKIN, LORD RUSSELL OF KILLOWEN, LORD MACMILLAN, LORD WRIGHT, LORD ROCHE and LORD PORTER, that the stipulation providing for a reasonable extension referred only to a temporary impossibility and not to the prolonged period of impossibility occasioned by the outbreak of war, and that the contract was, accordingly, frustrated: that the buyer was entitled to the recovery of the £1,000 paid in advance as money paid upon a consideration which had wholly failed.

VISCOUNT SIMON, L.C. The conclusion is that the rule in *Chandler* v. *Webster* is wrong, and that, the appellants can recover their £1,000. While this result obviates the harshness with which the previous view in some instances treated the party who had made a prepayment, it cannot be regarded as dealing fairly between the parties in all cases, and must sometimes have the result of leaving the recipient who has to return the money at a grave disadvantage. He may have incurred expenses in connection with the partial carrying out of the contract which are equivalent, or more than equivalent, to the money which he prudently stipulated should be prepaid, but which he now has to return for reasons which are no fault of his. He may have to repay the money, though he has executed almost the whole of the contractual work, which will be left on his hands. These results follow from the fact that the English common law does not undertake to apportion a prepaid sum in such circumstances. It must be for the legislature to decide whether provision should be made for an equitable apportionment of prepaid moneys which have to be returned by the recipient in view of the frustration of the contract in respect of which they were paid.

Law Reform (Frustrated Contracts) Act 1943

1. Adjustment of rights and liabilities of parties to frustrated contracts

(1) Where a contract governed by English law has become impossible of performance or been otherwise frustrated, and the parties thereto have for that reason been discharged from the further performance of the contract, the following provisions of this section shall, subject to the provisions of section two of this Act, have effect in relation thereto.

(2) All sums paid or payable to any party in pursuance of the contract before the time when the parties were so discharged (in this Act referred to as 'the time of discharge') shall, in the case of sums so paid, be recoverable from him as money received by him for the use of the party by whom the sums were paid, and, in the case of sums so payable, cease to be so payable:

Provided that, if the party to whom the sums were so paid or payable incurred expenses before the time of discharge in, or for the purpose of, the performance of the contract, the court may, if it considers it just to do so having regard to all the circumstances of the case, allow him to retain or, as the case may be, recover the whole or any part of the sums so paid or payable, not being an amount in excess of the expenses so incurred.

(3) Where any party to the contract has, by reason of anything done by any other party thereto in, or for the purpose of, the performance of the contract, obtained a valuable benefit (other than a payment of money to which the last foregoing subsection applies) before the time of discharge, there shall be recoverable from him by the said other party such sum (if any), not exceeding the value of the said benefit to the party obtaining it, as the court considers just, having regard to all the circumstances of the case and, in particular –

(*a*) the amount of any expenses incurred before the time of discharge by the benefited party in, or for the purpose of, the performance of the contract, including any sums paid or payable by him to any other party in pursuance of the contract and retained or recoverable by that party under the last foregoing subsection, and

(*b*) the effect, in relation to the said benefit, of the circumstances giving rise to the frustration of the contract.

(4) In estimating, for the purposes of the foregoing provisions of this section, the amount of any expenses incurred by any party to the contract, the court may, without prejudice to the generality of the said provisions, include such sums as appears to be reasonable in respect of overhead expenses and in respect of any work or services performed personally by the said party.

(5) In considering whether any sum ought to be recovered or retained under the foregoing provisions of this section by any party to the contract, the court shall not take into account any sums which have, by reason of the circumstances giving rise to the frustration of the contract, become payable to that party under any contract of insurance unless there was an obligation to insure imposed by an express term of the frustrated contract or by or under any enactment.

(6) Where any person has assumed obligations under the contract in consideration of the conferring of a benefit by any other party to the contract upon any other person, whether a party to the contract or not, the court may, if in all the circumstances of the case it considers it just to do so, treat for the purposes of subsection (3) of this section any benefit so conferred as a benefit obtained by the person who has assumed the obligations as aforesaid.

2. Provision as to application of this Act

(1) This Act shall apply to contracts, whether made before or after the commencement of this Act, as respects which the time of discharge is on or after the first day of July, nineteen hundred and forty-three, but not to contracts as respects which the time of discharge is before the said date.

(2) This Act shall apply to contracts to which the Crown is a party in like manner as to contracts between subjects.

(3) Where any contract to which this Act applies contains any provision which, upon the true construction of the contract, is intended to have effect in the event of circumstances arising which operate, or would but for the said provision operate, to frustrate the contract, or is intended to have effect whether such circumstances arise or not, the court shall give effect to the said provision and shall only give effect to the foregoing section of this Act to such extent, if any, as appears to the court to be consistent with the said provision.

(4) Where it appears to the court that a part of any contract to which this Act applies can properly be severed from the remainder of the contract, being a part wholly performed before the time of discharge, or so performed except for the payment in respect of that part of the contract of sums which are or can be ascertained under the contract, the court shall treat that part of the contract as if it were a separate contract and had not been frustrated and shall treat the foregoing section of this Act as only applicable to the remainder of that contract.

(5) This Act shall not apply —

(*a*) to any charterparty, except a time charterparty or a charterparty by way of demise, or to any contract (other than a charterparty) for the carriage of goods by sea; or

(*b*) to any contract of insurance, save as is provided by subsection (5) of the foregoing section; or

(*c*) to any contract to which section seven of the Sale of Goods Act, 1893 (which avoids contracts for the sale of specific goods which perish before the risk has passed to the buyer) applies, or to any other contract for the sale, or for the sale and delivery, of specific goods, where the contract is frustrated by reason of the fact that the goods have perished.

3. Short title and interpretation

(1) This Act may be cited as the Law Reform (Frustrated Contracts) Act 1943.

(2) In this Act the expression 'court' means, in relation to any matter, the court or arbitrator by or before whom the matter falls to be determined.

18. Discharge by acceptance of breach

When one party wrongly refuses to perform obligations, this
will not automatically bring the contract to an end. The
innocent party has an option. He may either accept the
wrongful repudiation as determining the contract and sue
for damages or he may ignore or reject the attempt to
determine the contract and affirm its continued existence:
The Simona per LORD ACKNER.

Summary

1. Fundamental breach or breach of condition

Where there is a fundamental breach or a breach of condition, the
aggrieved party may elect either to affirm the contract by treating it
as still in force, or treat it as being conclusively discharged by his
acceptance of the other party's breach: *General Billposting* v.
Atkinson [1908]; *Fercometal S.A.R.L.* v. *Mediterranean Shipping Co.,
The Simona* [1988]. Where there is an anticipatory breach, the aggrieved party may immediately accept it, treat himself as discharged
from further performance and sue for damages: he does not have to
wait for the date for performance under the contract: *Hochster* v. *De
la Tour* [1853]. An affirmation keeps the contract alive for the benefit
of both parties: *White and Carter (Councils)* v. *McGregor* [1962].
Furthermore, the affirming party is not absolved from tendering
further performance of his obligations under the contract.
Accordingly, where a repudiation by anticipatory breach is followed
by affirmation of the contract, the repudiating party can escape if the
affirming party subsequently breaks the contract: *The Simona* [1988].

2. Breach of warranty and wrongful notice

Where the breach does not amount to a fundamental breach or breach of condition, there is no right of election for there is no repudiation: *Hong Kong Fir Shipping Co.* v. *Kawasaki Kissen Kaisha* [1962]. In such a case, the remedy sounds in damages only and if the aggrieved party wrongfully gives notice of election to put an end to the contract, that notice, of itself, will be a serious breach and may be accepted by the other party as a repudiation: *Decro-Wall International S.A.* v. *Practitioners in Marketing* [1971]. Where, however, such a notice is sent in good faith, it does not necessarily constitute a repudiatory breach: its effect will depend on the circumstances and the conduct of the parties as a whole: *Woodar Investment Development* v. *Wimpey Construction* [1980]. A threatened breach which has the effect of a threat to deprive a party of substantially the whole of the benefit of the contract, may be accepted by the aggrieved party so as to put an end to the contract: *Federal Commerce and Navigation Ltd.* v. *Molena Alpha Inc.* [1979].

General Billposting Co. Ltd. v. Atkinson

[1909] A.C. 118; [1908–10] All E.R. Rep. 619

House of Lords

The defendant, a billposter, entered into a contract of employment with the plaintiff company, the contract being subject to termination by either party giving twelve months notice in writing. By the contract, the defendant undertook that he would not, within two years of leaving the plaintiff company's employment, engage as a billposter within a radius of fifty miles of the company's registered office. The company dismissed him without giving the agreed twelve months notice. He then set himself up as a billposter within fifty miles of the company's registered office. The company brought this action against him, claiming damages and an injunction to restrain him from working as a billposter within the range of fifty miles as agreed in the contract of employment. The action came before NEVILLE, J., who gave judgment for the plaintiff company. The defendant appealed and it was held by the Court of Appeal that the company, by dismissing the employee without the agreed period of notice had completely and totally repudiated the contract of employment and that, accordingly, the employee was entitled to accept the repudiation and regard himself as no longer bound by any of its terms. The company appealed to the House of Lords.

HELD, by the EARL OF HALSBURY, LORD COLLINS, LORD ROBERTSON and LORD LOREBURN, L.C., that the employers dismissed the defendant in deliberate disregard of the terms of the contract, and that he was thereupon justified in rescinding the contract and treating himself as absolved from further performance of it on his part.

LORD ROBERTSON. The respondent's position in entering into the contract is a very intelligible one. He says: 'I am a billposter, and I desire occupation, either on my own account or in the service of others. If I enter the employment of others, I am willing to give up the right to trade on my own account to the extent specified in this agreement. I do not desire to have it both ways.' The claim of the appellants, on the other hand, as now put forward, is that taking him at his word, as expressed in the contract, and getting his services, they are to be entitled both to deprive him (against the contract) of the right to serve them and also of the right to serve himself. It seems to me that the covenant not to set up business is not only germane to but ancillary to the contract of service, and that, once the contract of service is rescinded, the other falls with it.

NOTE

A contracting party may elect to put an end to all primary obligations of both parties remaining unperformed if (i) the other party is in fundamental breach or (ii) he is in breach of condition.

Fundamental breach occurs where the event resulting from the failure of one other party to perform a primary obligation has the effect of depriving the other party of substantially the whole benefit which it was the intention of the parties that he should obtain from the contract.

Breach of condition occurs where the contracting parties have agreed, expressly or by implication, that *any* failure by one party to perform a particular primary obligation (the condition), irrespective of the gravity of the event that has in fact resulted from the breach.

Where such an election is made, the consequences are two-fold. First, there is substituted by implication of law for the primary obligations of the party in default which remain unperformed, a secondary obligation to pay monetary compensation for the loss sustained due to their non-performance in the future. This substituted secondary obligation is called the anticipatory secondary obligation — it is additional to the general secondary obligation which arises when the breach is neither fundamental nor breach of condition. (For an explanation of primary and secondary obligations, see Lord Diplock's speech in *Photo Production* v. *Securicor* (1980).)

Fercometal S.A.R.L. v. Mediterranean Shipping Co., The Simona

[1988] 2 All E.R. 742
House of Lords
In June 1982 the charterers entered into a charterparty with shipowners for the carriage of a cargo of steel coils from Durban to Bilbao on the owner's vessel. Under the terms of the charterparty the charterers were entitled to cancel the charterparty if the vessel was not ready to load on or before 9 July. On 2 July the owners requested an extension of the cancellation date because the shipowners wished to load other cargo first, in which case the vessel

would not be ready to load the charterer's cargo until 13 July. The charterers cancelled the contract forthwith and engaged another vessel, then at Durban, to carry the cargo. The owners did not accept the charterers' repudiation, which was in any event premature because it was given in advance of the cancellation date, and on 5 July the owners notified the charterers that the vessel would start loading on 8 July. When the vessel arrived in Durban on that day the owners tendered notice of readiness although they were not in fact ready to load the charterers' cargo. The charterers rejected that notice and began loading their cargo into the substitute vessel. The owners brought a claim for deadfreight, which was upheld on arbitration on the ground that the charterers' wrongful repudiation of the contract relieved the owners from complying with their own obligations and that therefore the owners' failure to tender the vessel ready to load on time did not prevent them claiming damages for the charterers' wrongful repudiation. On appeal the judge set aside the award. On further appeal, the Court of Appeal held that the charterers' prior unaccepted repudiation did not prevent them cancelling the charterparty when the owners failed to tender a valid notice of readiness on 9 July. The owners appealed.

HELD, by LORD BRIDGE, LORD TEMPLEMAN, LORD ACKNER, LORD OLIVER and LORD JAUNCEY, that where a party to a contract wrongfully repudiated his contractual obligations before he was required to perform those obligations the innocent party could either affirm the contract by treating it as still in force or treat it as being conclusively discharged, but if he elected to affirm the contract he was not absolved from tendering further performance of his own obligations under the contract. Accordingly, if a repudiation by anticipatory breach was followed by affirmation of the contract the repudiating party could escape liability if the affirming party was subsequently in breach of the contract. On the facts, the owners, having affirmed the contract when they refused to accept the charterers' premature repudiation, could only avoid the operation of the cancellation provision in the charterparty by tendering the vessel ready to load on time (which they had failed to do) or by establishing (which they could not) that their failure was the result of their acting on a representation by the charterers that they had given up their option to cancel. Accordingly, the appeal would be dismissed.

LORD ACKNER. When one party wrongly refuses to perform

obligations, this will not automatically bring the contract to an end. The innocent party has an option. He may either accept the wrongful repudiation as determining the contract and sue for damages or he may ignore or reject the attempt to determine the contract and affirm its continued existence. Cockburn, C.J., in *Frost* v. *Knight* (1872) L.R. 7 Ex Ch 111 at 112–113, [1861–73] All E.R. Rep. 221 at 223–224 put the matter thus:

> 'The law with reference to a contract to be performed at a future time, where the party bound to performance announces prior to the time his intention not to perform it, as established by the cases of *Hochster* v. *De la Tour* ((1853) 2 E. & B. 678, [1843–60] All E.R. Rep. 12) and *The Danube and Black Sea Co.* v. *Xenos* ((1863) 13 C.B.N.S. 825, 143 E.R. 325) on the one hand, and *Avery* v. *Bowden* ((1855) 5 E. & B. 714, 119 E.R. 647), *Reid* v. *Hoskins*((1856) 6 E. & B. 953, 119 E.R. 1119), and *Barwick* v. *Buba* ((1857) 2 C.B.N.S. 563, 140 E.R. 536) on the other, may be this stated. The promisee, if he pleases, may treat the notice of intention as inoperative, and await the time when the contract is to be executed, and then hold the other party responsible for all the consequences of non-performance: but in that case he keeps the contract alive for the benefit of the other party as well as his own; he remains subject to all his own obligations and liabilities under it, and enables the other party not only to complete the contract, if so advised, notwithstanding his previous repudiation of it, but also to take advantage of any supervening circumstance which would justify him in declining to complete it. On the other hand, the promisee may, if he thinks proper, treat the repudiation of the other party as a wrongful putting an end to the contract, and may at once bring his action as on a breach of it; and in such action he will be entitled to such damages as would have arisen from the non-performance of the contract at the appointed time, subject, however, to abatement in respect of any circumstances which may have afforded him the means of mitigating his loss.'

This passage was adopted by Cotton, L.J. in *Johnstone* v. *Milling* (1886) 16 Q.B.D. at 460 at 470. In that case Lord Esher, M.R. described the situation thus (at 467):

> '. . . a renunciation of a contract, or, in other words, a total refusal to perform it by one party before the time for performance arrives, does not, by itself, amount to a breach of contract but may

be so acted upon and adopted by the other party as a rescission of a contract as to give an immediate right of action. When one party assumes to renounce the contract, that is, by anticipation refuses to perform it, he thereby, so far as he is concerned, declares his intention then and there to rescind the contract. . . The other party may adopt such renunciation of the contract by so acting upon it as in effect to declare that he too treats the contract as at an end, except for the purpose of bringing an action upon it for the damages sustained by him in consequence of such renunciation.'

The way in which a 'supervening circumstance' may turn out to be to the advantage of the party in default, thus relieving him from liability, is illustrated by *Avery* v. *Bowden*, where the outbreak of the Crimean war between England and Russia made performance of the charterparty no longer legally possible. The defendant, who prior to the outbreak of the war had in breach of contract refused to load, was provided with a good defence to an action for breach of contract, since his repudiation had been ignored. As pointed out by Parker, L.J. in his judgment ([1987] 2 Lloyd's Rep. 236 at 240), the law as stated in *Frost* v. *Knight* and *Johnstone* v. *Milling* has been reasserted in many cases since, and in particular in *Heyman* v. *Darwins Ltd.* [1942] 1 All E.R. 337 at 340, [1942] A.C. 356 at 361, where Viscount Simon L.C., said:

'The first head of claim in the writ appears to be advanced on the view that an agreement is automatically terminated if one party "repudiates" it. That is not so. As SCRUTTON, L.J., said in *Golding* v. *London & Edinburgh Insurance Co., Ltd.* ((1932) 43 Ll. L.R. 487 at 488): "I have never been able to understand what effect the repudiation by one party has unless the other accepts it." If one party so acts or so expresses himself, as to show that he does not mean to accept and discharge the obligations of a contract any further, the other party has an option as to the attitude he may take up. He may, notwithstanding the so-called repudiation, insist on holding his co-contractor to the bargain and continue to tender due performance on his part. In that event, the co-contractor *has the opportunity of withdrawing from his false position, and, even if he does not, may escape ultimate liability because of some supervening event not due to this own fault which excuses or puts an end to further performance.'* (Parker, L.J.'s emphasis.)

If an unaccepted repudiation has no legal effect ('a thing writ in water and of no value to anybody': per Asquith, L.J., in *Howard* v. *Pickford Tool Co. Ltd.* [1951] 1 K.B. 417 at 421), how can the unaccepted acts of repudiation by the charterers in this case provide the owners with any cause of action? It was accepted in the Court of Appeal by counsel then appearing for the owners that it was an inevitable inference from the findings made by the arbitrators that the Simona was not ready to load the charterers' steel at any time prior to the charterers notice of cancellation on 12 July. Counsel who has appeared before your Lordships for the owners has not been able to depart from this concession. Applying the well-established principles set out above, the anticipatory breaches by the charterers not having been accepted by the owners as terminating the contract, the charterparty survived intact with the right of cancellation unaffected. The vessel was not ready to load by close of business on the cancelling date, viz 9 July, and the charterers were therefore entitled to and did give what on the face of it was an effective notice of cancellation.

White and Carter (Councils), Ltd. v. McGregor
[1962] A.C. 413; [1961] 3 All E.R. 1178
House of Lords
A Scottish appeal. The appellant company's business was the supply of litter bins to local authorities in urban areas. It was the company's practice to attach advertisement plates to the bins, for which the advertisers would pay according to the terms of a standard form of contract. The respondent, who carried on a garage business, entered into a contract through his sales manager by which the company undertook to prepare and exhibit plates advertising McGregor's business for a period of three years. The contract form was headed by a notice that it was not to be cancelled by the advertiser and one of the express conditions provided to the same effect. Immediately after this contract was signed, the following letter was sent to the company: 'We regret that our Mr. Ward signed an order today continuing the lamp post advertisements for a further period of three years. He was unaware that our proprietor Mr. McGregor does not wish to continue this form of advertisement. Please therefore cancel the order.' The appellant company did not accept the attempted cancellation and displayed the advertisements during the ensuing

three years. The respondents refused to pay and the appellant sought to recover the sum due under the contract.

HELD, by LORD REID, LORD TUCKER and LORD HODSON (LORD MORTON OF HENRYTON and LORD KEITH OF AVONHOLM dissenting), that the contract remained unaffected by the unaccepted repudiation and the appellant company was entitled to recover the sums due under the contract.

LORD HODSON. It is settled as a fundamental rule of the law of contract, that repudiation by one of the parties to a contract does not itself discharge it ... . It follows that, if, as here, there was no acceptance, the contract remains alive for the benefit of both parties and the party who has repudiated can change his mind but it does not follow that the party at the receiving end of the proffered repudiation is bound to accept it before the time for performance and is left to his remedy in damages for breach.

Counsel for the respondent did not seek to dispute the general proposition of law to which I have referred but sought to argue that if at the date of performance by the innocent party the guilty party maintains his refusal to accept performance and the innocent party does not accept the repudiations, although the contract still survives, it does not survive so far as the right of the innocent party to perform it is concerned but survives only for the purpose of enforcing remedies open to him by way of damages or specific implement. This produces an impossible result; if the party is deprived of some of his rights it involves putting an end to the contract except in cases, unlike this, where, in the exercise of the court's discretion, the remedy of specific implement is available.

The true position is that the contract survives and does so not only where specific implement is available. When the assistance of the court is not required the innocent party can choose whether he will accept repudiation and sue for damages for anticipatory breach or await the date of performance by the guilty party. Then, if there is failure in performance, his rights are preserved.

It may be unfortunate that the appellants have saddled themselves with an unwanted contract causing an apparent waste of time and money. No doubt this aspect impressed the Court of Session but there is no equity which can assist the respondent. It is trite that equity will not rewrite an improvident contract where there is no disability on either side. There is no duty laid on a party to a subsisting contract to vary it at the behest of the other party so as to deprive himself of the benefit given to him by the contract. To hold otherwise would be to introduce a novel equitable doctrine that a party was not to be held to his contract unless the court in a given instance thought it reasonable so to do. In this case it would make an action for debt a claim for a discretionary remedy.

NOTE

Discharge occurs only where the aggrieved party exercises his right of election to treat the breach as a repudiation. Where the aggrieved party does not so elect, the contract is unaffected. In *Howard* v. *Pickford Tool Co.* (1951) Asquith, L.J., said that: 'An unaccepted repudiation is a thing writ in water and of no value to anybody: it confers no legal rights of any sort or kind'.

In *Johnson* v. *Agnew* (1980) it was held by the House of Lords that, a party having a right of election may sue for specific performance without, in so doing, irrevocably affirming the contract.

Where a contract has been repudiated by an anticipatory breach and the contract–breaker subsequently becomes entitled under the contract to cancel that contract, only nominal damages will be awarded: the *Mihalis Angelos* (1970).

Hong Kong Fir Shipping Co., Ltd. v. Kawasaki Kisen Kaisha, Ltd.

[1962] 2 Q.B. 26; [1962] 1 All E.R. 474
Court of Appeal

The owners of a ship undertook by charterparty to let it to the charterers for a period of twenty-four months. They undertook that the ship was fitted in every way for ordinary cargo service and that they would maintain her in a thoroughly efficient state in both hull and machinery. It was agreed that no payment should become due for time lost exceeding twenty-four hours in carrying out repairs to the vessel and that such off-hire periods might, at the option of the charterers, be added to the charter time. The charterers took delivery of the vessel at Liverpool on 13th February 1957, when she sailed in ballast for Newport News, U.S.A., where it was intended that she should pick up a cargo of coal and then proceed to Osaka via the Panama Canal. Between Liverpool and Osaka, the ship was at sea for eight and a half weeks, and for five weeks she was off-hire for repairs. When the ship arrived at Osaka on 15th May, it was discovered that her engines were in bad condition and that major repairs were necessary. The bad state of the engines on arrival at Osaka was due in part to the incompetence of the engine-room staff. On 15th September, the ship was once more ready to put to sea and the engine-room staff was by then adequate and efficient. In the meantime, the charterers wrote to the owners on 6th June, 27th July and 11th September, repudiating the charterparty and claiming for breach of contract. On each occasion, the owners replied that they would treat the contract as wrongfully repudiated and that they would claim damages accordingly. On 13th September, the owners formally accepted the charterers' repudiation and subsequently brought this action for damages for wrongful repudiation of the charterparty. The charterers counter-claimed for damages for breach of the charterparty. The owners succeeded before SALMON, J., and the charterers appealed.

HELD, by SELLERS, UPJOHN and DIPLOCK, L.JJ., that neither the unseaworthiness by itself nor the delay caused by the owners' breach of contract entitled the charterers to repudiate the charterparty.

UPJOHN, L.J. In my judgment, the remedies open to the innocent party for breach of a stipulation which is not a condition strictly so called, depend entirely on the nature of the breach and its foreseeable consequences. Breaches of stipulation fall, naturally, into two classes. First, there is the case where the owner by his conduct indicates that he considers himself no longer bound to perform his part of the contract; in that case, of course, the charterers may accept the repudiation and treat the contract as at an end. The second class of case is, of course, the more usual one, and that is where, due to misfortune such as the perils of the sea, engine failures, incompetence of the crew and so on, the owner is unable to perform a particular stipulation precisely in accordance with the terms of the contract try he never so hard to remedy it. In that case, the question to be answered is, does the breach of the stipulation go so much to the root of the contract that it makes further performance of the contract impossible, or, in other words, is the whole contract frustrated? If yea, the innocent party may treat the contract as at an end. If nay, his claim sounds in damages only.

Woodar Investment Development, Ltd. v. Wimpey Construction U.K., Ltd.

[1980] 1 W.L.R. 277; [1980] 1 All E.R. 571
House of Lords

Woodar (the vendors) agreed to sell and Wimpey (the purchasers) agreed to buy 14 acres of land for development. The price was £850,000 with provision for a further payment on completion of £150,000 to a third party. The contract contained a provision (condition E) by which Wimpey could rescind the contract 'if prior to the date of completion any Authority having a statutory power of compulsory acquisition shall have commenced the procedure required by law for the compulsory acquisition of the property or any part thereof'. In good faith Wimpey sent to Woodar a notice purporting to rescind under this condition citing a compulsory acquisition process. Wimpey conceded before the Court of Appeal that the process was not caught by the condition. Woodar contended that, by invoking condition E, Wimpey must be taken to have repudiated the contract. Woodar further contended that they accepted the repudiation and were entitled to sue for damages. On appeal to the House of Lords on the question whether Wimpey's attempted rescission amounted to a repudiation:
HELD, by LORD WILBERFORCE, LORD KEITH and LORD SCARMAN (LORD SALMON and LORD RUSSELL dissenting), that unjustified rescission did not always amount to repudiation: it is necessary to consider the circumstances and the parties conduct as a whole. Wimpey's attempt at rescission was a reliance (albeit mistaken) on contract condition E rather than a refusal to be bound by the contract. The erroneous and unsuccessful notice of rescission did not amount to repudiation.

LORD WILBERFORCE. My Lords, I have used the words 'in the circumstances' to indicate, as I think both sides accept, that in considering whether there has been a repudiation by one party, it is necessary to look at his conduct as a whole. Does this indicate an intention to abandon and to refuse performance of the contract? In the present case, without taking Wimpey's conduct generally into account, Woodar's contention, that Wimpey had repudiated, would be a difficult one. So far from repudiating the contract, Wimpey were relying on it and invoking one of its provisions, to which both parties had given their consent. And unless the invocation of that provision were totally abusive, or lacking in good faith (neither of which is contended for), the fact that it has proved to be wrong in law cannot turn it into a repudiation.

NOTE

In *Decro-Wall International S.A.* v. *Practitioners in Marketing* (1971) an oral agreement was made in March 1967 between the plaintiffs, a French manufacturing company, and the defendants, a marketing company. By this agrrement, the plaintiffs undertook (*a*) not to sell their goods in the United Kingdom to anyone other than the defendants, (*b*) to ship any goods ordered by the defendants with reasonable despatch, and (*c*) to supply the defendants with advertising material. In return for these undertakings, the defendants promised as part of the oral agreement (*a*) not to sell goods competing with the plaintiffs' goods, (*b*) to pay for the goods by means of bills of exchange due 90 days from the date of invoice and (*c*) to use their best endeavours to create and develop a market for the plaintiffs' goods. (The agreement made no express provision defining its duration and it was conceded by both parties at the trial that the agreement was terminable by reasonable notice on either side.)

The defendants succeeded in developing a market for the goods which, by April 1970, constituted 83 per cent of the defendants' business. The defendants were consistently late in payment, the delay in each instance varied from 2 to 20 days. At the beginning of April 1970, without warning the defendants, the plaintiffs appointed another company to be their sole concessionaires in the UK. On 9 April the plaintiffs wrote to the defendants contending that the delays in payment constituted a repudiation of contract and that they accepted the repudiation and that the contract was, accordingly, at an end. The plaintiffs brought this action (*a*) for moneys due under the contract, and (*b*) for a declaration that the defendants had ceased to be their sole concessionaires in the UK from 10 April 1970.

It was held by the Court of Appeal: (*a*) The failure to pay promptly and the likelihood of delays in the future did not constitute a repudiation of the agreement as time of payment was not expressed to be of the essence of the contract and the delays did not, therefore, go to the root of the contract. (*b*) The plaintiffs' breach by appointing another concessionaire and their repudiation of contract contained in the letter of 9 April did not automatically terminate the contract because the repudiation was not accepted by the defendants. (*c*) In the circumstances, 12 months was the reasonable period of notice required for termination of the agreement. (*d*) The plaintiffs' letter of 9 April wrongfully purported to accept the defendants' alleged repudiation of the agreement, constituted a repudiation of the agreement by the plaintiffs. (*e*) The plaintiffs should be released from their positive undertakings to supply goods to the defendants but they should remain bound by their undertaking not to sell goods to anyone in the UK other than the defendants, for otherwise it would enable the plaintiffs to inflict a ruinous blow to the defendants' business for which damages could not provide full compensation.

Federal Commerce and Navigation, Ltd. v. Molena Alpha, Inc.

[1979] A.C. 757; [1979] 1 All E.R. 307
House of Lords

By three time charterparties in identical form and dated 1st November 1974 the respective owners of three vessels let them to charterers for a period of six years. The intention was to use the vessels for the carriage of grain and steel on c.i.f. terms. Accordingly, the shippers would pay the freight for the carriage in advance and receive bills of lading marked 'freight pre-paid'. Because of slow steaming, the charterers deducted 47,122 dollars from the hire due on one of the vessels. In retaliation, the owners instructed the masters of the three ships (*i*) to withdraw all authority to the charterers to sign bills of lading, (*ii*) to refuse to sign any bill of lading endorsed 'freight pre-paid' and (*iii*) to insist that all bills of lading should be endorsed with the charterparty terms. The charterers were informed of these instructions on 4th October 1975. The owners knew that the carrying out of the instructions would result in serious difficulties to the charterers, whose sub-charterers would blacklist the vessels. The owners, having taken legal advice, believed that they were entitled to act in this way. On reference to arbitration, the umpire found in favour of the charterers, but stated his award in the form of a special case for the court. The judge held that the owners' action on 4th October had not validly terminated the charterparties. On appeal to the Court of Appeal, it was held that the action of the owners' on 4th October amounted to an anticipatory breach of the charterparties and that the charterers were therefore entitled to treat them as terminated. The owners appealed to the House of Lords.

HELD, by LORD WILBERFORCE, VISCOUNT DILHORNE, LORD FRASER, LORD RUSSELL and LORD SCARMAN, that the appeal should be dismissed. By the charterparties the charterers had the power to require the masters to sign freight pre-paid bills of lading and the owners' attempt to prevent the masters from doing so was an anticipatory or (per VISCOUNT DILHORNE and LORD RUSSELL) actual breach of the charterparties. The actual breach which had occurred, by threatening to deprive the charterers of substantially the whole of the benefit of the contract, had gone to the root of the contract, since the charterparties would then have become useless for the purpose for which they had been entered into, and the breach was therefore such as to entitle the charterers to terminate them.

LORD WILBERFORCE. My Lords, I do not think there can be any doubt that the owners' breach or threatened breach in the present case, consisting in their announcement that their masters would refuse to issue bills of lading freight pre-paid and not 'claused' so as to refer to the charters, *prima facie* went to the root of the contract as depriving the charterers of substantially the whole benefit of the contract. This is clear from the findings of the umpire to which I have already referred. It was in fact the owners' intention to put irresistible pressure on the charterers ('to compel the Charterers to pay over all sums deducted from hire by the Charterers which the Owners disputed, irrespective of whether such deductions should ultimately be determined to be valid or invalid': see the award, para 27), through the action they threatened to take. If the charterers had not given way, the charters would have become useless for the purpose for which they were granted. I do not think that this was disputed by the owners; in any event it was not disputable. What was said was that the action of the owners in the circumstances in which it was taken, should not be taken to be repudiatory.

NOTE

Section 11 of the Sale of Goods Act 1979 contains the following provision:

> (2) Where a contract of sale is subject to a condition to be fulfilled by the seller, the buyer may waive the condition, or may elect to treat

the breach of the condition as a breach of warranty and not as a ground for treating the contract as repudiated.

(3) Whether a stipulation in a contract of sale is a condition, the breach of which may give rise to a right to treat the contract as repudiated, or a warranty, the breach of which may give rise to a claim for damages but not to a right to reject the goods and treat the contract as repudiated, depends in each case on the construction of the contract; and a stipulation may be a condition, though called a warranty in the contract.

(4) Where a contract of sale is not severable and the buyer has accepted the goods or part of them, the breach of a condition to be fulfilled by the seller can only be treated as a breach of warranty, and not as a ground for rejecting the goods and treating the contract as repudiated, unless there is an express or implied term of the contract to that effect.

Thus, where there has been a breach of condition by the seller, the buyer may treat the contract as repudiated and refuse further performance. But the buyer may elect or be compelled, to treat the breach of condition as a breach of warranty sounding in damages only. Where a condition sinks to the level of a warranty, the breach is known as a breach of warranty *ex post facto*. These rules apply to express conditions and implied conditions equally.

By section 61(1) of the Sale of Goods Act, 'warranty' means an agreement with reference to goods which are the subject of a contract of sale, but collateral to the main purpose of such contract, the breach of which gives rise to a claim for damages, but not to a right to reject the goods and treat the contract as repudiated.

It is a fundamental breach for the buyer in a c.i.f. contract to refuse to pay the price on presentation of the shipping documents if the seller accepts such a breach, the contract is discharged, so that the buyer thereafter has no right to reject the goods as not conforming to contract description: *Berger & Co.* v. *Gill & Duffus* [1984], a House of Lords case.

Failure to pay in accordance with contract cannot be treated as repudiation unless it is expressly provided that full and punctual payment is of the essence of the contract: *Lombard North Central* v. *Butterworth* [1987].

19. Promissory estoppel

> Much as I am inclined to favour the principle of the High Trees case, it is important that it should not be stretched too far lest it should be endangered: Combe v. Combe, per DENNING, L.J.

Summary

1. Promissory estoppel as a defence

Where a party has waived his contractual rights against the other party, and that other party has changed his position in reliance on the waiver, it would be unjust to allow an action against him on the original contract. Thus, in equity, the party who waived his rights may, if he sues, be estopped from denying that he intended the waiver to be binding. *Central London Property Trust* v. *High Trees House* [1947]; *Tool Metal Manufacturing Co.* v. *Tungsten Electric Co.* [1955]. See also *Combe* v. *Combe* [1951].

2. Is the estoppel irrevocable?

In *W.J. Alan & Co.* v. *El Nasr Export and Import Co.* [1972] Lord Denning said that '. . . the one who waives his strict rights cannot afterwards insist on them. His strict rights are at any rate suspended so long as the waiver lasts. He may on occasion be able to revert to his strict legal rights for the future by giving reasonable notice in that behalf, or otherwise making it plain by his conduct that he will thereafter insist on them: *see* the Tool Metal case. But there are cases where no withdrawal is possible. It may be too late to withdraw; or it cannot be done without injustice to the other party. In that event he will be bound by his waiver. He can only enforce them subject to the waiver he has made.'

Central London Property Trust Ltd. v. High Trees House Ltd.

[1947] K.B. 130; [1956] 1 All E.R. 256

King's Bench Division

The plaintiff company (the landlords) let a new block of flats to the defendant company (the tenants) in 1937 for a term of ninety-nine years at a rent of £2,500 a year. The plaintiff company held all the shares of the defendant company. The block of flats was not fully occupied when war broke out in 1939, nor was there any possibility of letting all the flats with war conditions prevailing in London. It became clear that the defendants' profits would not be sufficient to pay the agreed rent and, as a result of discussions between the directors concerned, an arrangement was made by which the plaintiffs wrote to the defendants in the following terms: 'We confirm the arrangement made between us by which the ground rent should be reduced as from the commencement of the lease to £1,250 per annum'. The period during which the reduction was to operate was not specified, nor was there any consideration given by the defendant company in return for the reduction. The defendants paid the reduced rent, but by early in 1945 the flats were fully let and the rents received from them had been increased to a figure higher than that which had originally been anticipated. In 1941 the debenture-holders of the plaintiff company appointed a receiver who was still managing the affairs of the company at the time of this action. In September 1945 the receiver discovered for the first time that the rent reserved in the lease was £2,500 a year and he, accordingly, informed the defendants that this was the annual sum due. The plaintiffs brought this action to recover £625 rent for the quarter ended 29th September 1945, and also £625 for the quarter ended 25th December 1945. The defendants contended that the reduction was to apply throughout the term of ninety-nine years and, alternatively, that the reduction was to apply up to 24th September 1945, after when the original rent of £2,500 a year would become payable.

HELD, by DENNING, J., that the amounts claimed in the action were fully payable, the reduction arrangement not being binding after early 1945.

LORD DENNING. The courts have not gone so far as to give a cause of action in damages for the breach of such a promise, but they have refused to allow the party making it to act inconsistently with it. It is in that sense, and that sense only, that such a promise gives rise to an estoppel. The decisions are a natural result of the fusion of law and equity: for the cases of *Hughes* v. *Metropolitan Ry. Co.*, *Birmingham and District Land Co.* v. *London & North Western Ry. Co.* and *Salisbury (Marquess)* v. *Gilmore*, afford a sufficient basis for saying that a party would not be allowed in equity to go back on such a promise. In my opinion, the time has now come for the validity of such a promise to be recognized. The logical consequence, no doubt, is that a promise to accept a smaller sum in discharge of a larger sum, if acted upon, is binding notwithstanding the absence of consideration: and if the fusion of law and equity leads to this result, so much the better. That aspect was not considered in *Foakes* v. *Beer*. At this time of day however, when law and equity have been joined together for over seventy years, principles must be reconsidered in the light of their combined effect. It is to be noticed that in the Sixth Interim Report of the Law Revision Committee, pars. 35, 40, it is recommended that such a promise as that to which I have referred, should be enforceable in law even though no consideration for it has been given by the promisee. It seems to me that, to the extent I have mentioned, that result has now been achieved by the decisions of the courts.

I am satisfied that a promise such as that to which I have referred is binding and the only question remaining for my consideration is the scope of the promise in the present case. I am satisfied on all the evidence that the promise here was that the ground rent should be reduced to £1,250 a year as a temporary expedient while the block of flats was not fully, or substantially fully let, owing to the conditions prevailing. That means that the reduction in the rent applied throughout the years down to the end of 1944, but early in 1945 it is plain that the flats were fully let, and, indeed the rents received from them (many of them not being affected by the Rent Restrictions Acts) were increased beyond the figure at which it was originally contemplated that they would be let. At all events the rent from them must have been very considerable. I find that the conditions prevailing at the time when the reduction in rent was made, had completely passed away by the early months of 1945. I am satisfied that the promise was understood by all parties only to apply under the conditions prevailing at the time when it was made, namely, when the flats were only partially let, and that it did not extend any further than that. When the flats became fully let, early in 1945, the reduction ceased to apply.

In those circumstances, under the law as I hold it, it seems to me that rent is payable at the full rate for the quarters ending September 29 and December 25, 1945.

If the case had been one of estoppel, it might be said that in any event the estoppel would cease when the conditions to which the representation applied came to an end, or it also might be said that it would only come to an end on notice. In either case it is only a way of ascertaining what is the scope of the representation. I prefer to apply the principle that a promise intended to be binding, intended to be acted on and in fact acted on, is binding so far as its terms properly apply. Here it was binding as covering the period down to the early part of 1945, and as from that time full rent is payable.

I therefore give judgment for the plaintiff company for the amount claimed.

NOTE

In *Combe* v. *Combe* [1951] a wife obtained a decree nisi against her husband, in 1943 and immediately afterwards her solicitors wrote to her husband's solicitors asking whether the husband was prepared to make an allowance of £100 a year to the wife. The husband's solicitors replied that the husband agreed. The husband never paid the allowance. In 1950, the wife brought this action, claiming arrears of payment under the husband's promise. At first instance, the judge found for the wife. He held that, although the agreement was not supported by consideration, the husband's promise was enforceable because it was an absolute acceptance of liability, which was intended to be binding and acted on, and was in fact acted on by the wife. The husband appealed, contending that the judge had misapplied the High Trees principle, which could be used 'as a shield and not as a sword'. It was held by the Court of Appeal that the wife had given no consideration for the husband's promise, therefore she could not succeed in an action on it. Lord Denning said, 'It [the High Trees principle] does not create new causes of action where none existed before. It only prevents a party from insisting on his strict legal rights when it would be unjust to allow him to do so, having regard to the dealings which have taken place between the parties. Thus a creditor is not allowed to enforce a debt which he has deliberately agreed to waive if the debtor has carried on some business or in some other way changed his position in reliance on the waiver.'

Tool Metal Manufacturing Co., Ltd. v. Tungsten Electric Co., Ltd.

[1955] 1 W.L.R. 761; [1955] 2 All E.R. 657
House of Lords

TMMC granted by deed to TECO a non-exclusive licence under British letters patent to import, make, use and sell certain alloys made by means of inventions which were the subject of the patents. The licence was expressed to run from 1st June 1937 until 18th September 1947 and thereafter to be determinable by either party on the giving of six months' notice in writing. TECO agreed to pay a royalty on the sale of use of alloys made under the relevant patents. TECO also agreed by cl. 5 of the deed to pay 'compensation' to TMMC if the alloys sold or used under the licence exceeded a specified monthly quota. On the outbreak of war in 1939, TMMC voluntarily suspended their right to 'compensation,' it being understood between the parties that a new agreement would be entered into after the end of the war. In 1941 the patents covering certain of the grades of alloys (the iron grades), expired so that the iron grades did not thereafter bear royalty, although they continued to bear 'compensation' under cl. 5. In a previous action, commenced in July 1945, TECO claimed damages for fraud and breach of contract and TMMC counterclaimed for the payment of 'compensation' under cl. 5 as from 1st June 1945. The counterclaim failed because there was insufficient notice to determine the suspension of the payment of 'compensation'. TMMC brought this action to recover 'compensation' under cl. 5 as from 1st January 1947, and succeeded before PEARSON, J., who held that the counterclaim which had failed in the first action involved 'a reversal of the former attitude, and therefore it started running a reasonable time for resumption of compensation payments.' On appeal the decision was reversed, the Court of Appeal holding that the counterclaim 'did not purport to determine any existing agreement' and that it 'specified no date for the determination'. TMMC appealed to the House of Lords.

HELD, by VISCOUNT SIMONDS, LORD OAKSEY, LORD TUCKER and LORD COHEN, that equity required that any resumption of rights to 'compensation' under cl. 5 would be effective only after reasonable notice to TECO: and that the counterclaim in the previous action constituted notice, the nine months which elapsed between the date of the delivery of the counterclaim and the date from which compensation was now claimed, i.e. 1st January

1947, being a reasonable period of notice for this purpose. The decision of PEARSON, J., was restored.

VISCOUNT SIMONDS. My Lords, the decision of the Court of Appeal in the first action was based on nothing else than the principle of equity stated in this House in *Hughes* v. *Metropolitan Railway Co.* and interpreted by BOWEN, L.J., in *Birmingham and District Land Co.* v. *London & North Western Railway Co.* in these terms: 'It seems to me to amount to this, that if persons who have contractual rights against others induce by their conduct those against whom they have such rights to believe that such rights will either not be enforced or will be kept in suspense or abeyance for some particular time, those persons will not be allowed by a court of equity to enforce the rights until such time has elapsed, without at all events placing the parties in the same position as they were before.' These last words are important, for they emphasise that the gist of the equity lies in the fact that one party has by his conduct led the other to alter his position. I lay stress on this because I would not have it supposed, particularly in commercial transactions, that mere acts of indulgence are apt to create rights, and I do not wish to lend the authority of this House to the statement of the principle which is to be found in *Combe* v. *Combe* and may well be far too widely stated.

The difficulty in the present case lies in the fact that in the first action, in which it was held that between these parties the principle applies, neither of them in any pleading or other statement between the delivery of the counterclaim in March, 1946, and judgment in April, 1950, took their stand upon its existence. The respondents asserted a binding agreement for the complete and final abrogation of any compensation: the appellants, though willing to make some concession in regard to the past, denied any agreement in respect of any period at all. The position of neither of them was compatible with the existence of an equitable arrangement by which the right to receive and the obligation to pay compensation were suspended for a period which lasted at least until March, 1946, and for a debatable period thereafter.

My Lords, I think that at this point the issue is a very narrow one. On the one hand it is said that a plea resting on the denial of an agreement cannot be a notice determining that agreement. This is the view taken by ROMER, L.J. in which the other members of the Court of Appeal concurred. On the other hand, it is urged that, since the suspensory period is due to the gratuitous willingness of the one party to forgo their rights, nothing can be a clearer intimation that they propose no longer to forgo them than a claim which, though it may ask too much, can leave the other party in no doubt that they must not expect further indulgence. The problem may perhaps be stated in this way. Did equity require that the appellants should expressly and unequivocally refer to an equitable arrangement which the respondents had not pleaded and they did not recognise? Or was it sufficient for them by a reassertion of their legal rights to proclaim that the period of indulgence was over? In favour of the latter view it is added that such an attitude on the part of the appellants could not surprise the respondents who had not hesitated to bring against them a serious charge of fraud.

My Lords, it is not clear to me what conclusion the Court of Appeal would have reached but for the authority of the case of the *Canadian Pacific Railway Co.* v. *The King*, to which I must refer later. For my part I have, after some hesitation, formed the opinion that, as soon as the counterclaim was delivered, the respondents must be taken to know that the suspensory period was at an end and were bound to put their house in order. The position is a very artificial one, but it was their own ignorance of a suspensory period, or at least their failure to plead it, which created the difficulty, and I do not think that they can take advantage of their own ignorance or default and say that they were entitled to a further period of grace until a further notice was given. Equity demands that all the circumstances of the case should be regarded, and I think that the fair and reasonable view is that the respondents could not, after they had received the counterclaim, regard themselves as entitled to further indulgence.

It was, however, urged on behalf of the respondents that, even if the counterclaim could otherwise be regarded as a sufficient notice that the equitable arrangement was at an end, yet it was defective in that it did not name a certain future date at which it was to take effect. To this the reply was made that equity did not require a future date to be named in the notice, but that what it did require was that a reasonable time should be allowed to elapse before it was sought to enforce it. Here, too, the Court of Appeal favoured the view of the respondents, again feeling themselves constrained by the decision in the *Canadian Pacific Railway* case. And here, too, I am forced to the opposite conclusion. Equity is not held in a strait-jacket. There is no universal rule that an equitable arrangement must always be determined in one way. It may in some cases be right and fair that a dated notice should be given. But in this case what was the position in January, 1947, which I take to be the critical date? Then for nine months, the respondents must, in my opinion, be taken to have been aware that the appellants proposed to stand on their legal rights. It is not denied that those nine months gave them ample time to readjust their position. I cannot regard it as a requirement of equity that in such circumstances they should have been expressly notified in March, 1946, that they would have nine months and no more to take such steps as the altered circumstances required.

20. Part performance

> *The true rule is, in my view stated in* FRY ON SPECIFIC
> PERFORMANCE (6th Edn.), p.278, s. 582; *'The true
> principle, however, of the operation of acts of part
> performance seems only to require that the acts in question
> be such as must be referred to some contract, and may be
> referred to the alleged one; that they prove the existence of
> some contract, and are consistent with the contract alleged'*
> : Kingswood Estate *v.* Anderson, per UPJOHN, L.J.

Summary

1. The Law of Property Act 1925, s. 40 (1)

This sub-section provides that, 'No action may be brought upon any
contract for the sale or other disposition of land or any interest in
land, unless the agreement upon which such action is brought, or
some memorandum or note thereof, is in writing and signed by the
party to be charged or by some other person thereunto by him
lawfully authorised'.

Where the plaintiff cannot produce the required written evidence
and the defendant pleads the statute, the contract is unenforceable
at common law. But, in equity, there may be a sufficient act of part
performance of the contract which the court would accept as
evidence of the contract, thus rendering it specifically enforceable.
See Lord Reid's speech in *Steadman* v. *Steadman* [1976].

2. Sufficiency of the act of part performance

Not all of the acts done towards the execution of a contract are sufficient to invoke the doctrine of part performance. The important question is: what kind of an act must it be? The true principle seems only to require that the acts in question be such as must be referred to some contract, and may be referred to the alleged one: Fry on Specific Performance approved in *Kingswood Estate Co.* v. *Anderson* [1963].

Steadman v. Steadman

[1976] A.C. 536; [1974] 2 All E.R. 977
House of Lords
The husband and wife were joint owners of a house bought in 1963
for £3,600. Their marriage was dissolved in 1970. Prior to the divorce,
the husband had been ordered to pay maintenance of £2 per week
to the wife and £2 10s. per week for their child. The husband
continued to occupy the house after the wife left in 1968. In 1970 the
wife applied for an order under s. 17 of the *Married Women's Property
Act,* 1882 for an order for the sale of the house and division of the
proceeds. No further steps were taken until 1972, at which time the
husband was £194 in arrears with the maintenance. In 1972 the
matter came before the magistrates' court. The parties then agreed
orally as follows: the court was to be asked to discharge the
maintenance order, to order the husband to pay £100 of the arrears
and to order remission of the balance. The court was, by oral
agreement, to be informed at the same time that the parties had
agreed that, with regard to the house, the husband should pay £1,500
to the wife in return for which she would transfer to the husband her
interest in the house. The court made orders in accordance with the
agreement and the husband paid £100 to the wife. The husband then
borrowed £1,500 from a building society and paid it to his solicitor
who prepare a deed of transfer of the wife's interest and sent it to
her for signature. But the wife by then thought that £1,500 was not
enough and she refused to sign. She renewed her application under
s. 17 to have the house sold and the proceeds divided. The husband
contended that the compromise agreement was binding and the wife
pleaded that the agreement was unenforceable. She relied on s .40
(1) of the *Law of Property Act*, 1925. The husband relied on s. 40 (2).
The registrar held that there had been part performance and,
accordingly, s. 40 (1) did not apply. On appeal to the county court,
the registrar's decision was reversed. The husband appealed to the
Court of Appeal where it was allowed by a majority. The wife
appealed to the House of Lords.
HELD, by LORD REID, VISCOUNT DILHORNE, LORD
SIMON and LORD SALMON (LORD MORRIS dissenting), that
the agreement was enforceable against the wife for the following
reasons:

(*i*) In order to establish facts amounting to part performance it was
necessary for a plaintiff to show that he had acted to his detriment
and that the acts in question were such as to indicate on a balance of

probabilities that they had been performed in reliance on a contract with the defendant which was consistent with the contract alleged.

There was no general rule that the payment of a sum of money could never constitute part performance.

(*ii*) Although the payment by the husband to the wife of £100 would, by itself, have been insufficient to constitute part performance, that payment taken in conjunction with the announcement of the oral agreement to the justices, the abandonment by the husband of his right to claim full remission of arrears of maintenance and the preparation and delivery to the wife of a form of transfer for her signature amounted to acts of part performance by the husband in that the acts were such as to indicate that they had been carried out by him in reliance on a contract with the wife, a contract of the nature alleged. In these circumstances it would be inequitable to allow the wife to rely on the defence under s. 40 (1) of the 1925 Act. Oral and affidavit evidence was admissible to prove the contract.

LORD REID. Section 40 replaced a part of s. 4 of the Statute of Frauds (1677) and very soon after the passing of that Act authorities on this matter began to accumulate. It is now very difficult to find from them any clear guidance of general application. But it is not difficult to see at least one principle behind them. If one party to an agreement stands by and lets the other party incur expense or prejudice his position on the faith of the agreement being valid he will not then be allowed to turn round and assert that the agreement is unenforceable. Using fraud in its older and less precise sense, that would be fraudulent on his part and it has become proverbial that courts of equity will not permit the state to be made an instrument of fraud.

It must be remembered that this legislation did not and does not make oral contracts relating to land void: it only makes them unenforceable. And the statutory provision must be pleaded; otherwise the court does not apply it. So it is in keeping with equitable principles that in proper circumstances a person will not be allowed 'fraudulently' to take advantage of a defence of this kind. There is nothing about part performances in the Statute of Frauds. It is an invention of the Court of Chancery and in deciding any case not clearly covered by authority I think that the equitable nature of the remedy must be kept in mind.

A large number of the authorities are cases where a purchaser under an oral agreement has been permitted to take possession of or to do things on the land which he has agreed to buy. But sometimes rules appropriate to that situation have been sought to be applied to other cases of part performance where they are not appropriate. Indeed the courts have sometimes seemed disinclined to apply the principle at all to such other cases.

Normally the consideration for the purchase of land is a sum of money and there are statements that a sum of money can never be treated as part performance. Such statements would be reasonable if the person pleading the statute tendered repayment of any part of the price which he had received and was able thus to make restitutio in integrum. That would remove any 'fraud' or any equity on which the purchaser could properly rely. But to make a general rule that payment of money can never be part performance would seem to me to defeat the whole purpose of the doctrine and I do not think that we are compelled by authority to do that.

NOTE

Steadman v. *Steadman* was applied in *Sutton* v. *Sutton* [1984]. In this case a husband agreed orally to transfer the matrimonial home to his wife as part of their divorce arrangements. After obtaining a decree absolute of divorce, he refused to transfer the house contending, inter alia, that the agreement was not enforceable because there was no note or memorandum within s. 40 of the Law of Property Act. It was held that, although there was no note or memorandum, the agreement was binding on the husband because there had been a sufficient act of part performance on the part of the wife. The wife's consenting to the divorce as agreed was an act of part performance. Although she was quite content to be divorced, in the abstract, consenting to a divorce does not indicate any contract, let alone a contract about land. But in this case the term about the house was in the petition which must have been posted when her formal consent was sought under the postal procedure. This meant that her consent to the petition was in itself, in the circumstances, tied to the authority for that.

Kingswood Estate Co., Ltd. v. Anderson

[1963] 2 Q.B. 169; [1962] 3 All E.R. 593
Court of Appeal, Civil Division
In 1954 the landlords (the plaintiffs) acquired property which they wished to develop. This property included a house within the Rent

Restriction Acts, the weekly tenant of which was the defendant. The defendant's invalid son lived with her. In 1958 the landlords gave the tenant notice to quit, as a result of which, she became a statutory tenant. She was willing to give the landlords possession if she could move to suitable alternative accommodation. In 1959 the landlords purchased suitable alternative accommodation. But before the tenant moved, there were two conversations about the tenant's security of tenure in the new accommodation with a representative of the landlords. The first conversation was in the presence of one of the tenant's daughters, who knew, if the tenant did not, that she could not be evicted without suitable alternative accommodation being provided. The second conversation was by telephone with the tenant's other daughter. This daughter also knew that the tenant could not be evicted without suitable alternative accommodation being provided. On the strength of these conversations, the tenant moved to the new accommodation as a weekly tenant. The landlords later gave notice to quit the new accommodation and brought this action for possession. The county court judge gave judgment for the tenant and the landlords appealed.

HELD, by WILLMER, UPJOHN and RUSSELL, L.JJ., that the conversations constituted an oral agreement for a tenancy in equity for lives, there having been part performance, and the landlords' claim for possession failed.

WILLMER, L.J. On the question of part performance, I do not think that there is any room for doubt. Where the question is whether there was an agreement for a tenancy, I cannot imagine any better evidence of part performance than the fact of the tenant going into actual occupation. It is said, however, that the act of the tenant in going into occupation was equivocal, in that it might be referable to any kind of tenancy agreement. I do not understand, however, that part performance must necessarily be referable to the agreement, and only the particular agreement, relied on. I cite from ANSON'S LAW OF CONTRACT (21st Edn.) (1959), p. 75, where the principle is stated, as I think correctly, in the following terms:

'The acts of performance relied upon must of themselves suggest the existence of a contract such as it is desired to prove, although they need not establish the exact terms of that contract.'

As I understand it, if there is evidence of such part performance, that is sufficient to warrant the admission of oral evidence to prove what the exact terms of the contract were. I have no doubt that the evidence in the present case proved sufficient part performance within that principle. It follows that, notwithstanding the absence of any memorandum in writing, there was here sufficient proof of an agreement enforceable in equity on the basis of the principle established by *Walsh* v. *Lonsdale*.

The question whether the learned county court judge had jurisdiction to give effect to an agreement such as is here alleged gives rise to some difficulty. There is no doubt that, having regard to s. 52 (1) (d) of the County Courts Act, 1959, a claim by the tenant for specific performance of the agreement would have been clearly outside the county court jurisdiction. Our attention has been directed to the decision of this court in *Foster* v. *Reeves*, which is relied on for the proposition that, where the value of the property exceeds £500, the only jurisdiction which the county court judge possesses is his common law jurisdiction.

UPJOHN, L.J. Then it is said that, even if that was the contract, it was an oral contract and there is no written memorandum to satisfy s. 40 of the Law of Property Act, 1925. But leaving No. 91 and going into possession of No. 46 constitute acts of part performance which entitled the tenant to rely on a bare oral contract and which prevents the landlords from taking any objection of the want of writing. With all respect to the submission of counsel for the landlords, I should have thought that his argument founded on the want of writing was quite unarguable, for, in my judgment, this is a complete textbook case of part performance. However, counsel relies on the well-known conditions necessary to prevent the operation of the statute laid down by WARRINGTON, L.J., in *Chaproniere* v. *Lambert*, and says that the acts of part performance here do not satisfy the first condition, namely, that the acts of part performance must not only be referable to a contract such as that alleged, but be referable to no other title. So he says the acts of part performance here are equally consistent with a weekly tenancy and to a tenancy for lives, so that it cannot be said that the acts of part performance are referable to no other title. This, however, is a long exploded idea. The true rule is in my view, stated in FRY ON SPECIFIC PERFORMANCE (6th Edn.), p. 278, s. 582:

'The true principle, however, of the operation of acts of part performance seems only to require that the acts in question be such as must be referred to some contract, any may be referred to the alleged one; that they prove the existence of some contract, and are consistent with the contract alleged.'

In my judgment, this is plainly satisfied in this case, and the doctrine of part performance prevents the operation of the statute. Accordingly, in my judgment, the tenant having proved an oral contract by evidence accepted by the learned county court judge, is entitled to be rewarded as a tenant in possession having a right to specific performance.

Wakeham v. Mackenzie
[1968] 1 W.L.R. 1175; [1968] 2 All E.R. 783
Chancery Division
A 72-year-old widower, Ball, made an oral agreement with the plaintiff, a 67-year-old widow. By this agreement, Ball promised the plaintiff that if she would move into his house and look after him and the house for the rest of his life, she should have the house and its contents when he died. It was part of the agreement that the plaintiff should pay for her own board and coal. On the strength of Ball's promise, the plaintiff gave up her council flat and made her home in Ball's house, looking after Ball and the house, paying for her own board and coal. Ball died about two years later but he did not leave the house or its contents to the plaintiff, who brought this action for specific performance of Ball's promise under the oral agreement.
HELD, by STAMP, J., that the plaintiff's giving up of her flat, her moving into Ball's house, her acts in looking after Ball and the house and in paying for her board and coal, were acts of part performance which must be referred to some contract, and were referable to the contract that she alleged; accordingly she was entitled to specific performance of Ball's oral promise that she should have his house and its contents after his death.

STAMP, J. I conclude from *Kingswood Estate Co., Ltd.* v. *Anderson*, first that it is not the law that the acts of part performances relied on must be not only referable to a contract such as that alleged, but referable to no other title, the doctrine to that effect laid down by WARRINGTON, L.J., in *Chaproniere* v. *Lambert* having been exploded; and secondly, that the true rule is that the operation of acts of part performance requires only that the acts in question be such as must be referred to some contract and may be referred to some contract and may be referred to the alleged one: that they prove the existence of some contract and are consistent with the contract alleged.

The acts of part performance in this case, the giving up of the plaintiff's home to make her home at 172, Wilton Road, the moving into a new home, the acts which the plaintiff performed in looking after the deceased and looking after that home and putting £2 a week into the common pot clearly, in my judgment, raise an equity in her. Those acts were, in my judgment, such as must be referred to some contract. The expression 'must be referred to some contract,' used by UPJOHN, L.J., in the *Kingswood Estate* case, cannot exclude any act which could possibly be referable to love or affection, for whenever a man goes into possession of land he may be there by the grace and favour of another.

In the circumstances in which the plaintiff found herself at the relevant time I cannot suppose that she gave up her own home, took up residence at No. 172 and did what she did otherwise than by reference to some contract. If it were necessary to do so, I would further hold that the act in making her home at 172, Wilton Road during the whole of the residue of the life of Mr. Ball and keeping house, were acts of part performance relation to 172, Wilton Road.

NOTE

In equity, the question arises whether, in the absence of written evidence of a contract for the disposition of an interest in land, a party may obtain a decree of specific performance. The courts of equity have long sought to remedy the injustice that might be caused where the defendant pleads the statute and yet has, by his conduct, plainly admitted the existence of the contract. The courts of equity would dispense with the need for written evidence and accept instead evidence of acts of part performance. Section 40(1) of the Law of Property Act 1925 is a re-enactment of part of the Statute of Frauds 1677. The doctrine of part performance which developed as a result of the 1677 statute, remains unaffected by the passing of s. 40 (1) of the Law of Property Act. See s. 40 (2) of the 1925 Act.

21. Damages for breach

Where two parties have made a contract which one of them has broken the damages which the other party ought to receive in respect of such breach of contract should be such as may fairly and reasonably be considered as either arising naturally, i.e., according to the usual course of things, from such breach of contract itself, or such as may reasonably be supposed to have been in the contemplation of both parties at the time they made the contract as the probable result of the breach of it: Hadley v. Baxendale, per ALDERSON, B.

Summary

1. Damages

The usual common law remedy for breach of contract is damages, that is to say, monetary compensation. Unliquidated damages are those which are assessed by the court. Liquidated damages are agreed by the parties as part of their contract.

2. Unliquidated damages

In assessing unliquidated damages, the court will apply the rules governing remoteness of loss and measure of damages. These rules are contained in the cases, particularly *Hadley* v. *Baxendale* [1854], *Victoria Laundry* v. *Newman Industries* [1949] and The *Heron II* [1967]. Essentially, there are two kinds of loss which may be recoverable as damages: first, that which arises naturally, i.e., in the ordinary course of things: secondly, that which may reasonably be supposed to have been in the contemplation of both parties, to the supposed to have been in the contemplation of both parties, to the time they made the contract as the probable result of the breach of it.

A contracting party must take reasonable steps to minimise the effect of the other party's breach. He will be debarred from recovering any part of the damage which is due to his neglect to take such steps: *British Westinghouse Electric Co.* v. *Underground Electric Co.* [1912].

3. Liquidated damages

The parties may stipulate in their contract for the payment of an agreed amount of damages on the occurrence of a specified breach, e.g. delay in the completion of a building contract. The essence of liquidated damages is that the amount stipulated should be a genuine pre-assessment of the loss which flows from the breach. Any sum fixed in by way of punishment of the offending party (as opposed to the payment of compensation) will constitute a penalty which will be void and disregarded: *Dunlop Pneumatic Tyre Co.* v. *New Garage and Motor Co.* [1914].

Hadley v. Baxendale

[1854] 9 Exch. 341; [1843–60] All E.R. Rep. 461

Court of Exchequer

The plaintiffs were millers in Gloucestershire and the defendants were common carriers of goods. The crankshaft of the plaintiffs' steam engine was broken with the result that work in the mill had come to a halt. They had ordered a new shaft from an engineer in Greenwich and arranged with the defendants to carry the broken shaft from Gloucester to Greenwich to be used by the engineer as a model for the new shaft. The defendants did not know that the plaintiffs had no spare shaft and that the mill could not operate until the new shaft was installed. The defendants delayed delivery of the broken shaft to the engineer for several days, with resulting delay to the plaintiffs in getting their steam-mill working. The plaintiffs claimed damages for breach of contract. On the question whether damages should include loss of profits:

HELD, by PARKE, ALDERSON, PLATT and MARTIN, B.B., that the loss of profits was not recoverable as it could not reasonably be considered a consequence of the breach of contract as could have been fairly and reasonably contemplated by both the parties when they made the contract.

ALDERSON, B., [delivering the judgment of the court]. We think the proper rule in such a case as the present is this. Where two parties have made a contract which one of them has broken the damages which the other party ought to receive in respect of such breach of contract should be such as may fairly and reasonably be considered as either arising naturally, i.e. according to the usual course of things, from such breach of contract itself, or such as may reasonably be supposed to have been in the contemplation of both parties at the time they made the contract as the probable results of the breach of it. If special circumstances under which the contract was actually made were communicated by the plaintiffs to the defendants, and thus known to both parties, the damages resulting from the breach of such a contract which they would reasonably contemplate would be the amount of injury which would ordinarily follow from a breach of contract under the special circumstances so known and communicated. But, on the other hand, if these special circumstances were wholly unknown to the party breaking the contract, he, at the most, could only be supposed to have had in him contemplation the amount of injury which would arise generally, and in the great multitude of cases not affected by any special circumstances, from such a breach of contract. For, had the special circumstances been known, the parties might have specially provided for the breach of contract by special terms as to the damages in that case; and of this advantage it would be very unjust to deprive them . . . In the present case, if we are to apply the principles above laid down, we find that the only circumstances here communicated by the plaintiffs to the defendants at the time the contract was made were that the article to be carried was the broken shaft of a mill and that the plaintiffs were the millers of that mill. But how do these circumstances show reasonably that the profits of the mill must be stopped by an unreasonable delay in the delivery of the broken shaft by the carrier to the third person? Suppose the plaintiffs had another shaft in their possession put up or putting up at the time, and that they only wished to send back the broken shaft to the engineer who made it; it is clear that this would be quite consistent with the above circumstances, and yet the unreasonable delay in the delivery would have no effect upon the intermediate profits of the mill. Or, again, suppose that, at the time of the delivery to the carrier, the machinery of the mill had been in other respects defective, then, also, the same results would follow. Here it is true that the shaft was actually sent back to serve as a model for a new one, that the want of a new one was the only cause of the stoppage of the mill, and that the loss of profit really arose from not sending down the new shaft in proper time, and that this arose from the delay in delivering the broken one to serve as a model. But it is obvious that, in the great multitude of cases of millers sending off broken shafts to third persons by a carrier under ordinary circumstances, such consequences would not, in all probability, have occurred, and these special circumstances were here never communicated by the plaintiffs to the defendants.

It follows, therefore, that the loss of profits here cannot reasonably be considered such a consequence of the breach of contract as could have been fairly and reasonably contemplated by both the parties when they made this contract. For such loss would neither have flowed naturally from the breach of this contract in the great multitude of such cases occurring under ordinary circumstances, nor were the special circumstances, which, perhaps, would have made it a reasonable and natural consequence of such breach of contract, communicated to or known by the defendants.

Victoria Laundry Ltd. v. Newman Industries Ltd.

[1949] 2 K.B. 528; [1949] 1 All E.R. 997
Court of Appeal
The plaintiffs, who were launderers and dyers, decided to extend their business, and with this end in view, purchased a large boiler from the defendants. The defendants knew at the time of the contract that the plaintiffs were laundry-men and dyers and that they required the boiler for the purposes of their business. They also were aware that the plaintiffs wanted the boiler for immediate use. But the defendants did not know at the time the contract was made exactly how the plaintiffs planned to use the boiler in their business. They did not know whether (as the fact was) it was to function as a substitute for a smaller boiler already in operation, or as a replacement of an existing boiler of equal capacity, or as an extra unit to be operated in addition to any boilers already in use. The defendants, in breach of contract, delayed delivery of the boiler for five months. The plaintiffs brought this action for damages. The defendants disputed that the plaintiffs were entitled to damages for the loss of profits they would have earned if the boiler had been delivered on time. The plaintiffs contended that they could have taken on a large number of new customers in the course of their laundry business and that they could and would have accepted a number of highly lucrative dyeing contracts for the Ministry of Supply. STREATFEILD, J., awarded £110 damages under certain minor heads but no damages in respect of loss of profits on the grounds that this was too remote. The plaintiffs appealed to the Court of Appeal.
HELD, by TUCKER, ASQUITH and SINGLETON, L.JJ., that there were ample means of knowledge on the part of the defendants that business loss of some sort would be likely to result to the plaintiffs from the defendants' default in performing their contract; and that the appeal should, therefore, be allowed and the issue referred to an official referee as to what damage, if any, is recoverable in addition to the £110 awarded by the trial judge.

ASQUITH, L.J., [who read the judgment of the court]. What propositions applicable to the present case emerge from the authorities as a whole, including those analysed above? We think they include the following: (*i*) It is well settled that the governing purpose of damages is to put the party whose rights have been violated in the same position, so far as money can do so, as if his rights had been observed. This purpose, if relentlessly pursued, would provide him with a complete indemnity for all loss *de facto* resulting from a particular breach, however improbable, however unpredictable, This, in contract at least, is recognised as too harsh a rule. Hence, (*ii*): In cases of breach of contract the aggrieved party is only entitled to recover such part of the loss actually resulting as was at the time of the contract reasonably foreseeable as liable to result from the breach. (*iii*) What was at that time reasonably foreseeable depends on the knowledge then possessed by the parties, or, at all events, by the party who later commits the breach. (*iv*) For this purpose knowledge 'possessed' is of two kinds – one imputed, the other actual. Everyone, as a reasonable person, is taken to know the 'ordinary course of things' and consequently what loss is liable to result from a breach of that ordinary course. This is the subject matter of the 'first rule' in *Hadley* v. *Baxendale*, but to this knowledge, which the contract-breaker is assumed to possess whether he actually possesses it or not, there may have to be added in a particular case knowledge which he actually possesses of special circumstances outside the 'ordinary course of things' of such a kind that a breach in those special circumstances would be liable to cause more loss. Such a case attracts the operation of the 'second rule' so as to make additional loss also recoverable. (*v*) In order to make the contract-breaker liable under either rule it is not necessary that he should actually have asked himself what loss is liable to result from a breach. As has often been pointed out, parties at the time of contracting contemplate, not the breach of the contract, but its performance. It suffices that, if he had considered the question, he would as a reasonable man have concluded that the loss in question was liable to result. (*vi*) Nor, finally, to make a particular loss recoverable, need it be proved that on a given state of knowledge the defendant could, as a reasonable man, foresee that a breach must necessarily result in that loss. It is enough if he could foresee it was likely so to result ...

We agree that in order that the plaintiffs should recover specifically and as such the profits expected on these [government dyeing] contracts, the defendants would have had to know, at the time of their agreement with the plaintiffs, of the prospect and terms of such contracts. We also agree that they did not, in fact, know these things. If does not, however, follow that the plaintiffs are precluded from recovering some general (and perhaps conjectural) sum for loss of business in respect of dyeing contracts to be reasonably expected

any more than in respect of laundering contracts to be reasonably
expected.

The Heron II, Koufos v. Czarnikow Ltd.

[1967] 2 Lloyd's Rep. 457; [1967] 3 All E.R. 686
House of Lords

The respondents chartered the appellant's vessel, *Heron II*, to sail to
Constanza, and there to load a cargo of sugar and to carry this to
Basrah or to Jeddah, at the charterer's option. The option was not
exercised and the vessel arrived at Basrah with a delay of nine days
due to deviations made in breach of contract. The respondents had
intended to sell the sugar promptly after arrival at Basrah but the
appellant did not know this, although he was aware that there existed
a sugar market at Basrah. Shortly before the sugar was sold at
Basrah, the market price fell partly by reason of the arrival of another
cargo of sugar. If the appellant's vessel had not been in delay by nine
days, the sugar would have fetched £32 10s. per ton. The price
realised on the market was £31 2s. 9d. per ton. The respondent
charterers brought this action to recover the difference as damages
for breach of contract. The appellant shipowner, while admitting
liability to pay interest for nine days on the value of the sugar, denied
that the fall in market value should be taken into account in assessing
damages. It was held by the Court of Appeal that the loss due to the
fall in market price was not too remote and could be recovered as
damages. The shipowner appealed to the House of Lords.

HELD, by LORD REID, LORD MORRIS OF BORTH-Y-GEST,
LORD HODSON, LORD PEARCE and LORD UPJOHN, that the
case fell within the first branch of the rule in *Hadley* v. *Baxendale* and
that the difference was recoverable as damages for breach of
contract.

LORD MORRIS. The present case is one in which no special
information was given to the carrier as to what the charterers
intended to do with the goods after they arrived at Basrah. In those
circumstances in deciding what damages would fairly and reasonably
be regarded as arising, if the delivery of the goods was delayed, I
think that the reasonable contemplation of a reasonable shipowner
at the time of the making of the charterparty must be considered. I
think that such a shipowner must reasonably have contemplated that,
if he delivered the sugar at Basrah some nine or ten days later than

he could and should have delivered it, then a loss by reason of a fall in the market price for sugar at Basrah was one that was liable to result or at least was not unlikely to result. This results from the facts of this case. It is a question of what the parties contemplated. Even without notice of special circumstances or special considerations there may be situations where it is plain that there was a common contem- plation. In his dissenting judgment in *The Arpad*, SCRUTTON, L.J., said: 'I am inclined to think that in contracts of carriage from wheat-producing districts, it is always so probable that the shipper is sending for re-sale or for sale to a person who will re-sell, that the carrier will be liable if there is no market, for the effect on a contract of sale of his conversion or unjustifiable failure to deliver.' Whether this be so or not the shipowner in the present case must at least have appreciated that the charterers wanted to have the goods at Basrah at the date when they should have been delivered there. What could clearly be foreseen was that the charterers would be without their goods at the place where, and on the date when, they were entitled to expect to have them. Had there not been delivery at all, the damages would have been measured by relation to the market price of the goods at the date when they should have been delivered. In such an eventuality the charterers would have been entitled to acquire goods to replace those which, either by reason of their having been lost or for some other reason, were not delivered. By a parity of reasoning since the parties had not contracted on the basis that the shipowner could deliver as and when he liked but on the basis that he should proceed at all convenient speed and so should deliver on the date that could with reasonable accuracy be predicted, the charterers would be entitled, if it were necessary, to acquire goods to replace those which had not arrived. If when the goods later arrived the market price had advanced, the charterers would suffer no loss: if the market price had declined, they would suffer loss. If they actually suffered loss, it would *prima facie* be measured as the difference between the market price at the date when the goods should have been delivered and the market price at the date when they were delivered.

LORD UPJOHN. ASQUITH, L.J., in the *Victoria Laundry* case used the words 'likely to result' and he treated that as synonymous with a serious possibility or a real danger. He went on to equate that with the expression 'on the cards', but like all your lordships I deprecate the use of that phrase, which is far too imprecise and to my mind is capable of denoting a most improbable and unlikely event, such as winning a prize or a premium bond on any given drawing. ...

It is clear that on the one hand the test of foreseeability as laid down in the case of tort is not the test for breach of contract; nor on the other hand must the loser establish that the loss was a near certainty or an odds-on probability. I am content to adopt as the test a 'real danger' or a 'serious possibility'. There may be a shade of difference between these two phrases, but the assessment of damages is not an exact science and what to one judge or jury will appear a real danger may appear to another judge or jury to be a serious possibility. I do not think that the application of that test would have led to a different result in *Hadley* v. *Baxendale*. I cannot see why Pickfords in the absence of express mention should have contemplated as a real danger or serious possibility that work at the factory would be brought to a halt while the shaft was away.

Dunlop Pneumatic Tyre Co., Ltd. v. New Garage Co., Ltd.

[1915] A.C. 79; [1914–15] All E.R. Rep. 739
House of Lords

Dunlop, through an agent, entered into a contract with New Garage Co., by which they supplied them with their goods, consisting mainly of motor car tyres, covers and tubes. By this contract, New Garage Co. undertook not to do a number of things, including the following: Not to tamper with the manufacturer's marks; not to sell to any customer at prices less than the current list prices; not to supply to persons whose supplies Dunlop had decided to suspend; not to exhibit or to export without Dunlop's assent. The agreement contained the following clause: 'We agree to pay to the Dunlop company the sum of £5 for each and every tyre, cover or tube sold or offered in breach of this agreement, as and by way of liquidated damages and not as a penalty.' The New Garage Co. sold covers and tubes at prices below the list prices and Dunlop brought this action for liquidated damages. On the question whether the £5 stipulated in the agreement was penalty or liquidated damages:

HELD, by LORD DUNEDIN, LORD ATKINSON, LORD PARKER and LORD PARMOOR, that the stipulation was one for liquidated damages and that the New Garage Co. was liable to pay the sum specified in respect of each and every breach of the contract.

LORD PARMOOR. There is no question as to the competency of

parties to agree beforehand the amount of damages, uncertain in their nature, payable on the breach of a contract. There are cases, however, in which the courts have interfered with the free right of contract, although the parties have specified the definite sum agreed on by them to be in the nature of liquidated damages, and not of a penalty. If the court, after looking at the language of the contract, the character of the transaction, and the circumstances under which it was entered into, comes to the conclusion that the parties have made a mistake in calling the agreed sum liquidated damages, and that such sum is not really a pactional pre-estimate of loss within the contemplation of the parties at the time when the arrangement was made, but a penal sum inserted as a punishment on the defaulter irrespective of the amount of any loss which could at the time have been in contemplation of the parties, then such sum is a penalty, and the defaulter is only liable in respect of damages which can be proved against him.

LORD DUNEDIN. I shall content myself with stating succinctly the various propositions which I think are deducible from the decisions which rank as authoritative:

1. Though the parties to a contract who use the words 'penalty' or 'liquidated damages' may prima facie be supposed to mean what they say, yet the expression used is not conclusive. The Court must find out whether the payment stipulated is in truth a penalty or liquidated damages. This doctrine may be said to be found passim in nearly every case.

2. The essence of a penalty is a payment of money stipulated as in terrorem of the offending party; the essence of liquidated damages is a genuine covenanted pre-estimate of damage (*Clydebank Engineering and Shipbuilding Co.* v. *Don Jose Ramos Yzquierdo y Castaneda*).

3. The question whether a sum stipulated is penalty or liquidated damages is a question of construction to be decided upon the terms and inherent circumstances of each particular contract, judged of as at the time of the making of the contract, not as at the time of the breach (*Public Works Commissioner* v. *Hills* and *Webster* v. *Bosanquet*).

4. To assist this task of construction various tests have been suggested, which if applicable to the case under consideration may prove helpful, or even conclusive. Such as:

(*a*) It will be held to be penalty if the sum stipulated for is extravagant and unconscionable in amount in comparison with the greatest loss that could conceivably be proved to have followed from the breach. (Illustration given by LORD HALSBURY in *Clydebank Case*.)

(*b*) It will be held to be a penalty if the breach consists only in not paying a sum of money, and the sum stipulated is a sum greater than the sum which ought to have been paid (*Kemble* v. *Farren*). This though one of the most ancient instances is truly a corollary to the last test. Whether it had its historical origin in the doctrine of the common law that when A. promised to pay B. a sum of money on a certain day and did not do so, B. could only recover the sum with, in certain cases, interest, but could never recover further damages for non-timeous payment, or whether it was a survival or the time when equity reformed unconscionable bargains merely because they were unconscionable, – a subject which much exercised JESSEL, M.R. in *Wallis* v. *Smith* – is probably more interesting than material.

(*c*) There is a presumption (but no more) that it is penalty when 'a single lump sum is made payable by way of compensation, on the occurrence of one or more or all of several events, some of which may occasion serious and others but trifling damage' (LORD WATSON in *Lord Elphinstone* v. *Monkland Iron and Coal Co.*).

On the other hand:

(*d*) It is no obstacle to the sum stipulated being a genuine pre-estimate of damage, that the consequences of the breach are such as to make precise pre-estimation almost an impossibility. On the contrary, that is just the situation when it is probable that pre-estimated damage was the true bargain between the parties (*Clydebank Case*, LORD HALSBURY; *Webster* v. *Bosanquet*, LORD MERSEY).